D1221452

# Speech Style and Social Evaluation

# European Monographs in Social Psychology

*Series Editor* HENRI TAJFEL

EUROPEAN MONOGRAPHS IN SOCIAL PSYCHOLOGY 7
*Series Editor* HENRI TAJFEL

# Speech Style and Social Evaluation

HOWARD GILES
PETER F. POWESLAND
*University of Bristol, England*

1975

*Published in cooperation with the*
EUROPEAN ASSOCIATION OF EXPERIMENTAL
SOCIAL PSYCHOLOGY
*by*
ACADEMIC PRESS *London, New York and San Francisco*

ACADEMIC PRESS INC. (LONDON) LTD.
24/28 Oval Road
London NW1


*United States Edition published by*
ACADEMIC PRESS INC.
111 Fifth Avenue
New York, New York 10003

Library of Congress Catalog Card Number: 75 19638

ISBN 0 12 283750 9


PRINTED AND BOUND IN ENGLAND BY
HAZELL WATSON AND VINEY LTD
AYLESBURY, BUCKS

# Preface

One of the purposes of this monograph is to bring together from diverse sources evidence which shows that the characteristics of a person's speech influence the ways in which he is perceived and evaluated by his listeners. The main focus of attention is upon how social judgement is affected by a speaker's pronunciation, accent, dialect and language.

First we draw attention to the fact that within many communities a variety of language and speech forms can be found and that there are social norms with regard to their use. We suggest that such norms may be considered to have two kinds of application. One way in which a linguistic norm can take effect is in prescribing which language, dialect or speech style should be used on a given occasion or in given circumstances. Often a particular mode of language or speech is required for formal, public use. We refer to this as a "context-related standard". Another way in which speech norms can apply is in relation to social status: one particular form of speech may generally command greater prestige than others. We call this a "class-related standard".

In Chapter 3 we examine empirical findings, chiefly in the contexts of Britain, Canada and the United States of America, concerning the relation between speech and social status. Quite a large amount of evidence has accumulated to suggest that listeners readily use speech cues as a basis for attributing prestige or social class to speakers. In Chapters 4, 5 and 6 we extend the investigation to include a wide range of personality variables which listeners are prepared to judge from speech alone. We look at the stereotypes of character, competence and social attractiveness which are commonly associated with different ways of speaking and consider the possible consequences of these stereotypes for interpersonal influence.

In Chapters 7 and 8 we consider the concept of a repertoire of possible ways of speaking available to a particular speaker and the factors which influences his selection from this repertoire. We adduce evidence to suggest that one source of influence upon a person's speech patterns will be endogenous factors, such as his mood or state of health. But probably a more important set of constraints are the exogenous determinants. These influences include the topic of the speaker's utterance, the general context of the speech event, the degree of formality of the occasion and the characteristics and behaviour of the person or persons addressed.

In the final chapter we offer a somewhat rudimentary model of the individual speaker's diversity of speech possibilities. This "accommodation model" postulates that the speaker modifies his speech-style, either consciously or unconsciously, as a means of controlling the way in which he is perceived by the listener. The implications of the model are explored with particular regard to the use of accented speech in Britain. It is suggested that the speaker will vary his speech style along an accent dimension which is correlated with social status or prestige. His accent will, in certain circumstances, change so as to be more similar or less similar to the high-prestige speech form known as Received Pronunciation. Such variation will make the speaker appear more similar or less similar to his interlocutor and will represent either convergence or divergence with respect to the interlocutor's own speech style. The conditions favouring convergence and divergence are explored.

We suggest hypotheses which may be derived from the accommodation model and which might be experimentally tested; and we indicate the ways in which the model needs to be elaborated to account for the complexities of interpersonal speech.

We hope that the book will be useful for its collation of studies relating to interpersonal judgement on the basis of speech characteristics. We hope also that it will help to stimulate further research in this multidisciplinary field.

We wish to express out gratitude to all the colleagues with whom we have discussed the ideas with which this monograph is concerned. Howard Giles would like particularly to thank Wallace Lambert and Donald Taylor and members of the Language Research Unit at McGill University, Montreal, Canada, for their help and encouragement. Both authors greatly appreciate the value of discussions they have had with Colin Fraser, Guy Fielding and Richard Bourhis at the University of Bristol. We are also grateful to Henri Tajfel for his advice, encouragement and forbearance during the gestation of this book. Finally, we wish to thank Mrs Lesley Singleton for cheerfully deciphering and transcribing a series of heavily amended drafts.

HOWARD GILES
PETER F. POWESLAND

# Contents

# 1

# Introduction

Our perception of other people is not a passive process. When we meet someone for the first time we immediately begin to make judgements and inferences about him on the basis of what we see and hear. The nature of these inferences and the significance which we attach to them will depend upon our conscious or unconscious assumptions and beliefs. Whether we are aware of it or not we each have our own "implicit personality theories" which enable us, with varying degrees of validity, to construct impressions of people from whatever information about them is available.[1]

General appearance, facial expressions and gestures provide useful clues as to what sort of person we are dealing with. What he says to us, whether it is directly biographical or not and whether we accept it at face value or not, tells us a great deal about him. The manner in which he speaks can also be used as a basis of judgement, and it is with this source of information that this book is mainly concerned.

Since Pear (1931) wrote his entertaining and stimulating account of voice and personality, several studies have shown that a person's speech characteristics affect the way in which he is perceived and evaluated by others. Indeed there is some evidence which suggests that, for certain kinds of evaluation, noncontent cues have a more significant effect than the content of speech itself.

Mehrabian and Weiner (1967) studied the relative contributions of vocal qualities and verbal content to the impressions people form as to whether a speaker likes or dislikes the person he is addressing. Single word items connoting positive, neutral or negative affect were spoken in

1. For an account of person perception, see Cook (1971). For a theoretical discussion of social categorization see Eiser and Stroebe (1972).

a positive, neutral or negative tone of voice. All possible combinations of type of word and tone of voice were used. Subjects were asked to judge the speaker's feelings towards the person addressed. Some subjects were told to attend to the meanings of the words and ignore the tone of voice, some to attend to the tone and ignore the words, and some to "use all the information available". Under the latter instructions there was a significant effect of tone and no effect of content. When subjects were told to attend to tone only there was both a tone and a content effect. Even when subjects were instructed to attend to the content only the effect of tone of voice was noticeable although not statistically significant. It is also of interest that effects attributable to the use of two different speakers in the experiment are shown in several parts of the analysis of the data. In a further study, Mehrabian and Ferris (1967) suggest that the information judges receive about attitudes can be quantified as follows: 7% speech content, 38% vocal qualities and 55% facial.[2]

Some recent work conducted at Oxford using whole messages rather than just isolated words as stimuli, and in more realistic settings, also suggests that noncontent cues can under certain circumstances carry more weight than the content itself (Argyle, Salter, Nicholson, Williams and Burgess, 1970; Argyle, Alkema and Gilmour, 1971). Subjects were required to view videotapes of a performer making a speech which reflected a superior, neutral or inferior attitude towards participants in psychological experiments. Having observed one version, the subjects were required to rate the performer on ten bipolar rating scales. Both content and noncontent cues were varied in a $3 \times 3$ design. For example, one of these nine conditions represented a "superior" statement (approximately 20 seconds in length) performed in an "inferior" manner. That is, the statement was accompanied by nervous smiling, a lowered head and a tone of voice expressing an eagerness-to-please. The authors claim that their results indicate that the noncontent cues have 4·3 times more effect than the content cues. This study was repeated using a "hostile-friendly" dimension and this time it was found that the noncontent cues were six times as influential as the verbal content cues. Unfortunately, we cannot disentangle the relative weights of

---

2. Heinberg (1963) has suggested that the effectiveness of persuasive and other speeches is often far more dependent upon the manner of delivery than upon what is actually said.

factors relating to speech characteristics and those relating to appearance and gesture in these two experiments owing to the fact that they were employed in combination.

Seligman, Tucker and Lambert (1972) provide some evidence of the importance of noncontent speech cues for evaluation of personality. Student-teachers were asked to form subjective impressions of each of eight Grade III schoolboys on the basis of three types of information: a photograph, a tape-recorded speech sample and a sample of the pupil's work in the form of a composition and a drawing. The stimulus material had actually been carefully selected on the basis of previous assessments and combined to represent eight fictitious pupils showing all possible combinations of "good" and "bad" ratings for the three types of information. Subjects rated these hypothetical boys on six 7-point scales labelled: intelligent, good student, privileged, enthusiastic, self-confident, gentle. The results showed that "the boys with good voices were *always* evaluated significantly more favourably than those with poor voices. Not only were they judged to be more intelligent, more privileged, and better students, but they were also seen as being more enthusiastic, self-confident and gentle." There were interesting statistical interactions between voice and the other variables. The authors conclude that "speech style was an important cue to the teachers in their evaluations of students. Even when combined with other cues, its effect did not diminish."

Triandis, Loh and Levin (1966) also conducted an experiment which showed linguistic noncontent cues to be more influential in evaluation than visual ones. This time the visual cues were those of skin colour and dress. Subjects were shown photographs and played taperecordings of stimulus persons' comments about Civil Rights. Four variables were employed in the design: race (Negro/White); beliefs expressed (pro/anti Civil Rights); dress (suit/overalls); and voice (good/poor grammar). All four variables produced strong effects on the subjects' ratings of the stimulus persons but the grammatical variable accounted for over 70% of the variance on all scales.

Other workers who have shown the relative strength of linguistic noncontent cues over visual attributes in personality assessment are Dusenbury and Knower (1938) and Ellis (1964).

However, it seems from the results of a study by Hart and Brown (1974) that the question of the relative contribution of vocal qualities and verbal content to interpersonal judgements is dependent upon which dimension of judgements is involved. In their research, these workers used both spontaneous utterances by speakers and recitations of standard passages in order to separate the effects of verbal and vocal qualities upon the ratings given by judges. Various measures of inter-judge agreement and variance in ratings were used as indices of the amount of information transmitted. It was found that speech content contained more information than vocal qualities about speakers' "benevolence" (e.g. kindness, tolerance), while vocal qualities were found to provide more information than content for judgements on factors relating to "social attractiveness" (e.g. likeability, sociability) and "competence" (e.g. intelligence, confidence).

Some interesting experiments have recently been conducted at Brigham Young University on the effect of an individual's rate of speaking upon impression formation. Brown, Strong and Rencher (1973) used mechanically altered voices to study the separate effects of intonation and speech rate on interpersonal judgement, and in a later study, Brown, Strong, Rencher and Smith (1974) evaluated the interactions between rate, pitch and intonation in this respect. Both investigations revealed rate to be a better predictor of personality ratings than either of the other two. It was found that increasing the rate of a given speaker caused judges to mark him less favourably on traits of benevolence (e.g. kindness, tolerance), while decreasing speech rate resulted in less favourable ratings on traits of competence (e.g. intelligence, confidence). These experiments used only a narrow range of different speech rates and the voices were those of a rather homogeneous group of students and professors. The relationship between speech rate and competence evaluation appeared to be non-linear in that whereas a decrease in rate (as compared with the speaker's normal speed) led to a decrease in competence ratings, a corresponding increase in rate did not raise the ratings of competence. Smith, Brown, Strong and Rencher (1975) therefore set out to test the effects of manipulating nine levels of rate, using the voices of six subjects representing various social and educational backgrounds. It was found with this more diverse group of voices and wider range of rates that an increase in rate does indeed cause an increase in competence ratings as well as a decrease in benevolence ratings. Decreased rate was again found to decrease competence ratings, but this time it was also found to decrease benevolence ratings. Ratings of competence therefore appear to increase with speech rate in a monotonic, if not linear, fashion. Ratings of benevolence have an inverted-U relationship with speech rate with the highest benevolence ratings coinciding with the middle values of rate.

Other studies have shown that speakers who are hesitant (Lay and Burron, 1968) or whose speech contains a relatively high number of speech nonfluencies (such as repetitions and vocalized pauses) are perceived less favourably, particularly with regard to competence, than more fluent speakers (Miller and Hewgill, 1964; Sereno and Hawkins, 1967; McCroskey and Mehrley, 1969).

Pearce and Conklin (1971) had a speaker present a message on tape first in a "conversational" mode and then in a "dynamic" mode. The differences between these delivery patterns were characterized by degree rather than kind: conversational delivery involved a relatively smaller range of inflection, a greater consistency of rate and pitch, less volume and generally lower pitch levels than did dynamic delivery. Each style was designed to represent "good" but different delivery techniques comparable to those used by many speakers. It was found that when the speaker used the conversational style, he was evaluated by judges as more honest and person-oriented, whereas when he used dynamic delivery, he was rated as more tough minded, task-oriented, self-assured and assertive.

Addington (1968) has found that idiosyncratic characteristics of the voice, such as thinness, flatness, nasality, tenseness, throatiness and orotundity evoke stereotypes of personality. For instance, females who speak with a "breathy" voice are judged by listeners as feminine, pretty and effervescent. Vocal "thinness" is perceived as an indication of social, physical and mental immaturity. Orotundity is associated with heartiness and artistic inclination. A nasal voice implies a wide range of socially undesirable characteristics.[3]

Some indication as to which linguistic cues are more salient than others can be inferred from the findings of research by d'Anglejan and Tucker (1973). In their study, French-Canadian students, teachers and workers from three regions in Quebec were asked to indicate how their own speech style differed from the best form of French in Quebec. All the subject groups rated pronunciation and vocabulary as the most important sources of difference; grammar was rated least different by all groups. These subjects also reckoned that the form of French spoken in Quebec needed improvement and so they were asked which specific features of Quebec French were the "weakest". As in the previous

3. See also Addington (1971).

question, all subjects chose vocabulary and pronunciation most frequently; indeed the workers in all locations chose *pronunciation* more
frequently than vocabulary. Grammar emerged in third place followed
by intonation. Their findings were consistent with those of Chiasson-
Lavoie and Laberge (1971) on Montreal subjects: these workers found
that people are less conscious of deviant grammatical features than they
are of the phonological characteristics of their speech.

We have suggested that our impressions of others can very often be
based upon the characteristics of their speech style. The main focus of
attention in this book will be upon how social evaluation is affected by
pronunciation, accent, dialect and language usage. The need to distinguish operationally between these various linguistic levels has led to
much controversy, especially with regard to the distinction between
language and dialect (e.g. Haugen, 1966; Agard, 1971). The work of
Wolff (1959) in Africa has shown that one may use objective linguistic
criteria to justify the conclusion that two speech styles are dialects of the
same language rather than two separate languages, but find that this
decision does not correspond with the way the speakers themselves perceive the relationship between the two speech styles. Consider the
following quotation:

> The Okpe-Isoko dialects are rather divergent from the rest of Urhobo, but
> until recently there was a general agreement that mutual intelligibility
> was relatively high among all Urhobo dialects. Lately, however, speakers
> of Isoko have been claiming that their language is different from the rest
> of Urhobo, and that intelligibility between Urhobo and Isoko is not
> sufficient for normal linguistic communication. This claim has coincided
> with Isoko demands for greater political autonomy and ethnic self-
> sufficiency. Surprisingly enough, the speakers of the Okpe dialects—
> almost identical with Isoko—continue to consider themselves ethnically
> part of the Urhobo area and claim mutual intelligibility with the majority
> of Urhobo dialects. (Wolff, loc. cit.)

From this it seems that the distinction between language and dialect is
a "matter of degree" and partly subjective and contingent upon a
desire for social unity or separation. We shall endeavour in this book
to distinguish between language and dialect on the basis of both objective criteria and consensus opinion within the particular cultural context concerned.

The distinction between dialect and accent has given rise to less controversy. Nevertheless, as we shall see, social scientists in this field have
often been imprecise in their application of these terms. The term

"dialect" usually implies variation from a standard code at most levels of linguistic analysis, whereas "accent" implies a particular manner of pronunciation, intonation and rhythm, with the grammatical, syntactical and lexical levels remaining more or less consistent with the standard. Wells (1970) considers that an accent might be defined as "the phonetic aspect of a dialect or indeed a particular phonetic realization of Standard . . . interpreting the term 'phonetic' in its widest sense".

The experimental procedure which is frequently used in order to elicit people's evaluative reactions to various speech-styles, accents, dialects, and languages is known as the "matched-guise technique". The procedure is as follows. Judges are told that they are to hear the voices of different speakers, usually reading the same passage of "neutral" verbal material, and are asked to evaluate the speakers on a rating scale or bipolar adjective scale. The speech is actually produced by one person using realistic guises of different languages or speech characteristics. In his review of work involving this technique, Lambert (1967) suggests that it is "particularly valuable as a measure of group biases in evaluative reactions". He thinks that the method reveals more about listeners' feelings towards outgroups than can be found by direct attitude questionnaires. The vocal stereotypes which emerge often have "very good reliability in the sense that essentially the same profile of traits for a particular group appear when different samples of judges drawn from a particular population are used" (loc. cit.).

The main advantage of the matched-guise technique is that in experiments concerned with distinct language styles, such as different accents, it goes some way towards eliminating the effects of the more idiosyncratic variations in speech discussed above. The effects of these individual differences are interesting in themselves but would tend to confound the results in studies designed to elicit evaluative reactions to group differences.

In the following chapters we shall first examine and discuss research relating to the effects of speech characteristics upon listeners' evaluations of the speaker and then consider the ways in which a person's speech varies according to the circumstances in which he finds himself. Finally we shall discuss a tentative theoretical model based upon the proposition that the function of speech changes is in many cases to control the way in which the speaker is perceived by others.

The work to be discussed comes from many different branches of the social sciences and is reported in a wide variety of scientific journals.

Workers in the fields of education, sociology, social anthropology, psychology and linguistics have all made contributions.

Robinson (1972) has said of this area of research: "At the present time it is fair to say that we have no adequate theoretical framework or paradigm within which work is being carried on" and "we are still at the stage of finding out what variables are relevant and are collecting this information in a relatively haphazard way". This remains very largely true, but we hope this book may make some contribution to the formulation of descriptive laws which, as Robinson says, "will constitute a challenge that will eventually lead to explanations and theories".

# 2

# Speech Style and Perceived Status (I): Some Conceptual Distinctions

Fishman (1970) stresses that language "is not merely a *carrier* of content, whether latent or manifest. Language itself *is* content, a referent for loyalties and animosities, an indicator of social statuses and personal relationships, a marker of situations and topics as well as of the societal goals and the large-scale value-laden arenas of interaction that typify every speech community." In this and the succeeding chapter, we shall limit ourselves to a consideration of speech as a reflection of social status.

## The standardization process

Stewart (1968) claims that language undergoes, in the history of many cultures, a process of "standardization". This he defines as "the codification and acceptance within a community of users of a formal set of norms defining 'correct' usage", and it usually finds expression in a so-called "standard" dialect or accent. Indeed, many present-day developing nations in Africa and in South-East Asia have recently been considering the setting up of standard languages or dialects in order to facilitate communications between speakers of the numerous, mutually unintelligible languages and dialects spoken by those who reside within their borders. Moreover, such a national code can often serve as a symbol of national identity when it is a language or speech style indigenous to that culture (Fishman, 1969; 1972).[1] Interestingly enough,

1. For a detailed account of a single case, see the discussion by Omar (1971) of the standardization of Malay.

Jones (1973) has provided empirical evidence which suggests that countries which have undergone a linguistic standardization process advance economically at a much faster rate than those which have not. Commenting upon this relationship Jones says: "It does seem eminently reasonable that commonality of language among peoples would facilitate the kinds of behaviour required to improve economic and social conditions in developing countries."

But let us concentrate on dialects that have already been established as prestige forms of their languages for generations now, such as Parisian French or Standard British English. Why is it that one dialect achieves superiority over other dialects in that language, not only in status but often in terms of aesthetic quality as well? Giles, Bourhis and Davies (1975), concentrating on the phonic levels, suggest two possible answers to this question by reference to "inherent value" and "imposed norm" hypotheses.

The inherent value hypothesis claims that a dialect or accent is elevated to its prestige position owing to the fact that it is inherently the most pleasing form of that language. For instance, Wyld (1934) has commented on the inherent aesthetic quality of the Standard British accent, Received Pronunciation (RP), in the following manner:

> If it were possible to compare systematically every vowel sound in Received Standard with the corresponding sound in a number of provincial and other dialects, assuming that a comparison could be made, as is only fair, between speakers who possessed equal qualities of voice, and the knowledge how to use it, I believe no unbiased listener would hesitate in preferring Received Standard as the most pleasing and sonorous form, and the best suited to be the medium of poetry and oratory.

It has been shown in Britain (Giles, 1970)[2] that people are able to assign accents to positions along a continuum of pleasantness-unpleasantness, with the nonstandard forms in this respect inferior to the standard. The inherent value hypothesis appears to be closely related to the "deficit" theory of nonstandard speech usage. Advocates of this latter view (e.g. Deutsch, 1967; Hunt, 1964), which is mainly concerned with grammatical aspects of language, have argued that nonstandard dialects are substandard forms of the prestige variety. They suggest that a nonstandard dialect contains many irregularities and is limited in its expressive power. These arguments suggest, then, that a

2. See also Stanley (1971) who has considered the aesthetic aspects of a West Texan dialect.

standard dialect has attained its prestige over other varieties because it is objectively the most aesthetically pleasing and linguistically sophisticated form of that language.

The imposed norm hypothesis, on the other hand, suggests that the prestige speech style has gained acceptance as the most pleasing form simply because of cultural norms. It claims that a standard code attains its prestige from the status of the social group which happened by chance to speak in this manner. We may consider as an example of this the Received Pronunciation of English—sometimes popularly referred to as "B.B.C. English". This pronunciation derives from a form which was originally characteristic of the south-east of England (and, in particular, London) and which acquired prestige some time in the Middle Ages. Its ascendency over other regional forms has been attributed to its use in commerce and politics, and the presence of the Royal Court in the capital. Indeed, many other standard varieties of languages (e.g. Parisian French) are likely to have gained their eminence simply through being codes associated with the cultural and political centres of the states concerned.[3] As Fishman (1970) points out, the formal acceptance of such a standard variety of a language is usually advanced by such agencies as the government, the educational system and the mass media. Therefore, because of social pressures upon people to emulate the standard, it has come to be regarded as the superior form on many dimensions including the aesthetic. According to this argument, the emergence of a particular variety of speech or language as "standard" is somewhat arbitrary and does not necessarily indicate qualitative superiority over other forms. Had the Courts of England and France been situated in Liverpool and Marseilles rather than London and Paris, then in all probability it would have been the pronunciation

---

3. An unusual standardization process appears to be operating in Italy according to Galli de' Paratesi (1974). In this context, the most likely poles of standardization in the sense considered above are thought to be Rome, because of its political role as a capital, or Florence because of its traditional cultural prestige and because the written language on which the normative pronunciation is based is of Florentine origin. It appears, however, that the most accepted variety is that spoken in Milan—the *industrial* centre of Italy. It will be interesting to see whether, and by what social processes, the speech styles associated with technological and industrial centres come to assume greater prestige than those of the cultural centres of states. See Labov (1965) for a discussion of the mechanisms of linguistic change, Trudgill (1974) for a model concerned with the geographical diffusion of linguistic innovations, and Bender, Cooper and Ferguson (1972) for a discussion of language spread.

and intonation patterns peculiar to these areas that would have attained pre-eminence.

The imposed norm hypothesis would seem to be linked theoretically to the "difference" view of speech usage. Advocates of this position (e.g. Baratz, 1970; Stewart, 1970) would suggest that a nonstandard dialect is not at all "substandard" but is merely a different variety of the language, having its own complex and equally rich rule system. Arguments of this kind, then, suggest that a standard dialect has attained its prestige over other varieties on the basis of a cultural "accident" and that it is in fact no more aesthetically pleasing or linguistically sophisticated than nonstandard varieties of that language.

Giles, Bourhis and Davies (loc. cit.) attempted to test the relative merits of the inherent value and imposed norm hypotheses. More specifically, they were interested in determining whether people who had virtually no knowledge of the French language would be able to differentiate the various forms of French spoken in Quebec on aesthetic and prestige dimensions. In this cultural context, speakers of European-style French are perceived by French Canadians to be more intelligent, ambitious and likeable but less tough than speakers of their own Canadian-style French (d'Anglejan and Tucker, 1973). Moreover, French Canadians regard their dialects of French to be aesthetically less pleasing than the European model. However, when these French dialects, spoken by the same tridialectal speaker, were played to people in Wales who were totally unfamiliar with that language, subjects were unable to differentiate between the speech varieties on aesthetic grounds. Furthermore, they did not attribute any more prestige or favourable personality characteristics to the European-style speakers than to the Canadian French speakers. The authors suggest that these results support an imposed norm hypothesis since it appeared that the prestige speech style was not perceived any more favourably than the (culturally-determined) nonstandard varieties. Giles *et al.* claim that the social implications of this finding should "provide nonstandard dialect users with a more positive self-image and identity and a feeling that their mode of communication is undeniably as pleasant and as rich as the more prestigious variety".

In a follow-up study using the same method, Giles, Bourhis, Trudgill and Lewis (1974) asked British undergraduates to evaluate, amongst other speech samples, two forms of Greek (the Athenian and Cretan dialects) which were in fact spoken by the same bidialectal, female speaker using the matched-guise technique. The Athenian dialect is the prestige form of the Greek language, possessing considerable advantages over other varieties within that language community in terms of perceived pleasantness. From informal questioning of a number of Greek informants, it was ascertained that speakers of the Cretan dialect are steretyped as less intelligent and less sophisticated but more amusing and tough than speakers of the Athenian dialect. Once again, listeners who had absolutely no knowledge of Greek were unable to differentiate between the two varieties on aesthetic, prestige and personality trait scales, and it was considered that this lent further support to the imposed norm hypothesis. These workers state:

> Educationally, teachers and others should be encouraged to recognize their (apparently aesthetically based) attitudes to children's accents for what they are, and to allow for this factor in their evaluation of children with low status linguistic varieties. It suggests too, that arguments in favour of changing ("improving") children's accents cannot be legitimately couched in aesthetic terms.

Nevertheless, despite the fact that support for the imposed norm hypothesis has been gained from two studies using entirely different language varieties, it may be premature to suggest unconditionally that all prestige speech styles acquire their status and favourable aesthetic ratings by means of cultural norms. Further studies, perhaps using non-European languages, with many more bidialectal stimulus speakers, should be conducted before any such conclusion can be confidently drawn.

Indeed, some recent research by Brown, Strong and Rencher (1975) could be interpreted as providing evidence against the imposed norm hypothesis, or as suggesting that both the imposed norm and inherent value hypotheses may be necessary. Brown et al. compiled a tape of French Canadian speakers from a variety of social class backgrounds reciting a standard passage of prose. He found that not only could other French Canadians broadly differentiate between the speakers on tape on the basis of social class, but so too could Anglo-American students who had no knowledge of the French language. (In addition, he found that his working class speakers were judged by French Canadian listeners to be "hoarse" and "breathy" and lacking in both "articulation" and "intonation variety". We must note these labels particularly since it is known that paralinguistic features such as voice quality may relate to social class (Laver, 1968). As pejorative labels, however, they may be well explicable in terms of the imposed norm hypothesis.)

The important point is that Americans with no knowledge of French correctly assigned French speakers to their social background. Certainly this research needs to be replicated with stimulus speakers using languages less familiar to American ears than French, but we still have to attempt to explain why Americans were able to do this. First, since the matched-guise technique used in the experiments by Giles and others was not employed, there may have been class-related differences in recitation skills. Second, it could simply have been that there were, as was suggested above, perceptible differences in voice quality. This requires careful consideration, however. There are two main determinants of voice quality. One is the "anatomical and physiological foundation of a speaker's vocal equipment" (Laver, loc. cit.). If there were differences of this type amongst Brown's speakers, and if it so happened coincidentally that his working class speakers were born with more unpleasant voices than the others, this could explain the results. This possibility could be checked by replications of the experiment with other speakers. The second component of voice quality can be called "setting". Settings are long-term muscular adjustments of the vocal tract, which are acquired, usually by social imitation, and are unconsciously and habitually maintained. Thus, whereas the first component of voice quality is constitutional, settings are *learned*. Many male Americans, for example, appear to have deeper voices than male British speakers. This, however, is due, not to constitutional physiology, but to the fact that they have learned to use a lower part of their possible pitch range than most British men. It is a cultural, not a strictly physical phenomenon.[4] It might well be therefore that there is a relation between setting and social class in Canadian French and that the Americans reacted to this. Even if this were the case however, it does not necessarily imply support for an inherent value interpretation, since there may happen to be a relationship between the same paralinguistic features and social class in some varieties of American English —which would lead American listeners to react as they did in the experiment of Brown *et al*. We cannot assume that certain types of voice quality are universally perceived as pleasant or unpleasant, across cultures or across languages. Indeed, there is some evidence to the contrary. Nasalization, for example, is a component of voice quality commonly associated with many "unpleasant" Australian accents—but it is also a feature of most "nice" RP speakers. Similarly, pharyngealization is a

4. See also Sachs, Lieberman and Erickson (1973).

component of working class Norwich voice quality, which middle class Norwich people describe as very unpleasant (Trudgill, 1974a) but it is also a feature of some high status Arabic and German accents (Honikman, 1964). We also need to be careful about the cross-cultural implications of labels such as "breathy", since a "breathy voice" has different implications in different languages (Catford, 1964), and it is not necessarily related to sociological parameters. Clearly more research needs to be done in this area. In particular it would be instructive to have the reactions of listeners with no knowledge of English to different varieties of this language. But the work of Brown *et al.* does suggest that there may be a need in studies of this type to distinguish nonstandard accents from voice qualities which may be associated with them.

This empirical work on the cultural determinants of prestige speech styles seems to be related to cross-cultural research on the social psychology of aesthetics.[5] People across a number of societies who are actively engaged in creative pursuits such as pottery, abstract painting and music, and who are apparently isolated from each other's cultural norms, agree to a remarkable degree as regards the aesthetic quality of certain art forms. This is particularly evident when the works of art are structured in a cognitively simple manner. On the other hand, these studies also show little, if any, agreement cross-culturally between *non*-experts on the qualities of art forms. Therefore, it may be worthwhile to investigate whether the imposed norm hypothesis is still supported when linguistic experts (e.g. phoneticians, speech therapists) are asked to evaluate varieties of a language totally unfamiliar to them.

## Two types of standard speech styles

We shall distinguish very broadly between two functionally different types of standard language varieties: context-related and class-related standards. A *context-related* standard is the style of speech considered appropriate in certain socially-definable situations, usually the more formal and public, and can usually be found to some degree spoken by all social groups in that culture. A *class-related* standard can be defined as a style of speech regarded as the most prestigious variant of the language in a given culture, largely irrespective of context, and characteristic of one social group, usually the highest in socio-economic status.

5. See Ford, Prothro and Child (1966); Iwao and Child (1966); Francès and Tamba (1973).

CONTEXT-RELATED STANDARDS

A context-related "standard" often appears in cultures where speakers have two or more varieties of the same language at their disposal. Cultural norms prescribe the use of a standard variety in formal, public situations and "nonstandard" varieties appear in less formal contexts. John Gumperz, a social anthropologist, reports the occurrence of this sociolinguistic phenomenon among various societies in South-East Asia[6] and Northern Norway, and has tried to establish the implicit rules underlying the elicitation of these different codes (Gumperz, 1958; 1964; 1964a; 1964b). He distinguishes between the *vernacular*— the speech used within the home and with peers—and the *superposed* (or "standard") variety—the norm in other, more formal, situations. A special type of vernacular-superposed paradigm is that described by Ferguson (1959) as "diglossia". Here the standard dialect is taught in schools and is regarded as in some sense false since it is not expected that the children will ever use it as a medium for ordinary conversation. It is taught only for written purposes and for formal occasions such as speeches and ritual performance. This phenomenon is common in many Arab states, Greece and amongst speakers of the Haitian Creole languages and Swiss German. The standard is often referred to as the *High* dialect and the vernacular as the *Low* dialect. Geertz (1963) and Tanner (1967) report an apparently unique form of diglossia (which perhaps should be called "triglossia") in Java where the rules of linguistic etiquette require shifts between High Javanese, Low Javanese and the local vernacular. It can be seen that a context-related standard does not imply that its speakers are a specially privileged group socio-economically, neither does its production have connotations of high social status. It is simply the code thought more appropriate than its rivals for the more public kind of communication.

In cultures where two or more distinct languages are available (rather than dialects of the same language) one of them may emerge as "standard". For instance, Rubin (1962) has shown that the use of two languages in Paraguay—Spanish and Guarani—is determined by cultural norms and she gives the example of a couple speaking Spanish whilst courting but switching to Guarani after the marriage ceremony. A similar pattern of culturally-prescribed verbal sex-roles is reflected in

6. For a discussion of some sociolinguistic aspects of interlingual communication in India, see Apte (1970); for a discussion of linguistic variation in caste dialects, see Ramanujan (1967) and Ullrich (1971).

a study by Sechrest, Flores and Arellano (1968) in the Philippines. It was found on a college campus that mixed-sex couples were more likely than same-sex pairs to be found speaking English. The Philippine culture is one which strictly controls the free expression of emotionally-toned involvement between boy and girl in public. The local language (Tagalog) is used as the mode of intimate communication, whereas English is regarded as the "voice of intellect", and thus as more desirable as a mode of expression for mixed-sex interactions.

In a setting such as Israel or the United States of America, where there is a large immigrant population, the use of a standard mode of communication may be governed by powerful context-related norms. For the immigrant in this situation, the standard language would be that of the majority culture (which, for him, in most cases would be a second language) whereas his native language would be regarded as the nonstandard variety (see Kimple, Cooper and Fishman, 1969). Again the norms of the society at large require the use of the standard tongue in intergroup and formal, public contexts whilst the minority language is demanded by certain domestic and within-group situations. Change of context involves appropriate code-switching. The rules underlying the use of English amongst Spanish and Swedish immigrants in the United States have been studied by Barker (1947) and Hasselmo (1951) and those governing the use of Hebrew in Israel by Herman (1961).

Against this background of generally-accepted implicit rules governing the use of languages and dialects, some interesting examples of deviation from the norms may be seen. Fishman et al. (1966) have shown, in the case of immigrant communities in the United States, that some bilingual members of minority groups may possess so strong an emotional attachment to their native language that they may refrain from code-switching in social situations which, according to the "rules", demand the use of the standard code. Gumperz (1964a) has given an example of a similar "dialect-loyalty" with regard to the Hemnes settlement of northern Norway. People in this community refuse to conform to the norm which demands that they should use the standard code (Bokmål) outside the confines of the home. They insist on using the local dialect (Ranamål), on the grounds that they are "not ashamed of their origin". Fishman (1969) comments on the fact that there are urban-rural differences in the extent of code-loyalty.[7]

7. For discussions of the sociolinguistic correlates of urbanization and modernization, see Cadora (1970), Cooper and Horvath (1973) and Timm (1973).

The intelligentsia and middle class elements, both of which are almost exclusively urban, have frequently been the prime movers of language maintenance in those societies which possess both urban and rural populations. Indeed, urban groups have been the prime movers, organizers or mobilizers more generally, that is in connection with other language behaviour and behaviour toward language. Thus, whereas small rural groups have been more successful in establishing relatively self-contained communities which reveal language maintenance through preservation of traditional interaction patterns and social structure, urban groups, exposed to interaction in more fragmented and specialized networks, may reveal more conscious organized and novel attempts to preserve or revise or change their traditional language. The urban environment does facilitate change.

Miller (1924), emphasising social class differences in code-maintenance, claimed that "when languages have given way ... it has been the intellectual class that has yielded while the simple, uneducated class has clung to its language". Fishman and Hofman (1964) also suggest, from several studies of immigrants in the United States, that the lower classes have been more "language-loyal" than middle-class immigrants.

The connection between language-loyalty and group-loyalty is not always as close as one might suppose, for, as Hymes (1962) comments, "some languages do not enjoy the status of a symbol crucial to group identity". An example of this particular relationship can be illustrated with respect to the Italian Swiss who, according to Weinreich (1963) "cultivate the fullest loyalty to their language without aspiring to such nationalistic goals as political independence". The converse of this can be observed in many new, developing and highly nationalistic African states. Brosnaham (1963), Spencer (1963) and Fishman (1969) have reported that although many newly-formed African countries may be characterized by strong drives towards political and economic nationhood, language-loyalty is low. The relationship between code and group loyalty is thus seen to be a very complex one.

The choice of a standard or nonstandard language or dialect has thus far been considered within the framework of culturally-prescribed norms of verbal behaviour for different social situations. This is closely related to what Gumperz calls "transactional code-switching" (Gumperz, 1964a). He characterizes transactional situations as those concerned with socially defined goals. These situations would include religious services, job interviews and so on. He claims that "participants in such interactions in a sense suspend their individuality in order to act out the rights and obligations of relevant statuses. Hence their linguistic and other modes of behaviour must be predictable from the social definition of these statuses".

Herman (1961) considers factors associated with language choice in transactional situations in multilingual societies under three main headings: the background situation, the personal needs system of the speaker and the immediate situation. Unfortunately, these categories are not entirely distinct.

"Background situation" seems in Herman's account to refer to the speaker's acceptance or rejection of the culturally-prescribed, verbal role behaviours implicit in specific social situations. If, for example, the speaker accepts the prevailing norms of verbal usage and the patterns of social identification they imply, he will adopt the "appropriate" code for a particular situation, regardless of his relative language or dialect fluency. On the other hand, his emotional involvement with a particular code (code-loyalty) may cause him to use it in defiance of culturally-prescribed norms. It is also conceivable that newly-acquired group affiliations may require loyalty to a code in which he is not very proficient. Thus the "background situation" may be regarded basically as the speaker's attitude (positive or negative) towards the cultural norms of verbal usage.

In relatively private settings, or situations provoking tension or frustration, the "personal needs system" will assume salience. Then, irrespective of the background situation (or attitude towards appropriate verbal usage), the speaker will select the code which satisfies his emotional needs for immediate and fluent expression. Often, in these circumstances, the bilingual or bidialectal person needs, in order to express himself adequately, to select a code in which he is not only most fluent but also is best able to "be himself".

Conditions under which the "immediate situation" might assume greater salience than background situation and personal needs would be when:

(i) The speaker is unconcerned about both culturally-prescribed verbal usage and the demands of code-loyalty.

(ii) Well-established patterns of verbal behaviour characterize a relationship.

(iii) The behaviour is task-oriented.

The ambiguity in Herman's three categories can be seen when it is considered that the background situation may include facets of the other two categories. For instance, adapting to the prevailing verbal norms of a culture or to a particular reference group (as in code-loyalty) both involve the personal needs of the speaker in terms of desires for social identification with a particular group. Similarly, the acceptance of these cultural norms of behaviour also involves the speaker complying with the demands of the immediate situation. Hunt (1967) gives concrete examples of most of Herman's categories from data obtained in the multilingual setting of the Philippines but comments:

> Herman would hardly claim that [his] paper is the final word on this topic, but it does have the merit of focussing and bringing to conscious analysis at least some of the elements involved in selecting a medium of communication in a multilanguage setting.

This conceptualization of code choice, then, revolves around a consideration of the speaker's socio-verbal attitudes and motives. However, Ervin-Tripp (1964) and Hymes (1967) attempt to describe speech change by using a *taxonomic* approach. In other words, they are content merely to list factors (e.g. topic, setting and participant) which have been found to influence a speaker's choice of a language variety. They do not offer an explanatory account. Unfortunately, this sort of conceptual framework cannot readily include a consideration of the speaker's motivational state, which would seem to be fundamental in determining conscious, transactional decisions. The structure of Herman's theoretical framework, despite its inadequacies, would seem potentially more useful as a starting point in explaining a speaker's choice, in a given context, of a standard or nonstandard code.

While it is deemed necessary to construct a model to describe and (more hopefully) explain the lack of adherence to culturally-prescribed norms for the use of the context-related standard language variety, it is dubious and perhaps even a little simpleminded to suppose that pure and mutually exclusive class- and context-related standard paradigms actually exist. Let us consider for a moment the notion of relative language or dialect fluency introduced by Herman. In a situation such as described by Gumperz in the context of certain Indian societies, individuals, almost irrespective of their social position, are more or less balanced bidialectals: their communicational efficiency is almost equal in standard and nonstandard usage. In the absence of empirical evidence we may suppose that the low status person's use of the standard dialect has little if any social class significance and is equivalent to the use of this variety by a high status person. However, in the case of immigrant groups in, say, the United States or Britain, the situation is somewhat different. Admittedly, the majority of these people are able to switch successfully to English in the "correct" setting and suffer no social sanctions on this count, yet the medium through which they attempt to express the appropriate "standard" is often *"nonstandard"*. In other words, the accent (or even dialect) with which an immigrant speaks the standard language could easily be perceived as "foreign" and characteristic of an outgroup thereby being less prestigious than native usage. Thus, a context-related paradigm could in certain circumstances be confounded with a more consequential, underlying *class*-related structure.

## CLASS-RELATED STANDARDS

We have discussed context-related standard speech in terms of generally accepted norms as to what is "correct" usage in particular social situations. Class-related standard speech, on the other hand, occurs where a particular language variety is generally accepted as the most socially-desirable, regardless of context. Standard speech, in this sense, can usually be equated with that which is characteristic of those at the highest socioeconomic level of a society. Argyle (1967) says, with regard to British speech, that "regional accent is one of the main clues to social class" implying that a regional accent tends to label the speaker as working class. Similar stereotypes probably exist in other cultures, yet it would be extremely surprising to find in any of them a one-to-one relationship between standard language use and social class. Because of social mobility, nonstandard speech is often found amongst people quite high in socioeconomic status. Likewise some "down-and-outs" exhibit speech characteristics usually associated with the more successful levels of society.

The distinction between standard and nonstandard speech is not always clearcut either. This is particularly true of dialects and accents. For instance, speakers in Britain may be placed on a continuum with respect to accent in terms of the degree to which they exhibit the characteristics of RP (Received Pronunciation) or exhibit various degrees of "broadness" of regional accent. This accent continuum is roughly correlated with judgements of social status such that the more a speaker deviates from the standard accent (RP) the lower will be the social prestige attributed to him.

Just as context-related standards of speech are found to be operative in multilingual societies so too are status-related standards. One language may be considered generally more "correct" or socially desirable than other available languages. This differentiation may have its root in somewhat arbitrary historical factors or may occur for current political reasons. Let us again consider the Philippines. Although English is regarded as a context-related standard by people in the Islands, Tagalog has been accorded a privileged position among the various native languages. Many other languages have more speakers than Tagalog has, but this particular language is associated with a politically and economically powerful group and has high prestige for this reason. Similarly in Quebec, English has become the prestige form through the influence of a powerful minority group.

Herman (loc. cit.) has provided data suggesting that in Israel the various languages can be considered hierarchically in terms of social prestige. Hebrew, besides being the context-related standard, is probably the status-related standard as well. Herman presented 84 Hebrew-speaking students with a list of the major languages spoken in Israel and asked them to indicate beside each language whether it had "very high", "high", "medium", "low" or "very low" prestige in their eyes. The order which emerged was as follows: (1) Hebrew, (2) English, (3) French, (4) Russian, (5) German, (6) Arabic, (7) Spanish, (8) Yiddish, (9) Polish, (10) Ladino and Hungarian, (12) Turkish, (13) Roumanian, (14) Persian. When these students were asked in similar terms how they thought these languages would be rated by the public, the rank order correlation between their own assessments and those which they attributed to the public was +0·89. The same question concerning the "prestige of the languages in your own eyes" was given to a group of 56 nurses attending a country-wide seminar, and the rank order correlation between this group's responses and those of the students was +0·93. The students were also presented with a list of settlers from various countries (groups using the languages on the previous list) and were asked to rate their prestige. A rank order correlation of +0·84 was found between prestige of the languages and prestige of settler groups speaking these languages.

A similar hierarchical structure will be shown to exist with regard to the prestige attributed to nonstandard *accents* in Britain. Research conducted on standard accent usage has been concentrated around three cultures—Britain, the United States of America and French Canada, and we shall discuss each of these unique situations in turn. First, however, it is necessary to make yet another reservation about our definitions. Earlier we pointed out that context-related standards could also be status-based in some instances. Now it is important to stress that the prestige of a status-related standard cannot be entirely free of context. For instance, if a large company's managing director informally appeals to some of his factory workers about greater productivity without increased bonuses, he is unlikely to help his cause by distancing himself from them by means of standard language use. Admittedly neither is he likely to win their sympathy by some phoney identification with them through nonstandard usage. Nevertheless, the point remains that in certain social situations, not only can standard accent usage have no influence at all but it can be thoroughly disadvantageous. (We shall discuss the *persuasive* power and behavioural consequences of standard usage in Chapter 6.) Similarly, speakers of White American "network-style" English are unlikely to create a favourable impression amongst adherents of the Black Power movement nor would cultured European French receive much sympathy at a Free Quebec rally. Indeed, it is worthwhile bearing in mind Weinreich's (1963) recommendation that "as a technical term ... 'prestige' had better be restricted to a language's [and accent's] value in social advancement, or dispensed with altogether as too imprecise". Clearly, in the types of situation outlined above, the social advancement of a standard speaker in these contexts would be severely limited. With this restriction of our definition about class-related standards borne in mind, let us now proceed in the next chapter to consider the three accent situations mentioned.

# 3

# Speech Style and Perceived Status (II): Empirical Studies

We shall discuss the empirical studies concerning the relationship between speech styles and perceived social status in the three cultural contexts of Britain, the United States of America and French Canada separately.

## Britain

The English are regarded as being particularly sensitive to variations in the pronunciation of their language. As Spencer (1958) remarked, "it is apparent to any careful observer of the English scene that many pronunciation differences are socially highly significant, and appear to be related in some way to the English class structure". Moreover, according to Nicolson (1955) this extreme sensitivity is not paralleled in any other country or even in other parts of the English-speaking world. "One can detect" he says "by the accent of Frenchmen and Germans from what provinces they originate, but not to what social class they belong; in England, the several layers of society are as it were labelled by intonation". A standard British accent has never been imposed officially but appears to command fairly general acceptance. A consideration of the origins and present nature of this unofficial standard may help to explain some of the controversies and emotions it arouses and also provide a frame of reference for the series of inquiries to be presented later.

Gimson (1962) has stated that the conventions of grammatical forms and constructions as well as the greater part of the vocabulary have, for a long time, been accepted and adhered to by the majority of speakers at any given time, as has also the spelling of English. But there has always existed a greater diversity in the spoken realizations of the language in terms of the sounds used in different parts of the country. Also, since the sounds of the language are constantly in process of change, there have always been at any one time disparities between the speech sounds of the younger and older generations; the "advanced speech" of the young is traditionally characterized by old people as slovenly and debased. When communications between regions were poor, the speech of various communities did not develop at the same rate nor necessarily in the same way. Moreover, different parts of the country were exposed to different external influences (e.g. foreign invasion) which probably affected the phonetic evolution of the language. English therefore has always had its regional pronunciations for basically geographical and historical reasons. Nevertheless, there has existed in Britain, especially since mediaeval times, the notion that one kind of pronunciation of English is preferable socially to others; one regional accent began to acquire social prestige. For reasons of politics, commerce and the presence of the Court it was to the pronunciation of the south-east of England, and more particularly to that of the London region that this prestige was attached.

In 1569, the early phonetician, John Hart, noted that it was in the Court and London that "the flower of the English tongue is used ... Though some would say it were not so, reason would we should grant no less: for that unto these two places, do daily resort from all towns and countries, of the best of all professions". (Quoted by Gimson, 1962.) Puttenham, in his "The Arte of Englishe Poesie" (1589) recommended as the best type of English "the usual speach of the Court, and that of London and the shires lying about London within lx myles, and not much above" and commented that the speech of Northernmen "whether they be noble men or gentlemen, or of their best clarkes" and "in effect any speach used beyond the river of Trent ... is not so Courtly nor so currant as our Southerne English is, no more is the far Westerne mans speach" (from the edition by Willcock and Walker, 1936).

Nevertheless, many courtiers continued to use the pronunciation of their own region. We are told for instance, that Sir Walter Raleigh kept his own Devon accent. The speech of the Court increasingly acquired a prestige value and in time lost some of the local characteristics of London speech. It may be said to have been finally fixed as the speech of the ruling class through the conformist influence of the public schools of the nineteenth century. It became disseminated as a class pronunciation throughout the country and came to be recognized as characteristic not so much of a region as of a social stratum. As Spencer (loc. cit.) has commented, "the prestige [of the standard pronunciation] . . . is due directly and solely to the prestige of the class or group which possesses it". And so, many people eager for social advancement felt obliged to modify their accent in the direction of the social standard. Pronunciation became therefore a marker of position in society.

In more recent times, the lexical and grammatical features which characterize "dialect" have been disappearing from the speech of an ever increasing proportion of the population, whereas regional accent (in terms of phonic characteristics) has remained. Prestige still seems to be attached to the implicitly accepted social standard of pronunciation which is often called (as previously mentioned) "Received Pronunciation" (RP), a term suggesting that it is the result of a social judgement rather than of an official decision as to what is "correct" or "wrong". Abercrombie (1953) has noted other, more ambiguous, terms for RP such as "Educated English", "Southern English", "London English", "British Standard" and "Standard English". The British Broadcasting Corporation has traditionally favoured this form of pronunciation for its announcers, mainly because it is the type which is most widely understood and which is presumed to excite least prejudice of a regional kind, and so RP is often associated in the public mind with "B.B.C. English". This special position occupied by RP has led to its being the form of pronunciation most commonly described in the phonetics of British English (e.g. Jones, 1956; 1956a; 1956b) and traditionally taught to foreigners.

Twenty years ago, Abercrombie (1953) referred to the prestige value of RP thus:

> The division between RP speakers as we may call them, on the one hand, and educated English people who speak Standard English with some different accent, on the other, is a social one . . . It is an accent of privilege and prestige, conferring considerable advantages on those who speak it. In brief RP is a "status symbol". Its non-regional character, which is a necessary condition of being able to serve as such a status symbol, arises from, and is largely maintained by the great English Public Schools.

Since that passage was written many social and cultural changes have taken place in Great Britain. The erosion of social class boundaries, which had already been proceeding for many years, has continued. Broadcasting, which was then about thirty years old, has increased considerably in its scope and output, taking RP more frequently to the ears of more people but also promulgating regional accents throughout the nation. Secondary and higher education have become more generally available and more people of working-class origin are involved in teaching. Subtle modifications have undoubtedly occurred in RP itself (see Brook, 1973, pp. 165–166). In view of these developments it is of interest to examine current attitudes towards RP and regional accents and to assess their relative prestige.

Some writers consider that certain regional accents possess more prestige than others. Brook (1963) for instance, claims that "Scottish and Irish dialects enjoy greater prestige in England than do the dialects of the North of England, and it may be that the reason for this is that they are national, and not merely regional dialects". Wilkinson (1965) suggests that there are three levels of "accent prestige" in Britain. The "first class accents" comprise RP, certain unnamed foreign accents and forms of Scottish and Irish. "Second class accents" are considered to be the British regional accents, which may themselves constitute a sub-hierarchy. The lowest prestige accents, "third class accents", are those of certain large industrial towns.

Wells (1970) suggests that the local accents of England and Wales fall into three distinct groups. These are (i) the Southern English, (ii) the Northern English and (iii) the Welsh accents. The dividing line between the North and South (with reservations about Herefordshire and West Shropshire) runs from the Severn to the Wash. He also distinguishes a number of subvarieties within these Southern and Northern categories. For instance, the two main areas of the Southern complex are the South-west and the South-east, whilst he considers there are seven major regional varieties of the Northern complex. In the series of investigations about to be presented we shall describe how people react to the status of a number of those varieties Wells has made explicit and some he has not. These studies and others to be mentioned later, could be considered a response to Spencer's (loc. cit.) call for further research in this area:

> Because RP still possesses great prestige in England, it is a norm towards which many people strive, or would wish their children to strive. Too little is known about the changes which occur in the transition from dialect to standard and from regional accents to RP in individuals and groups . . .

Careful studies of how people speak in different contexts and varying situations, and their judgements about the way other people speak, are capable of throwing much light, not only upon linguistic habits and changes, but also on the social pressures which affect speech habits.

Giles (1970; 1971) investigated the perceived status of various accents heard in the British Isles using three evaluative techniques. By means of the matched-guise technique, Giles (1970) presented thirteen accents to 177 local-accented South Welsh and Somerset schoolchildren of two age levels—12 and 17 years. These subjects were told that they would hear 13 entirely different speakers. In fact they heard the tape-recorded voice of one male speaker reading the same neutral passage of prose in different, realistic guises. These included the regional, town and foreign accents shown in Table 1. The speaker attempted to control for para-linguistic and pronunciation broadness differences between the voices.

TABLE 1

The generalized accent prestige continuum: mean ratings of 13 accents

| | |
|---|---|
| 1. RP (2·1)* | 8. Italian (4·7) |
| 2. Affected RP (2·9)*[1] | 9. Northern English (4·8) |
| 3. N. American and French (3·6)* | 10. Somerset (5·1) |
| 5. German (4.2)* | 11. Cockney and Indian (5·2) |
| 6. South Welsh (4·3) | 13. Birmingham (5·3) |
| 7. Irish (4·6) | |

* Mean for 17 year olds (see text).

Despite the large number of guises produced by this speaker the listeners did not appear to recognize their common source. In fact some subjects, when informed of the true nature of the experiment at the end of the procedure, seemed completely surprised and unbelieving. After the presentation of each of the stimulus voices, the listeners were required to rate the accent on a number of scales, including the pleasantness of the voice and the status or prestige of the speaker. The results for prestige can be summarized by means of the mean ratings for each of the accents in Table 1. The ratings suggest that these accents can be considered as occupying positions along a value continuum of social prestige. The structure of this continuum must of course be "genera-

1. "Affected RP" can be considered popularly as a more exaggerated or "affected" form of the Standard, commonly associated with the aristocracy.

lized" for the following reasons: (1) The ratings of the Welsh accent were derived from the Somerset sample whilst the ratings for the Somerset accent were obtained only from the Welsh sample so that tendencies towards accent loyalty could be eliminated. (2) Where age differences were apparent (the asterisked accents), the mean scores for the older sample (the 17 year olds) were used. Nevertheless, the ordering of the judgements for each age group was found to be consistent as between listeners according to Kendall's test of concordance. Interestingly enough, there was greater consistency with regard to the status content than in the case of the aesthetic component (perceived pleasantness), particularly for the 17 year olds.

The subjects were also required to name the accents they had rated, and it was evident that they were fairly successful at this task. Nevertheless, age differences in error scores appeared at the 1 per cent level of significance in that 17 year olds were better able to attain the very strict criteria which were used for identification: the 12 year olds' mean error was 35·6 per cent as against 17·1 per cent for the 17 year olds. The coefficient of rank correlation between ages for frequency of correct identification was +0·77 indicating that, although errors are fewer at the older age, both groups had similar difficulties. A rank ordering of frequency of correct identification of accents was used as a rather crude index of accent familiarity. To determine whether this measure of familiarity was associated with objective evaluations of the accents, rank-order correlation coefficients were computed in respect of identification and evaluations. This showed that for the younger subjects there was a strong tendency to rate highly those accents with which they were most familiar, and to rate poorly those accents with which they were less familiar. This was not the case with the older subjects who appeared to be far more objective in their assessments: the rank-order coefficient for identification and perceived pleasantness for this group was +0·46 (not significant) and for status and identification, +0·30 (not significant). Thus familiarity would not seem an important factor in determining the status of the accents listed in Table 1.

As a form of validation of the matched-guise procedure Giles asked subjects to rate accents presented by name-label only (e.g. "Irish", "Birmingham") in the absence of a sample of the related speech. Some listeners undertook this task before the matched-guise presentation and others after it. Subjects were presented with the names of most of the accents given in Table 1 above together with others not listed and the

item, "an accent identical to my own". "Affected RP" was omitted
and RP was referred to as "B.B.C. accent". The rank correlations of
mean accent ratings for material presented both vocally and "conceptually" was $+0.79$ in the case of aesthetic evaluation and $+0.88$ for
status.

As mentioned previously, the accent prestige continuum was "generalized" and many interesting differences in evaluation emerged as between the two age groups. Many studies have claimed (e.g. Centers,
1950; Estvan and Estvan, 1959) that for most children, the perception
of status differences develops rapidly during the childhood years
attaining a good approximation to the adult level by early adolescence.
However, the results of this study cast serious doubts on this. For instance, 17 year olds attributed significantly more prestige to RP speech
than did the younger adolescents. The 12 year olds also gave lower
ratings to the prestige of Affected RP and German accented-speech.
These differences could perhaps be attributed to a less developed
awareness of status on the part of the younger children. A lack of social
conformity or awareness was again reflected in the 12 year olds' rating
of "an accent identical to your own": this was evaluated with a rather
unrealistic and positive bias. Moreover, members of this age group
(from both regions) tended to assess their "own accent" more favourably
than RP on both pleasantness and prestige dimensions. The 17 year
olds on the other hand rated RP more pleasant and more prestigious
than their "own accent".

Similar age differences were apparent with the ratings of the local
accent presented vocally or by name-label, i.e. when the South Welsh
children evaluated the South Welsh accent and the Somerset children
evaluated the Somerset accent. The 17 year olds (although still displaying strong tendencies of accent-loyalty) had moved some way in
the direction of the conventional evaluation in comparison with 12
year olds. An alternative explanation of these age differences could be
that they reflect a process of social change. Perhaps the 17 year olds
were exhibiting the "old-fashioned" views of their own "generation"
or age-cohort in contrast to the "modern" views of the 12 year old age-
cohort. Only a longitudinal study could test this hypothesis by assessing
the stability of these differences over time.

While South Welsh and Somerset subjects showed accent-loyalty in
the sense that each group reacted more favourably to its own local
accent than did the other regional group, they were still able to attribute

more prestige to RP than to their own local variety. Even the younger subjects tended to evaluate in this manner. It is interesting to note that while the 12 year olds would not concede that the "accent identical to their own" was inferior to RP they nonetheless rated the relevant local accent (Somerset or South Welsh) inferior to RP. This suggests that people consider their own individual accent as distinct from that of the local vernacular or at least fail to recognize the "broadness" of their own accent. Wilkinson (loc. cit.) reports this phenomenon with regard to Birmingham secondary school pupils and states that "very many English people who have not heard their voices on tape imagine that they have RP whilst their neighbours have an "accent". Even when they have heard themselves the prestige of RP is so high that they are often unwilling to admit to themselves that they deviate from it". He found a tendency for working class and male listeners to show more accent loyalty in rating the local accent than middle class and female subjects.

The results of Giles's study strongly resemble the pattern outlined by Wilkinson. His claim that the accents of lowest prestige are those of industrial towns was corroborated. Contrary to his expectations, however, no accent was found to be equal to RP in status value. The accent a listener himself possessed did not seem to affect the superior prestige value assigned to RP. However, it must be borne in mind that this study examined the reactions of listeners from two specific regions of southern Britain only. The possibility remains that RP has relatively less prestige to northern ears.

In addition, although the use of the matched-guise technique was considered necessary to eliminate variations in paralinguistic features likely to occur as between different speakers, it could be argued that the variants presented were no more than stereotyped impressions of the relevant accents. The "validation" of judgements of speech samples against judgements of accents identified by name-label alone could be cited in favour of such an argument. Cowan (1936) points out that actors typically employ a cultural stereotype of emotional expression and that these simulated stage emotions have voice characteristics different from responses spontaneously evoked in real life situations. The accent guises used in Giles's experiment may likewise have lacked verisimilitude in some respects and consequently there was room for doubt as to whether "natural" accents would give rise to the same ordering of prestige values. Another limitation of Giles's study may be

proposed with regard to the subjects. It was suggested that the continuum of accent prestige for the 17 year old subjects reflected "an
adult-oriented framework of evaluation". However, it is possible that
beyond this age people may develop even more status consciousness
which could disturb the relative positions.

For these reasons Giles (1971) repeated the earlier study with slightly
more mature subjects, 21 year old college students who were *heterogeneous* in their regional affiliations. This time the vocal stimuli were
produced by thirteen different speakers using their normal accents.
Except for an Italian priest, all the speakers were University staff or
students. A number of interesting methodological problems were encountered in obtaining this type of natural speech data and these are
discussed elsewhere (Giles, 1971). The use of many different speakers
introduces an enormous amount of variability amongst the voices in
paralinguistic features. It was this problem which the previous study
was designed to avoid. Nevertheless, it seemed important to determine
whether accent-prestige was reproducible despite these differences in
voice quality, perceived personality and so forth. In fact, the results
confirmed that such was indeed the case. The test of concordance again
showed that there was significant agreement between listeners' evaluations of the stimuli and the rank-order correlation for status content
for the two studies was extremely high, $+0.94$. The rank-order correlation between studies in terms of perceived pleasantness was rather
lower, $+0.64$. This might have been expected from the lack of control
of paralinguistic features amongst the various speakers.

Thus the three different techniques used by Giles—presenting subjects with accent guises, names of accents and "natural" accents—all
show that, of the accents sampled, RP speech attracts the highest ratings
for prestige.

Interestingly enough, however, there was a tendency for subjects in
the follow-up study to rate the prestige of most accents more favourably
than did the 17 year olds in the matched-guise study. This differential
evaluation by the two age groups, although admittedly to different
stimuli, could perhaps be explained in terms of the more cosmopolitan
social environment surrounding the older subjects. In other words,
it could be argued that the social qualities of college life are now, perhaps
more than ever before, such as to promote less ethnocentric and more
liberal attitudes towards the characteristics of outgroups. Support for
this notion comes from a number of studies. Webster, Freedman and

Heist (1962) provide a review of the early American work conducted to determine whether college life affected students' social attitudes and values. They conclude that the consensus appears to be that student behaviour has changed in the direction of a "more liberal attitude on social issues and a more tolerant attitude towards persons". In Britain, Butcher (1965) and McIntyre and Morrison (1967) found that the educational opinions of student teachers tend to change in the direction of radicalism and liberalism during their courses. Similarly, Smithers (1970) found that British engineering and social science undergraduates begame more "open-minded" after two years at university. Webster (1956) and Plant (1958; 1958a) have found that college students become less ethnocentric during the course of their studies.

Kramer (1964) points out that "various studies on voice have dealt with differences among speakers, but individual differences among listeners have been ignored". He suggests that personality differences amongst listeners could be quite important. Accordingly, Giles (1971a) hypothesized that highly ethnocentric (E+) listeners would react more favourably (in terms of prestige and pleasantness ratings) to the standard accent, and less favourably towards the regional varieties than would subjects who were low in ethnocentrism (E−).

A group of 63 sixth-formers (17 and 18 years of age) from South Welsh and Somerset schools were given the 24-item British Ethnocentrism (E) Scale constructed by Warr, Faust and Harrison (1967). From this original pool of subjects, selection was made as follows. From each region were taken five males and five females who showed the highest E-scores and similar numbers for the lowest E-scores. All were considered by their teachers to be representative members of the two accent communities concerned. Thus there were 20 E+ and 20 E− subjects, matched for age, sex and region. All E+ scores obtained were higher than 83 while all E− scores were below 73, yielding group means of 99·0 and 60·3 respectively.

These listeners were then required to rate six of the voices used in the previous matched-guise study, namely, RP, Irish, South Welsh, Birmingham, Somerset and Northern English accented speech. The rating scales included the same prestige and pleasantness dimensions. The results tended to support the hypothesis. There was a general tendency (not in all cases statistically significant) for the E+ subjects to rate regional accents less favourably in terms of pleasantness and prestige than the E− individuals, thereby displaying less tolerance towards regional variations in accent. Moreover, this lack of tolerance was accompanied by a more favourable reaction to RP than that shown by the E— group.

A number of studies have related personality characteristics of individuals to their style of speech.[2] For instance, Markel (1969) in an examination of the voice quality profiles of 78 psychiatric patients found that three different personality types were associated with high pitch, loud voice and fast speech rate. Thus, while personality differences occur with regard to individual variations in the encoding mechanisms of speech, this last study by Giles on ethnocentrism and evaluation suggests no less a status for personality differences in the decoding process.

In a further follow-up to these evaluation studies, Giles (1972) attempted to determine the effect of pronunciation mildness-broadness on the evaluation of regional accented speech. In other words, is the degree of broadness of an accent (i.e. the extent to which it diverges from the prestigious "standard") related to the listener's evaluation of it in terms of prestige? The study involved two groups of subjects: 12 year old schoolchildren (17 Welsh and 26 non-Welsh) and 21 year old college students (18 Welsh and 16 non-Welsh). The subjects were required to listen to and evaluate the pleasantness and prestige of six different voices. These voices were produced by one male speaker using the matched-guise technique and they included the mild and broad variants of three regional accents—South Welsh, Irish and Birmingham accented speech. The passage was identical with that used in the author's previous studies. After this evaluation task, subjects were required to carry out a perceptual task. This time they were told to listen to each of three pairs of voices similar to the ones they had already rated (they were in fact the very same ones). Each accent of each pair was to be evaluated on a 7-point scale from extremely mild to extremely broad in pronunciation. The subjects were informed that the voices within a pair might represent a large difference in pronunciation broadness, a very small difference or even no difference whatsoever. They were required to listen to both variants of a pair before rating either. This procedure was considered necessary as a kind of validation of the speaker's guises. As expected, the supposedly milder variants of each accent were so perceived by the subjects and the results were statistically significant

2. For citations, see Footnote 3 in Chapter 7.

for each accent.[3] The milder variants were generally rated more favourably in terms of pleasantness and higher in terms of status. This trend was found to be the case even among Welsh listeners rating their own local variants.

Interesting age differences again emerged in this study. The older group tended to be more sensitive to differences in accent broadness than the younger group. Yet on the other hand the 12 year olds appeared to be more discriminative in their *evaluations*. Although both age groups were able to detect acoustic differences between the mild and broad Irish variants, only the 12 year sample committed themselves to a significant differentiation in evaluation as well. It would appear therefore that as the adolescent matures he develops an increasing sensitivity to vocal differences in accent, but concomitantly a greater tolerance of these differences. The fact that the older subjects were college students must, however, be taken into account in the light of the previous discussion of tolerance and open-mindedness amongst students.

Past research has not considered the possibility of stimulus mildness-broadness affecting the evaluation of spoken accents and dialects.[4] It can clearly be seen that some form of control for this variable is desirable in all studies involving the evaluation of spoken language. The speaker in the first study by Giles, mentioned above, in which a generalized accent prestige continuum was obtained, attempted to control for accent broadness throughout his different guises. He tried to maintain an intermediate degree of broadness for each accent. In other words, he could have produced either milder or broader accented guises than the ones offered to the listeners. As the same speaker was used in the

3. Related research has been conducted by Brennan, Ryan and Dawson (1974) on the speech of Mexican-Americans in the south west, the vast majority of whom speak English with an unmistakable influence from Spanish phonology. In other words, their English is "Mexican-accented". It was found in this study that non-linguistic-ally-trained students were sensitive to small differences in the amount of accentedness in the English of eight Mexican bilinguals. Subjects gave magnitude estimates and also squeezed a hand dynamometer to indicate the amount of accentedness in the reading of an English passage by each of the speakers. There was significant agreement among speakers regarding the speech samples with each scaling method. In addition, interscale agreement was good and power functions fitted to the data had exponents falling in the range expected from earlier psychophysical studies. Moreover, the scale values correlated significantly with the frequency of accented pronunciations by the speakers as assessed by two independent judges. For a detailed discussion of the notion of accentedness, see Ryan (1973).

4. A recent exception is a study by Ryan, Carranza and Moffie (1974); see Chapter 5, p. 86.

later study by Giles (1972), the effect on evaluation of these milder and broader variants can be seen in relation to the previous accent prestige ratings. The information given in Table 2 suggests that the speaker was successful in producing three distinct levels of accent broadness, and that the levels were reflected in subjects' evaluations of prestige. It can be appreciated that if accents are to be placed on a continuum of accent prestige they must be matched for pronunciation broadness, otherwise misrepresentation may result.

TABLE 2

A comparison of the mean accent prestige values for the mild and broad variants of three regional accents (after Giles, 1970, 1972)

| Accents | Mean ratings of *mild* variants (Giles, 1972) | Mean ratings of *intermediate* variants (Giles, 1970) | Mean ratings of *broad* variants (Giles, 1972) |
|---|---|---|---|
| Irish | 4·4 | 4·6 | 4·8 |
| Birmingham | 5·1 | 5·3 | 5·9 |
| South Welsh | 3·9 | 4·3 | 4·7 |

In contrast to the above research, Trudgill (1972) has argued that British nonstandard speech is in a very real sense highly valued and prestigious in a manner that is not usually expressed. For instance, he claims:

> Many informants who initially stated that they did not speak properly and would like to do so, admitted, if pressed, that they perhaps would not *really* like to, and that they would almost certainly be considered foolish, arrogant or disloyal by their friends and family if they did.

And so, by means of a variation of the self-evaluation test (Labov, 1966), Trudgill has presented empirical evidence from speakers in the city of Norwich, East Anglia, which suggests that nonstandard speech has a "covert prestige". In this test, subjects were read aloud twelve lexical items each with two or more different pronunciations (prestige and nonstandard variants). The informants were asked after each item to choose which of the variants most closely resembled the way in which they normally said the word. Having already taperecorded an extensive interview with each subject, Trudgill was able to make a comparison between the forms they claimed to speak and those they actually used. In brief, it was found that male informants (both working class and middle class), and also female informants under the age of 30 years, reported using more *non*standard pronunciations than they really did. Trudgill argued that:

> if it is true that informants perceive their own speech in terms of the norms at which they are aiming rather than the sound actually produced, then the norm at which a large number of Norwich males are aiming is *nonstandard working class speech*. This favourable attitude is never overtly expressed, but the responses to these tests show that statements about "bad speech" are for public consumption only.

The notion of covert prestige is an interesting one, but an alternative explanation of these findings may lie in a possible methodological artifact in the interview situation. Awareness of the taperecorder and that the interrogation (perhaps by a middle class interviewer) was connected with "research" may have led the informants to adopt a more standardized speech style than they would have used in less artificial encounters with peer-group members. If this is true, it would not be surprising to find that they "over-report" in the self-evaluation task the use of nonstandard variants, since their interview speech (the comparison point) may not have adequately represented their everyday speech usage. It would be very useful, however, with this methodological problem borne in mind, to replicate Trudgill's study across a number of regions in Britain. If covert prestige associated with nonstandard speech were substantiated, it would be interesting to know whether it is a stable characteristic of this speech style across time, or whether on the other hand, Trudgill has discovered the initial signs of a linguistic change in the community towards the nonstandard.

The research reported from Britain confirms the notion discussed earlier that a vocal dimension involving standard and nonstandard pronunciation is, at least overtly, related to a dimension of prestige or social status. It has also indicated that a number of variables need to be taken into account, including the speaker's pronunciation broadness and the listener's age and personality.

Let us now consider the results of similar research in North America.

## United States of America

In the United States, it appears that no one regional dialect has become the recognized national "standard". In the nineteenth century however, some people did value a "Harvard accent" because it was perceived as indicating that the speaker came from a part of the country which had become associated with culture and wealth. Today such treasures are not concentrated in one place. No regional dialect or accent predominates as more "correct" than others. Linguistic geographers have discovered three main dialect areas according to Malmstrom (1967)— Northern, Midland and Southern—stretching from east to west across the continent.[5] These dialect areas are most distinct on the Atlantic coast where they reflect the original patterns of settlement. The further west one goes, the more the dialect areas blend and fuse, presumably as a result of the intermingling of settlers during the westward migration. These three dialect areas are defined by consistent differences in pronunciation, vocabulary and grammar, but they appear to be less marked than regional variations in Great Britain. Ellis (1967) has claimed that "listeners may be able to recognize social status cues in a person's speech in spite of the speaker's regional dialect". Thus, although regional variations in speech do not themselves appear to carry status connotations, it would seem that the inclusion or absence of certain "standard" or prestigious features in a speaker's vocal output may be a reliable guide to his social class origins. Labov (1964) mentions five pronunciation characteristics as being important as social class correlates in the speech of New Yorkers:

> The five phonological variables are:— (r), registering the presence or absence of final and preconsonantal /r/; (eh), indicating the height of the vowel in the word class of *bad, ask, half, dance* (as opposed to *bat, back, lap*); (oh), indicating the height of the vowel in the word class of *off, chocolate, all*; (th), the realization of the first consonant of *thing, thought, three*, as stop, affricate, or fricative; and (dh), a corresponding index for the voiced initial consonant of *then, this, the*, etc. (Labov, 1964).

Putnam and O'Hern (1955) recorded one-minute samples of speech from twelve Negroes of different educational levels and social and geographical origins telling a fable. Fifty-five White listeners evaluated the social status of these speakers, and their ratings yielded a correlation coefficient of $+0 \cdot 80$ with speakers' social positions as determined on an objective index. The high correspondence showed that status evaluation was possible despite a wide variety of regional dialects. Because all the listeners in this study were residents of Washington, D.C., the experiment was repeated (see Ellis, 1967) using exactly the same

5. For more detailed social dialectological discussions of North American English see Berger (1968) and Davis (1970).

tapes with Mid-Western judges, and a similar correlation was found between perceived and actual social status. Similarly, in an earlier study, Harms (1961) using Mid-Western White speakers found that listeners were well able to identify high, middle and low status speakers from their taped voices alone.

Ellis (loc. cit.) reports three studies on the perception of status from the voice, the first of which is basically a replication of Putnam's and O'Hern's findings. Twelve college freshmen were requested to relate a fable for 40 seconds, and the correlation between perceived status and an objective assessment was again +0·8. A follow-up study by Ellis involved the strategy of role-playing, whereby speakers were told to envisage themselves as honoured undergraduates who had been selected to conduct the University President and his guests on a tour of a new dormitory. The speakers were told to use their best grammar and voice quality, and to fake upper-class speech as best they could. The perceived-actual relationship in this situation was lower, but still very high, with a correlation coefficient of +0·65 indicating that status judgements based upon the voice seem to be largely immune from attempted disguise, thereby reflecting a stable characteristic of an individual's speech pattern. Harms (1961) had commented earlier that the judgements made in all the studies up to that date which had shown this correspondence between perceived and objective status "could be based on word choice, pronunciation, grammatical structure, voice quality, articulation and several other observable variables". Therefore, in order to investigate the salience of phonological patterns, Ellis's third study eliminated the influence of verbal structure by requiring speakers to count from one to twenty, and he still found a high correlation between perceived and actual status of +0·65. It would seem, then, that a speaker's pronunciation pattern (and perhaps tonal qualities) are fundamental determinants of perceived social status as judged from voice.

However, this somewhat simple view of the relationship does not comprehend the full range of intricacies involved. Labov (1966) found that the ability to identify correctly prestigious forms of American speech was dependent upon the listener's own social status and linguistic usage. In his study of the social and stylistic stratification of New York speech, Labov also developed a test which successfully isolated and measured unconscious subjective reactions of the informant to individual variables in the speech of others. The uniformity of the results proved surprising for although New Yorkers vary widely in their use of the /th/ variant, most of them can apparently detect low prestige variants of this feature in the speech of others and downgrade the speaker who uses nonstandard forms: 82% of the informants showed this ability to detect and stigmatize nonstandard /th/ forms. Moreover, it was found that those who showed the highest use of the nonstandard forms in their own speech were very often among the most sensitive in detecting these forms in the speech of others. For example, although the informants of Italian background showed many more nonstandard forms in their speech than those of Jewish background, they included only half as many who were insensitive to /th/; 14% of the Italians as against 27% for the Jewish group. An even more striking comparison can be made between the sexes. Men, on average, used more than twice as many nonstandard forms of speech as women did but only 9% of the former were insensitive to /th/ as compared with 30% of the latter. Thus it would appear that, on the whole, subjective responses of speakers are more uniform than performance. When a new prestige pattern enters the language, it may be accepted on the level of conscious subjective response before it achieves uniformity in actual use.

An interesting finding in the study by Harms (1961), which he did not discuss, was that lower status listeners rated middle status speakers significantly lower in terms of perceived status than did either middle or higher status listeners. This phenomenon perhaps could be explained either as a reflection of social strivings in that lower status people consider this group's speech within the limits of their attainments, or alternatively it may reflect an attitude of perceived social equality, such that, colloquially speaking, middle class people "aint much better than us". Nevertheless whatever explanation may be more appealing the perception of social status from the voice of others appears to be interwoven (as in Britain) with the listener's own cognitive structuring and his relative position in society. Indeed, a study of the social evaluation of Detroit speech by Shuy, Baratz and Wolfram (1969) has shown that middle-class listeners are more accurate judges of objective social status in speech than are working-class listeners. This is not surprising since Deutsch (1964) has shown that people from a working-class background have inferior auditory discrimination, owing, she believes, to certain environmental deficiencies.[6] Nevertheless, Shuy et al. found that the

6. A recent discussion of the "deficiency" and "difference" theorists' relative positions with regard to working class language usage has been produced by Bruck and Tucker (1972).

lower a speaker's status the more accurately he is identified as such, regardless of the listener's own socioeconomic status, and they argued that such lower class speakers may provide more salient cues. In this respect, McKay (1969) suggests that in social evaluation, listeners do not react reliably to the frequency of non-standard speech features but tend to pick out the lowest ranking feature (even if it appears rarely) as an indicator of the speaker's social status.

So far we have discussed characteristics of the stimuli and of listeners in the evaluation of American speech; but what of the characteristics of the judgemental process itself? Frederick Williams and his co-workers at the University of Texas have conducted a series of experiments which give us important information about the types of evaluative dimensions judges use when forming impressions of speakers. In the initial stage of his research, Williams attempted to construct a set of semantic differential scales on the basis of interview data provided by eight urban teachers. The teachers were asked to describe the speech and language differences of children of varying social status and ethnicity. Such adjectives as "nonstandard", "disadvantaged" and so on emerged from their descriptions. Williams (1970), in determining the relevance of all the adjectives elicited, required teachers to evaluate actual speech samples of children of varying social status and ethnicity. A testing procedure was devised in which tapes of 11 and 12 year old Negro and White children of low and high status were played to 33 Chicago teachers (12 Negro and 21 White). The children talked freely about games and television for about 250 words. A factor analysis of the teachers' ratings of these speech samples revealed two gross dimensions of judgement which were labelled, *confidence-eagerness* and *ethnicity-non-standardness*. Within these two dimensions, scales relating to social status judgements were incorporated mainly within the dimension of ethnicity-nonstandardness and to a lesser degree within the dimension of confidence-eagerness. In general, judgements on the latter dimension appeared to be related to the child's fluency, and his tendency to maintain a conversation. Ethnicity-nonstandardness seemed to be the recognition by the teacher that the child was non-White or spoke other than a standard version of English. Williams, Whitehead and Miller (1971) also found that there was a tendency to evaluate speakers on this dimension first before using the confidence-eagerness scales. In other studies in their report, these workers found that the two-factor judgemental model was applicable not only to audio tapes, but also to audio-visual presentations and visual-only presentations. Furthermore, it was also applicable when evaluations were made of the stereotyped written descriptions of Anglo, Black and Mexican-American children. Indeed, the two factor model also applied in the differentiation of children identified only by stereotyped labels (e.g. "Black"). The pervasiveness of the two dimensions was demonstrated even more convincingly when they showed that the model was independent both of judges' race and of the length of their experience in teaching children.

Naremore (1971) examined the extent to which teachers could be grouped in terms of the commonality of judges' evaluations, using Williams's data. She found that there appeared to be several different types of teachers in terms of what they attended to in the speech samples. For instance, one type was characterized as a "detail-oriented rater", another as a "communication-oriented rater". The latter implies a tendency to be concerned with the totality of the situation and the topic rather than to dwell on specific features of pronunciation or dialect. In general, Naremore found that White teachers tended to belong to the class of detail-oriented raters.

The work of Williams and his associates raises questions concerning the status of minority group speech in the United States. But first we need to know how well people can actually identify ethnic group membership from speech styles alone. A large number of studies have documented objective differences between the speech patterns of American Blacks and Whites. Differences have been reported on many linguistic levels including syntax (Stewart, 1967), pronunciation (Markel and Sharpless, 1972), fluency and thematic content (von Raffler Engel and Sigelman, 1971). Differences in nonverbal behaviour also have been reported by von Raffler Engel (1972). Nevertheless, McDavid and Davis (1972) have pointed to a methodological flaw in many studies investigating Black-White speech differences: "It is unfortunate that conclusions are based on a lack of comparable evidence so that the basic distinctiveness, so-called, of lower-class Negro speech is extrapolated from a comparison of lower-class Negro and middle-class White usage of different regional origins." In addition, many studies have obtained their Black speech data by means of White interviewers—another possible confounding factor (Sattler, 1970; Ledvinka, 1971; 1972).

Although many studies describing objective differences between Black and White speech styles may be regarded as methodologically dubious, the research on people's *subjective* impressions of such differences is supportive. For example, studies by Stroud (1961), Shuy, Baratz and Wolfram (1969) and Koustaal and Jackson (1972) have shown that racial identification of an individual by speech alone is usually between 80 and 90 per cent accurate. However, Shuy *et al.* (loc. cit.) did show that accuracy increases the lower the socioeconomic level of the speaker. Indeed, it is important to stress that racial identification from voice is not absolutely perfect.[7] Studies by Buck (1968), Williams, (1970) Davis (1970a) Fraser (1973) testify to the fact that some middle class Blacks' racial origins are not easily identifiable from voice cues alone. For example, in the study by Buck (loc. cit.) women college students were asked to classify four speakers reading a neutral passage of prose on tape. One of these speakers had previously been identified by a group of five expert speech teachers as a Negro, Standard Dialect speaker from New York. Nevertheless, out of the 26 listeners who rated the speaker, 24 considered him to be White.

Williams (1970) commented that "sounding White is equated with high status" and the studies mentioned so far have been concerned only with verbal and voice cues. How do people evaluate speakers whom they *hear* as standard but whom they *see* as belonging to a particular ethnic minority? Williams, Whitehead and Miller (1971a) provide us with a tentative answer to this question, at least as it relates to children's speech. They prepared a set of 90-second videotape segments each showing a Black, White or Mexican-American child assembling a plastic model car. The child was heard describing his actions and saying what he would do with his new toy. Some of the tapes showing Black or Mexican-American children were dubbed with the voice of a White child. The subjects were 44 trainee teachers undergoing a speech course at the University of Texas. Forty-two of them were female and presumably most, if not all, were White. These subjects each viewed (1) either a Black or a Mexican-American child whose nonstandard speech had been replaced by dubbing in the speech of a standard-English-speaking child; (2) either a Black or a Mexican-American child speaking nonstandard English (i.e. the tapes had their original sound tracks); and (3) a White child speaking standard English. Subjects rated the

---

7. A study by Giles and Bourhis (in press) shows that second generation Black immigrants in Cardiff, Britain, cannot be racially discriminated by local White listeners from speech cues alone. For a discussion of Black speech in Australia, see Sommer and Marsh (1969) and Jernudd (1971).

children represented by these "ethnic guises" on scales related to the factors of "confidence-eagerness" and "ethnicity-nonstandardness". The experiment was designed so that statistical analysis would show the effects of visual and auditory cues upon these ratings. One of the findings was that the ratings accorded to dubbed tapes representing a Black or Mexican-American child apparently speaking standard English indicated significantly more "ethnicity-nonstandardness" than the judgements of tapes with the same sound track but showing a White child. Thus visual evidence of the child's ethnic identity apparently influenced the subjects' judgements. However, ratings of tapes in which Black and Mexican American-children's own nonstandard speech was retained received more extreme "ethnic-nonstandard" ratings, indicating that speech style also influenced judgements to some extent. The authors conclude that:

> In general, findings indicated that the videotape image showing the child's ethnicity affects ratings of his language in the direction of racial stereotyping expectations. For Black children the bias was in the direction of expecting them to sound more nonstandard and ethnic than their White peers. For Mexican-American children, the bias was not only toward expecting greater ethnicity-nonstandardness but also more reticence and nonconfidence.

Clearly, if these findings have generality, there are important educational implications. They also raise questions concerning bias in the perception of adult, middle class members of various ethnic groups by members of the majority culture.[8]

With regard to Britain, it was suggested that regional and foreign accented speech could be placed along a continuum from high to low prestige, but it was stated above that it does not appear to be possible to order regional language varieties in the United States in this way. It is conceivable, however, that the speech of various *ethnic minorities* might be ranked for prestige. Evidence on this question is as yet inconclusive. From data given in another article by Williams, Whitehead and Miller (1971) it may be seen that the White teachers in their sample rated Black and Mexican-American children as more "nonstandard" than White children and that Black and Mexican-American teachers gave similar judgements. However, the White teachers found the Mexican-American children less "ethnic-nonstandard" than the Black children whereas the Black and Mexican-American teachers did not

8. Research on this problem by H. Giles and R. Bourhis is now in progress.

differentiate significantly between the two ethnic groups on this gross dimension. Nevertheless, not all ethnic minority speech has been found to possess inferior social prestige. Lambert, Giles and Picard (1975) asked Franco-American and Anglo-American students in Northern Maine to rate (*inter alia*) the social class of several taperecorded speakers. Various kinds of European, Canadian and local accented speech were represented, together with standard American English. Speakers were matched for objective social class. No differences at all emerged with regard to perceived status. Thus, it would seem that, at least in certain parts of the United States, some minority-group speech can be as prestigious as the standard version of a majority culture's language.

The discussion so far has been concerned with the attribution of prestige to others' speech forms, but how do people in America evaluate the prestige of their *own* speech? As mentioned previously, Labov (1966) constructed the "self-evaluation test" which required the informant to choose one of several pronunciations as the one he considered most "correct", and also to choose the one he actually employed most often. The number of items in which the choices were different formed the "index of linguistic insecurity", and it would appear that the speaker usually hears his own speech as conforming closely to the norm. The index itself represents to some extent the willingness of the speaker to recognize an exterior standard of correctness. For upper-middle and lower class speakers, the index was low, but for lower-middle class informants (white collar workers and the higher ranks of skilled manual workers), the indices were higher. The term "insecurity" expresses only one aspect of the situation: the recognition of an external standard of correctness could be regarded as a concomitant of upward social aspiration or mobility. Labov (1966a) found that upwardly mobile New Yorkers tended to adopt the linguistic norms and emulate the speech style of those one step above themselves socioeconomically.

Whereas in Britain the mere possession of a regional accent tends to be regarded as a mark of low status, there appears to be no such discrimination against regional accents *per se* in the United States of America. Neither is there any exact equivalent of English Received Pronunciation (RP): it seems that the user of any regional variety of speech is capable of exhibiting "standard" or "nonstandard" features of that particular regional speech form. It is not clear to what extent these prestigious features are common to all the regional varieties. Although there is no evidence that one regional variety has more prestige than any other, it seems unlikely that there is absolutely no regional stratification in this respect. One feels that there must be some areas of the United States whose inhabitants suffer from a reputation of having low economic and educational standards and whose characteristic regional accents accordingly evoke a low-status stereotype.

## French Canada

Let us now turn our attention to another unique type of class-related standard language situation, that of French Canada. French is today the mother tongue of more than five million Canadians, 75% of whom live in the Province of Quebec. Although enclaves of French-speaking Canadians occur throughout the country, English has been rapidly replacing French as the language of the French Canadian ethnic group in all areas other than Quebec. (There is a similar trend in the French-speaking areas of the northern United States.) The high proportion of French Canadians in Quebec, with their strong loyalty to the French language (only 1·6% of Quebec's French ethnic population reported English as their mother tongue in 1961) has served to maintain the position of French as one of Canada's two official languages and to provide an important shield against linguistic and cultural assimilation (Lieberson, 1970).

Although the British North America Act of 1867 recognized both French and English as the official languages of Canada there is abundant evidence (Royal Commission on Bilingualism and Biculturalism, 1965) that for many years the French language occupied a minor status in Canada. Even in Quebec, English became firmly entrenched as the working language and French Canadians were underrepresented in the higher echelons of business. The eruption of terrorist activities in the early 1960s brought to light the feelings of resentment held by many French Canadians with respect to their inferior status. The following ten years, which have been marked by sporadic outbursts of terrorism and the birth of an official Quebec separatist party, have seen a parallel acceleration in language policy developments at both federal and provincial levels.

In their historical survey of the development of language policy in Quebec, Pinault and Ladouceur (1971) pointed out that more had been done in the past ten years to guarantee the maintenance and development of French as the working language of the province than during the preceding 190 years. For example, it is now mandatory in Quebec for all English-speaking children to acquire a working knowledge of French within their school curriculum. A working knowledge of French has replaced Canadian citizenship as a requirement for certain professional licensing and pressure has been exerted on large businesses and industries to collaborate with the government to make French the working language of employees at all levels.

In view of the significant role which French has played in preserving the people of Quebec and their culture from assimilation, and the relationship between language and nationalistic movements throughout the world, it is not surprising to find that matters of language occupy a position of priority on the Quebec political and educational scene. However, the French spoken in Quebec today by all but a small academic and professional elite differs at all levels of linguistic analysis from the accepted form of the language as spoken in France. This standard model, which has evolved from the Ile-de-France dialect, commands high prestige which is attributed by Spilka (1970) to three main factors: (1) early and successful efforts at language standardization on the part of the French State (the Académie Française, which is entrusted with the defence and preservation of the French language, was founded in 1635 and published its first dictionary in 1644): (2) the considerable prestige enjoyed by France and French culture throughout the world; and (3) the absence of any serious political and economic challenge to France's superior position by other French-speaking nations.

Denis (1949) has described the evolution of the French language in Canada following the British conquest and the departure of the French-speaking elite. Cut off from contact with other French-speaking centres, Canadian French became archaiac and offered little resistance to the influence of English. By the end of the nineteenth century the contamination of French by borrowings from English reached such proportions that public campaigns were organized to awaken French Canadians to the fact that their language was in danger. Unfortunately, these campaigns and corrective movements were ineffective in the face of the growing influence of the English language press, and eventually, of radio and television. These events led Valin (1970) to remark that if Quebec French were left to evolve naturally it would become unintelligible to speakers of standard French.

In 1961, the Quebec government established an Office de la Langue Française (OLF). This agency was assigned the task of revitalizing

French in Quebec by bringing it closer to standard French and by upgrading the language of the under-privileged classes. The OLF regularly disseminates normative bulletins to educational institutions, businesses and the mass media, drawing attention to specific differences between Quebec French and standard French and providing appropriate standard French vocabulary lists to replace certain Canadianisms and anglicisms in common use. In its first official publication (Cahier No. 1), the OLF stated that if the French language in Quebec is to survive the pressures of an English-speaking North American milieu, it must adhere to the same norms which prevail in other large francophone countries. No variation in morphology or syntax should be tolerated; phonetic and lexical variation should be reduced to an absolute minimum.

According to Harmer (1954), the French at all levels of society display an intense interest in their own language and show remarkably little tolerance or sympathy towards either regional or social class deviations from the prestige standard. It is understandable therefore, that French Canadians, who are now attempting to establish and strengthen cultural ties with France as a bulwark against the pressures of North America, may feel sensitive and somewhat insecure with regard to their "nonstandard" dialect. Indeed, as long as thirty-five years ago Miner (1939) remarked that the rural French Canadian was usually apologetic about his speech. Corrective measures have succeeded in making him lose pride in his language and he has no real basis for judging which of the words he uses are standard French and which are not. And so, French Canadians tend, as minority groups often do, to downgrade their own mode of speaking. Political movements for an independent Quebec have apparently not as yet succeeded in removing this feeling of inferiority (Lazure, 1970). One might suggest that particular attention should be paid to the psychological condition of people who have thus been exposed to continual negative value judgements about the quality of their speech. To date, however, researchers have concentrated on the identification and description of the speech style of French Canadians from different regions and social strata (e.g. Charbonneau, 1955; Ellis, 1965; Gendron, 1966). Brown (1969) presented subjects with the taped voices of male and female speakers of Canadian French from a large number of socioeconomic levels, reading extracts from Le Petit Prince. French Canadian listeners were then asked to rate the social status of each of the speakers presented to them.

It was found that listeners' assessments of social class from speech cues were limited to two gross categories—upper and lower class. Brown also gave evidence of the phenomenon, reported by Labov (1966a) in the case of New York speech, that people who are upwardly mobile tend to emulate and adopt the speech style of those one step above them socioeconomically. Nevertheless, very few studies have examined the sociolinguistic correlates of French usage in Canada. Preliminary investigations which have done so have found evidence of linguistic insecurity among lower-class French Canadians in Montreal (Chiasson-Lavoie and Laberge, 1971) and a tendency among teenagers to possess a more favourable impression of the formal, more educated French Canadian style of speech over the more informal, popular form.

The scarcity of data motivated d'Anglejan and Tucker (1973) to conduct a fairly comprehensive series of inquiries into the status of the various styles of Canadian French. Their sample consisted of 243 students, teachers and factory workers from three areas of Quebec and they used two techniques of inquiry. Subjects were first given a questionnaire comprising 40 multiple-choice and semantic-differential items. In brief it was found that subjects appeared to be moderately satisfied with their own speech yet there was a consensus that Quebec French needed improvement. At the same time, there appeared a strong tendency for subjects to refuse to accept the cliché that Quebec French was actually "not as nice as" European or Continental French or that the Parisian dialect was the best. Moreover, while 87% said that they would generally accept correction of their speech by other Quebecers, only 50% would tolerate linguistic guidance from a European. Subjects were then presented with tape-recordings of twelve different male speakers: four working-class and four middle-class French Canadian and four European speakers. They each were heard for about 40 seconds talking spontaneously about a recent blizzard. Despite the fact that subjects had earlier tended to reject the European French model, they nevertheless rated the Continental speakers higher on the occupational scale than any of the eight French Canadian speakers. Indeed, as we shall see in the next chapter, listeners also attributed more favourable personality characteristics to the Continental speakers. In another part of the study, the twelve stimulus speakers were required to count from one to twenty. Even from this content-free speech, subjects again rated the European French speakers higher in occupational status than the Canadian speakers, and rated their speech style to be more socially advantageous than the local speech. This finding, it may be recalled, is consonant with the work of Ellis (1967) reported in the context of the United States.

The research findings of Rémillard, Tucker and Bruck (1973) would suggest that the prestige of the European model holds for most social situations. In their experiment, French Canadians were asked to listen to the same phrases spoken in the European and Canadian French dialects and were asked to evaluate how "correct" or "incorrect" they perceived them to be in five distinct social contexts of varying degrees of formality and informality. The authors concluded that the European French phrases were rated more "correct" than their Canadian counterparts in all situations. Subjects did, however, admit to using more Canadian phrases at home and at school but claimed that in those same situations they would prefer to use the European models. Nevertheless, before we can entirely accept the proposition that the prestige of European French does not depend upon context at all, many more types of social context need to be studied in perhaps a more realistic way.

Thus, it appears that French Canada presents an interesting class-related standard speech style situation. Unlike the previous contexts described, its prestige speech style is derived from a source exterior to its own domestic cultural environment. French Canadians regard their own French Canadian speech styles (even the upper-class version) as socially less desirable than the European standard. However, at the conscious level of expressed attitude (in d'Anglejan's and Tucker's questionnaire survey), subjects displayed a reluctance to accept this standard as the more prestigious variant. It is possible that the investigation referred to was carried out during a period of considerable social change, and it may be that later research will show that Canadian standards of speech have been adopted and "internalized" rather than simply subscribed to at a conscious level.

*     *     *

We have discussed two types of standard language situation: the context- and class-related standards. We shall discuss the former again in chapters 7 and 8 showing that the possession of standard and non-standard variants in a speaker's repertoire can be part and parcel of a speaker's more general facility to modify his speech to suit a particular situation. But more immediately, in chapters 4, 5 and 6, the class-related standard situation will be discussed in terms of the psychosocial concomitants of standard-nonstandard usage. For instance, evidence has accrued that perceived social status is consonant with perceived favourability of personality. In a study reviewed earlier, Harms (1961) found that high status speakers were perceived as being more competent and trustworthy than lower status speakers, while Ellis (1967) in his first study, found a correlation of $+0.60$ between perceived status and perceived likeability, and a correlation of $+0.76$ between perceived likeability and objectively assessed status. The next chapter looks into this situation more closely and considers whether personality can be as validly perceived from the voice as status can.

# 4

# Speech Style and Perceived Personality (I): The Canadian Studies

The term "personality" is thought to be derived from the Latin *per*, through, *sonare*, to sound—hence, "to sound through"—apparently referring to the mouth opening in the mask worn by an actor. Later the term came to mean the actor himself and eventually any particular individual. It is interesting that the etymological origin of "personality" is associated with the voice of the speaker. However, as a *valid* reflection of what we now understand as personality the voice has been shown to be less than perfect.

The earliest studies (Herzog, 1933; Pear, 1931) found that listeners are able to judge accurately the sex of the speaker, and curiously enough, are moderately good at estimating occupation, weight, height, and appearance. In terms of size of sample, the study by Pear (1931) was quite impressive: he analyzed over 4,000 reports from British radio listeners who had responded to questions about nine different readers they had heard on the air. Subsequent studies (Taylor, 1934; Bonaventura, 1935; Stagner, 1936) also found that subjects were moderately successful in estimating speakers' appearances. Cantril and Allport (1935) reported on a series of 14 experiments involving 24 speakers and 600 judges. The judges were asked to match the voices presented to them with features of personality. These features included age, height, complexion, appearance, handwriting, vocation, political preferences, extraversion-introversion, ascendence-submission, dominant values and a summary sketch of personality. Some success was found with regard to age, vocation, extraversion, ascendence-submission, values and summary sketch. However, no characteristic was consistently revealed correctly, and in general, judges showed more agreement than accuracy.

A series of studies by Fay and Middleton (1939–43) investigated judgements of a number of personality characteristics from voices transmitted over a public address system. The characteristics judged with some success were the Spranger personality types (1939), occupation (1939a), intelligence (1940), sociability (1941), introversion (1942) and leadership (1943). The authors in their 1939 study claimed that: "certain voices are stereotypes; they definitely impress listeners as being the voice of persons who might be classified (according to one or another personality types)." Other studies which have investigated the relationship between personality traits perceived from speakers' voices and their scores on certain personality test batteries have all echoed this statement (Taylor, loc. cit.; Stagner, loc. cit.; Eisenberg and Zalowitz, 1938; Wolff, 1943), as have the subsequent reviews (Sanford, 1942; Licklider and Miller, 1951; Kramer, 1963: Starkweather, 1964). Indeed, as Kramer (loc. cit.) has commented, "such vocal stereotypes have remained the most frequent findings in all studies of the relationships between voice and personality."

The role of expert judgement in determining personality from voice was investigated by Jones (1942). He gave the Rorschach protocol from an adolescent boy to a well-known Rorschach analyst and also gave a recording of the boy's voice to Moses, a laryngologist who has had a strong interest in the interrelationship of voice and personality. The two independent analyses were considered to match well with each other. Moreover, a more recent study has shown, in contrast to the early work in this field, that inexperienced listeners can give accurate judgements of personality attributes from speech. This study by Hunt and Lin (1967) showed some evidence of consistency of individual performance across samples of speech expressive of quite different personalities, along with a demonstration of significant individual differences in accuracy. Accuracy was defined in terms of the correspondence between listeners' reactions and speakers' self-ratings. The data revealed variations in accuracy as a function of the attribute being judged: accuracy was greater for affective-conative attributes than for behaviour-physical ones. Speakers, besides reading in-character parts, were required also to read out-of-character passages and accuracy was unaffected by this variable, nor was there any relation between accuracy of judgements and interpersonal similarity between speaker and judge. This finding that speakers may not be able to disguise their personality very successfully when speaking is consonant with the finding of Ellis (1967; see Chap. 3) that speakers have difficulty in disguising their social status effectively. Unfortunately, Hunt and Lin do not attempt to explain the discrepancy between their study and those conducted earlier in the century. *Ad hoc* explanations could be formulated in terms of the more sophisticated judgements of present day listeners, or on the grounds that speakers now are less inhibited or more ready to reveal their true selves than they have been hitherto.

Kramer (1964) has suggested a refinement for future investigations in this area. He claims that the voice samples used in all studies have been monologues whereas many of the personality traits requiring judgements are associated with interactions, e.g. dominance-submission, introversion-extraversion, and thus might be more appropriately perceived from dialogue. Also, speakers in these types of studies have usually known the purpose for which their voices were being tape-recorded and therefore may not have given entirely natural samples. A recent study by Scherer (1972) has taken account of both these previous methodological shortcomings by taperecording a group discussion and then editing selected voice samples from it. In this situation, speakers (American and German) had no idea that their voices would be subsequently used for personality assessment. It was found that there was, as usual, little agreement between listeners' assessments and speakers' self-ratings. However, there was a better-than-chance agreement between listeners' assessments and *peer* ratings for the American and German speakers on traits of extraversion/sociability and assertiveness/dominance respectively. A similar study has been conducted by Bourhis, Giles and Lambert (1974) and will be discussed in the succeeding chapter. Other studies concerned with interaction between ethnic groups, are now beginning to emerge (Tucker, Taylor and Reyes, 1970; Taylor, Tucker and Gaboriault, 1971).

Thus, the results in this area would appear to be somewhat inconclusive and we cannot say, at the moment, that the various dimensions of a speaker's personality can be validly assessed by listening to his voice. Nevertheless, Kramer (loc. cit.) has commented upon the usefulness and validity of this type of study:

> The personality traits being judged in such studies—those traits for which some voices provide presumably erroneous stereotypes—are not definable by a set of laboratory operations. They come from common experience or

expert judges' reactions to persons, as do most of our personality-trait labels. Only part of any such personality construct is operationally defined by a test designed to measure it; part of the trait remains unmeasured. The validity criteria, such as the Bernreuter Personality Inventory . . . are often highly imperfect measures of those traits that they are used to validate . . . Seen within this framework, the listeners' judgements are as valid a measure of a trait as are the test scores which have been used for the external criteria.

Lambert (1967) in his theoretical review of the work using the "matched-guise" technique has shown how listeners' personality judgements from voice, even though they may be objectively inaccurate, are "particularly valuable as a measure of group biases in evaluative reactions."[1] By examining this and related work, we may gain insight into the question raised at the end of Chapter 3: In a class-related standard language situation, is a speaker perceived more favourably in terms of personality traits if he speaks a standard rather than a nonstandard language, dialect or accent? It would seem appropriate to commence with the work of Wallace Lambert, the methodological innovator in this field. Most of the work has been conducted in the context of English and French intergroup tension in Canada.

Until the present time, the Canadian language situation could perhaps have been regarded as a class-related standard language situation. In this cultural context, English has been historically regarded by many as the standard language with French occupying an inferior position, even in the province of Quebec where, in these terms, "nonstandard" speakers would outnumber the "standard" speakers. In 1958–59, Lambert and his associates set about investigating how each group perceived the other in evaluative, personality terms. They (Lambert, Hodgson, Gardner and Fillenbaum, 1960) asked two groups of university students, French-Canadians (FC) and English-Canadians(EC) to rate four male bilingual speakers reading the same two and a half minute passage of prose once in English and once in French, on 14 bipolar-adjective, six-point rating scales. The subjects were lead to believe that they were

1. Traditional studies have involved presenting subjects with ethnic group labels in some form of questionnaire to elicit judgements about ethnic groups. Methodologically a trend can be noted in the literature from the use of relatively artificial to more realistic judgemental situations. For example, Secord, Bevan and Katz (1956) and Secord (1959) reported consistent reactions to photographs of ethnic group members, while Razran (1950) reported similar results when subjects rated pictures accompanied by ethnic surnames. Tajfel, Sheikh and Gardner (1964) and Yackley (1969) both report in their studies stimulus speakers who were actually physically present.

actually eight different personalities and so this procedure involved the so-called "matched-guise" technique for the first time. The results indicated that both groups of judges rated the speakers in their English guises more favourably than in their corresponding French guises. The EC subjects, for instance, rated the English guises superior on seven traits (good looks, height, intelligence, dependability, kindness, ambition and having character), with the French being rated superior on only one trait—a sense of humour. The FC group, however, rated the English guises more favourably on *ten* traits, with the French guises superior on only two—kindness and religiousness. It was argued therefore that the EC viewed their own group as superior to the French group, and that the FC seemed to have adopted the inferior position assigned to them by the majority culture around them—a kind of self-denigration. Preston (1963) on the other hand, has shown a different type of relationship when the French guise was of a "Continental" (i.e. European) nature—as indeed did Lambert *et al.* (loc. cit.) in the case of one particular speaker. The EC listeners in the Preston study did not downgrade the speakers in their Continental French guises appreciably as compared with the English guises except for a few minor deviations. In contrast to the main findings of Lambert *et al.* (loc. cit.), the FC subjects generally rated the European French guises more favourably than they did the EC matched-guises. This difference between European and Canadian French dialects in terms of personality correlates will be discussed more fully later in this chapter.

Tajfel (1959) attempts to explain Lambert's results in terms other than self-denigration. He points out that the FCs accentuate the differences between the groups more than the EC subjects do on certain dimensions related to socioeconomic success: leadership, intelligence, self-confidence, dependability, character and ambition. He offers the following reasons:

> There exists in the Montreal community a discrepancy in socio-economic status in favour of the English group. Both groups of subjects are aware of this: when estimating the likely occupations of the speakers, they ascribe significantly higher status to the English than to the French guises . . . It is a fair assumption that this discrepancy causes more concern, is in a sense more salient, worrying and relevant to the French than to the English subjects . . . If this is so, some differences between the French and the English are of greater impact to them than to their English counterparts.

This explanation accounts very well for Lambert's data, but the more general hypothesis that people from a socioeconomically deprived group will tend to downgrade members of that group only or mainly on traits related to socioeconomic success is not unequivocally supported by the results of other studies.

Let us take for example the work carried out in the Philippines by Tucker (1968). In the Philippines, English can be regarded as having superior status over the many local languages, including the somewhat prestigious language, Tagalog. Tucker required a group of Tagalog listeners to rate three types of taped speakers on 12 personality traits. The stimulus speakers were native American, local Filipino-accented American and Tagalog speakers. The last two voices were presented by the same speakers using the matched-guise technique. The results indicated that the Tagalog listeners rated the American voices more favourably than the Filipino-accented American voices on 11 out of the 12 scales, and the latter more favourably than the Tagalog speakers on four scales. Tucker discusses his results in the following manner:

> The general downgrading of Filipino Tagalog relative to American English and to Filipino-English probably represents harsh economic reality. In the Philippines social mobility now depends upon the acquisition of skill in English. Higher education, better employment opportunities and travel abroad are easily accessible only to those who possess the necessary skills in English. The subjects, all prospective teachers, were particularly sensitive to these facts of life. It is not at all surprising, therefore, that judges downgraded the Filipino-Tagalog speakers, especially on those rating scales relevant to success and advancement. What is perhaps surprising is that this downgrading also extended to the more personal characteristics. There may exist then, not only an acceptance of economic reality but also a type of ethnic inferiority complex . . .

Thus a self-denigration phenomenon would seem to occur in this culture as in Canada. Nevertheless, if we return to the Canadian context we shall see that, when the variable of sex of speaker is taken into account, neither Tajfel's nor Lambert's explanatory notions are entirely adequate to explain the complexity of ingroup-outgroup evaluation.

Preston (loc cit.) investigated whether judges react similarly to male and female speakers in the FC and EC guises. In general, it was found that the EC listeners viewed the female speakers more favourably in their French guises but the male speakers more favourably in their English guises. EC female listeners were not quite as resolute as male listeners in their upgrading of FC female speakers but there was still a strong tendency in the same direction. Lambert (1967) commented that:

this tendency to downgrade the FC male, already noted in the basic study, may well be the expression of an unfavourable stereotyped and prejudiced attitude toward FCs, but, apparently, this prejudice is selectively directed towards FC males, possibly because they are better known than females as power figures who control local and regional governments and who thereby can be viewed as sources of threat or frustration, (or as the guardians of FC women, keeping them all to themselves).

The result of Preston's study with regard to FC listeners indicated not only that judges react differently to male and female speakers, but also that male and female listeners differ in their reactions. For instance, the tendency found in the case of FC male listeners to prefer both male and female representatives of the EC group is not found to the same extent in the case of FC female listeners. According to their judgements of the guises, the females appeared to view FC men as more competent (intelligent, industrious, etc.) and socially attractive (likeable, entertaining, etc.) than EC men. Lambert (loc. cit.) comments:

> the FC women, in contrast, appear to be guardians of FC culture in the sense that they favoured male representatives of their own cultural group . . . FC women may be particularly anxious to preserve FC values and to pass these on in their own families through language, religion and tradition.

From the studies so far considered, it is possible to summarize the findings as in Table 3 below, in terms of listeners' relative evaluations of speakers representing each subculture. In the table a positive sign indicates a relatively more favourable personality assessment accorded a given speaker by a particular group of listeners in comparison with a speaker of the same sex in the opposing language community. It is interesting to speculate why sex of speaker is such an important variable in this cultural context whereas in others, as will become apparent, it is not.

Webster and Kramer (1968) in a similar study of the Canadian situation, have produced evidence which at least suggests that attitudinal differences between judges affect their evaluations. They administered a prejudice questionnaire to a small sample of EC judges, and classified responses in terms of three levels of prejudice—low, middle and high. In a subsequent evaluation of FC guises, the middle-prejudice group rated the FC guises much more favourably than either low or high prejudiced listeners. Unfortunately, these findings can be no more than tentative since the total of judges over all three groups was only 22. The authors attempted to explain the results by suggesting that low-prejudiced judges would exhibit prejudice which they did not recognize, that high-prejudiced judges would recognize their negative attitudes but regard them as justified and that the middle-prejudice group would recognize their prejudice and over-compensate for it.

TABLE 3

Relative favourableness of evaluations of FC and EC speakers

| Listeners | Speakers | | | |
|---|---|---|---|---|
| | Males | | Females | |
| | FC | EC | FC | EC |
| FC Males | − | + | − | + |
| FC Females | + | − | − | + |
| EC Males | − | + | + | − |
| EC Females | − | + | + | − |

Anisfeld and Lambert (1964) have shown that the listener's language background is another factor affecting evaluation of personality from speech. These authors used 10 year old monolingual and bilingual FCs, who were instructed to listen to tape-recordings of children's voices, some in English and some in French, from children of the same age. Subjects then rated each speaker's personality on 15 different traits. Differences were found in the stereotypes held by these two groups of children such that French-speaking monolinguals upgraded the personalities of the FC speakers on all traits, whereas the bilinguals tended to see fewer differences, between the personalities of French and English speakers. The results indicate that, unlike college-age students, FC bilingual children at the age of ten do not have a negative bias against their own group. Lambert, Frankel and Tucker (1966) found in a massive developmental study investigating the evaluative reactions of French-Canadian girls to English- and French-Canadian speakers, that the negative bias against their own group emerged at about 12 years of age. These workers in fact found that the girls' social background was an important variable in that upper middle class girls were expecially biased in favour of the English-Canadian guises on tape.

Lambert (1967) comments with regard to evaluative reactions to spoken language that:

the type and strength of impression depends on characteristics of the speakers—their sex, age, the dialect they use, and very likely the social class background as this is revealed in speech style. The impression also seems to depend on characteristics of the audience of judges—their age, sex, socioeconomic background, their bilinguality and their own speech style.

Thus the interaction between speaker variables and listener variables mentioned in the preceding chapter with regard to the perception of social status from language variety appears again in relation to person-ality evaluation. The complexity of the interactions is such that it would be difficult to account for them all in terms of a single concept such as self-depreciation. Nevertheless, these studies seem to indicate (with certain exceptions) a general tendency for the French Canadian minority group to accept an evaluation of themselves derived from majority group opinion. However, as will be observed from some of Lambert's other work to be discussed in the next chapter, this pheno-menon is largely culturally-specific or, to use Wober's (1969) termino-logy, "centri-cultural".

The investigations conducted more recently into the relationship be-tween perceived personality and speech style in Canada were carried out at the University of Western Ontario by Donald Taylor and Robert Gardner. But before proceeding directly to a discussion of this work it is important first to mention an earlier study of theirs (Gardner, Wonnacott and Taylor, 1968). They were interested in investigating the dimensions of French Canadian stereotypy and had a group of 108 EC students rate the concept of "French Canadians" on 39 bipolar adjectives. From a factor analysis of these ratings, one large factor emerged (the "stereotype" factor) which was independent of subjects' own attitudes towards FCs as assessed by a separate 15-item French-Canadian attitude scale, and, according to the authors, largely "non-evaluative". The adjectives from this stereotype factor described the FC as talkative, excitable, proud, religious, sensitive, colourful, emo-tional and artistic. It is important to note that the studies to be cited from the Western Ontario group of Taylor and Gardner used this "nonevaluative" stereotype dimension as the dependent measure of their voice studies. This measure is thus distinct from the more evalu-ative traits employed by Lambert and his co-workers at McGill Uni-versity.

In the matched-guise studies mentioned so far, care was taken by the experimenters to ensure that the content of the spoken material was neutral and likely to be regarded by listeners as irrelevant to the assessment of the speaker's personality. Gardner and Taylor (1968) designed an experiment with the express purpose of investigating how voice characteristics and relevant speech-content might interact with each other in affecting listeners' judgements. At the same time they investigated possible group-conformity effects upon person perception. Their EC subjects undertook the experimental task in groups of five. Each subject listened to tape-recordings and made his responses in a separate cubicle, but in each cubicle was a display panel which, in some of the experimental conditions, gave purported information about the responses of the other four subjects. The information given was actually controlled by the experimenters. Subjects were told that the tape-recordings were of people in an interview situation talking about themselves. There were three different recordings all of the same FC speaker. In one version the speaker gave information about himself which tended to confirm the previously-established FC stereotype (talkative, excitable, proud, religious, etc.). In a second version the speaker gave information which tended to contradict the stereotype and in the third (neutral) version the speaker spoke of irrelevant matters. There were also three experimental conditions relating to group conformity. In one, subjects were given false information suggesting that their colleagues' assessments were in accordance with the FC stereotype, in a second condition other subjects' ratings were shown as contrary to stereotype and in the third condition no information was given.

The results showed that when the content of the speech confirmed the stereotype, subjects' ratings, not surprisingly, confirmed it too. Information purporting to give other subjects' responses also had predictable effects in this condition, leading to ratings which were either more or less close to the stereotype according to the direction of the "pressure". When the speaker disconfirmed the stereotype by the content of his speech, subjects tended to give neutral or moderate judgements of the various traits. Conformity-pressure in the direction contrary to stereotype had little effect on those judgements. This suggests that subjects were not entirely persuaded, either by the speaker himself or by the opinions of "others", to abandon the stereotype completely. When the speaker offered no information about himself, stereotyped responses, modifiable by conformity-pressure, tended to be given.

The same experimenters carried out a further study (Taylor and Gardner, 1969) in which the stimulus-material was presented as being part of a public lecture. It was thought that, in this setting, speakers might be less credible in their self-evaluations than in the interview setting. This supposition was confirmed by the finding that speech content tending to disconfirm the FC stereotype was even less effective in reducing the stereotypy of subjects' judgements than it had been in the previous experiment.

In addition to obtaining ratings of the speakers on five stereotypical scales, Taylor and Gardner required their EC subjects to rate speakers on three evaluative ones—likeability, friendliness and peace-lovingness. These three evaluations, provided interesting results. For example, when a speaker contradicted his group stereotype he tended to be judged more neutrally on the stereotypical scales than a speaker who confirmed the stereotype but was evaluated less favourably in terms of likeability, friendliness and peace-lovingness. As the authors point out, "it may be that ethnic group representatives bent on changing people's views of them, may have varying degrees of success, but at the same time generate unfavourable attitudes towards themselves". Conversely, when a speaker confirms what is expected of him, it seems that he is "rewarded" for maintaining the status quo and is seen as more agreeable, possibly because he causes no cognitive strain.

The impression is sometimes given by social psychologists that they regard stereotyped beliefs and attitudes as socially objectionable on the grounds that they are (a) derogatory to the groups to which they refer and (b) invalid. As it happens, the FC stereotype described by Gardner, Wonnacott and Taylor (1968), including as it does such attributes as religious, sensitive, colourful and artistic, is not particularly derogatory. It is possible, too, that the stereotype may have some statistical validity: perhaps French Canadians are, *in general*, more religious, sensitive etc., than English-speaking Canadians. There are, however, good reasons for regarding stereotypes as undesirable. They tend to be applied to any members of the relevant group immediately upon recognition of his group membership and in the absence of any evidence as to applicability in his particular case. Evidence of statistical validity of the stereotype, i.e. that it represents a correct generalization about most members of the group, does not justify this automatic application to individuals. It is characteristic of stereotypes that not only are they applied unthinkingly to individuals in the absence of supporting evidence but they are also peculiarly resistant to contrary evidence. Both these invidious features are revealed by the research discussed above.

These studies by Taylor and Gardner suggest that if a stranger's voice evokes a negative stereotype of himself in his listener, there is little he can say at that time which can make the impression positive. How, then, would it be possible to change such a negative impression? Unfortunately, there is little empirical research to suggest what specific types of information would overcome a negative stereotype, how much is needed or in what contexts it could be most effectively presented.

In Chapter 3 it was stated that the standard French dialect in Quebec appears to be derived from a source external to the culture itself, i.e. it is the European model. Thus it is likely that the French Canadian will not only compare himself unfavourably with English-Canadian speakers in some respects but will also take a poor view of himself in comparison with standard European-French style speakers. Indeed, initial support for this notion comes from the basic study by Lambert in the case of one of his bilingual stimulus speakers ("Tri") who was in fact a European-style French speaker. Lambert *et al.* (1960) state that:

> it can be seen ... that speaker Tri was not downgraded by the French subjects when speaking French as were the other speakers; in fact he was considered significantly more self-confident in French than in English. Nor do the English subjects treat him adversely in French, for they perceive him as having reliably more humour, entertainingness, and sociability in French than English. Clearly more than one speaker with a Parisian style is needed to test this notion, but the data suggest that the Montreal community may differentiate between Parisian and Canadian French in their attitudes.

This finding was corroborated later by d'Anglejan and Tucker (1973) using more than one voice sample of European French speech for French Canadian listeners to evaluate. This study was referred to in Chapter 3 and it may be recalled that European French and upper and lower class Canadian French were each represented by four tape-recorded speakers talking spontaneously about a recent blizzard. In addition to ratings of socioeconomic status that have been mentioned already, subjects were asked to rate the stimulus speakers on four personality traits. It was found, as expected, that the standard European French speakers were consistently rated as more intelligent, more likeable and more ambitious than either the upper or lower class Canadian French speakers. However, these latter voices were rated as superior to the European model in one trait, that of toughness. This was a finding that the authors did not discuss. It is interesting because it is similar to a finding by Labov *et al.* (1968) with working class speech in New York.

There are no data from any culture to indicate which personality components working class people, minority groups or nonstandard speakers value most highly. Is it of greater value within a community of nonstandard speakers to be perceived by one's ingroup as intelligent and ambitious or as tough? Intuitively, it could be suggested that in many cases the latter would be true. It is important that we should investigate this question empirically rather than impose our own value system on the situation by the biased selection of traits for examination.[2]

Although rated as superior on toughness, the Canadian French speakers were downgraded on likeability. If toughness is regarded as a virtue, this suggests some degree of ambivalence. Clearly, much more information is needed about cognitive structures relating to FCs before we can make sense of these isolated evaluations.

A study by Aboud, Clément and Taylor (1974) shows that the downgrading of nonstandard speech styles in Quebec depends not only upon the evaluative dimensions chosen but also upon the social context. Methodologically, this research is very interesting as it employed the matched-guise technique in relation to both speech and visual presentation of the stimulus material. Photographs of the same person enacting different occupational roles were used in conjunction with taperecordings. French Canadians have strong expectations that middle class French Canadians should speak standard Canadian French whereas the working class are expected to speak a more colloquial form of French called *Joual*. The subjects in this study were presented with stimulus guises of persons who were either working class or middle class and who spoke one of three styles of Quebec French varying in social prestige. After the presentation of each of the stimulus guises the subjects were asked to indicate their willingness to interact with the person (a) as a superior, (b) as a subordinate and (c) as an equal. It was found that subjects rated those stimulus persons who disconfirmed their expectations (i.e. middle class persons speaking *Joual* and working class persons speaking standard French) more favourably than those who confirmed their expectations (i.e. middle class persons speaking standard French and working class persons speaking *Joual*). The situation was perceived differently, however, when the subjects had been asked to envisage interactions where the roles were more specific, formal and normative, that is, with a superior or subordinate. In these con-

2. In a recent matched-guise experiment, Bourhis, Giles and Tajfel (1973) (see Chapter 5, p. 75f) took into account this bias in their selection of dependent measures.

texts, departures from expectations as regards social class and speech style were generally not favourably evaluated except in the case where a person's characteristics were more socially desirable than expected (a working class person speaking standard French).[3] The important point in the present discussion is that in peer relationships the use of *Joual* by a middle class speaker can make him perhaps more interesting[4] a character than he would have been had he maintained his expected and more prestigious speech style. Often, then, a particular context dictates how favourably a speech style will be received irrespective of the superiority generally attached to it.

Despite the advantages of nonstandard Quebec French, along certain evaluative dimensions and in particular social contexts, the speaker of European French appears to be generally the most favourably perceived on most personality dimensions at the present time. d'Anglejan and Tucker (loc. cit.) commented:

> Among the subjects whom we studied, Quebec style speech does not as yet serve as a symbol of national identity differentiating French Canadians from other North Americans and also from European speakers of French. We speculated that they might reject Standard European French as a form of "cultural imperialism" and show preference for the upper class French Canadian model. They did not and the consistent pattern of downgrading both upper and lower class French Canadian speech in favour of a Standard European French style . . . again emerged.

However, as Lawson and Giles (1973) have pointed out in their study of the perception of world powers, studies of stereotypical behaviour need to be replicated continually because of changes in sociopolitical situations. In other words, the French Canadian situation needs to be carefully monitored over the course of the next few years by means of voice evaluation studies. If the French Canadian self-image becomes more favourable it would seem important to relate any such change to factors occurring in the sociopolitical situation. Such information would allow us a better understanding of the causal factors underlying changes in group self-esteem. Indeed, in the next chapter we shall tentatively propose that such a re-evaluation of native speech style may have occurred in Wales.

3. The findings of the study by Aboud *et al.* are interestingly interpreted in the framework of consistency and discrepancy theories.
4. For a rationale for the choice of this dimension see Aboud and Taylor (1972), Aboud and Taylor (1973).

# 5

# Speech Style and Perceived Personality (II): Other Cultures

Although the original work on the social evaluation of speech was pioneered in Quebec in the early 1960s, work has been conducted in many other cultural contexts, most notably in the United Kingdom and the United States.[1]

## Britain

In Chapter 3 we saw that RP was considered the high prestige accent in Britain in relation to various regional forms. The early research in this culture (see Table 4) was conducted by Strongman and Woosley (1967) and Cheyne (1970). The former studied the reactions of Northern and Southern English listeners to the matched-guises of Yorkshire and London accents. Few differences between the two groups of subjects emerged; this may have been due to the fact that all subjects were attending a southern university. Judges showed considerable agreement that the London speakers were more self-confident, while the Yorkshire (Northern) accented speakers seemed more honest and reliable. The Northern judges themselves perceived their own group as significantly more generous, good-natured and kind-hearted. Cheyne

1. In addition to studies of social evaluation of speech styles in Canada, Britain and the United States of America, there has been some rather sporadic research in other cultural contexts such as the Philippines (Tucker, 1968) and Peru (Wölck, 1973). Systematic programmes of research have now begun in the Middle East and many interesting projects have recently been undertaken by Robert Cooper in Israel and by Richard Tucker in the Arab states. See Fellman (1973) for a discussion of the language situation in the Middle East. See also Lambert, Anisfeld and Yeni-Komshian (1965) with regard to Israel and El-Dash and Tucker (1975) with regard to Egypt.

(1970) looked at the evaluations of Scottish and English voices and found that both Scottish and English listeners rated male English speakers as possessing more leadership, intelligence, ambition and self-confidence than Scottish speakers. The Scottish listeners, like the Northern judges, showed some *accent loyalty*, evaluating their own group as more generous, goodhearted, friendly, humorous and likeable. The English judges also conceded friendliness to the Scottish voices.

TABLE 4

Results of two studies (Strongman and Woosley, 1967; Cheyne, 1970)

| Strongman and Woosley | Cheyne |
|---|---|
| Traits on which LONDON voices were rated more favourably by both Southern and Northern listeners: | Traits on which ENGLISH voices were rated more favourably by both Scottish and English listeners: |
| Self-confidence | Self-confidence<br>Intelligence<br>Ambition |
| Traits on which YORKSHIRE voices were rated more favourably | Leadership<br>Prestige and wealth |
| by Northern listeners:     by Southern listeners: | Good looks and height<br>Occupational status<br>Cleanliness |
| Honesty      Honesty | |
| Reliability      Reliability | Traits on which SCOTTISH voices |
| Generosity      Generosity | were rated more favourably by |
| Goodnaturedness | Scottish listeners:    English listeners: |
| Kindheartedness | Friendliness     Friendliness |
| Irritability | Sense of humour |
| Industriousness | Generosity<br>Goodnaturedness<br>Likeability<br>Nervousness |

Assuming that the loosely-termed "London" and "English" accents in these studies could be regarded as representative of Southern Standard English (RP) then a trend in evaluation may be discerned from the results in Table 4. For instance, it would seem that speakers of RP may attract stereotyped personality impressions of greater *competence* from listeners than speakers of nonstandard regional accents. This impression appears to transcend accent loyalty. However, both regional accented judges and to a lesser extent RP judges seem to consider nonstandard speakers as possessing greater personal integrity and social attractiveness than RP speakers.

With these findings in mind, Giles (1971b) designed a matched-guise study to determine whether this same evaluative trend would be reflected in personality assessments based upon two other regional accents relative to RP—South Welsh and Somerset. Since previous work had shown (as mentioned in Chapter 3) that RP, South Welsh and Somerset accented speech represented high, intermediate and low status positions respectively, it was further hypothesized that a similar ranking would emerge in respect of the personality traits of competence, integrity and attractiveness.

Matched groups of listeners from South Wales and Somerset who were considered to be representative of the accent communities concerned, rated the matched-guises of two speakers reading a neutral passage of prose in RP, South Welsh and Somerset accented speech. The hypotheses were confirmed. The RP speakers were perceived as relatively more ambitious, intelligent, self-confident, determined and industrious than the regional accented speakers. Moreover, it appeared that these competence impressions were to a certain extent a function of relative accent prestige. Nevertheless, nonstandard accented speakers were found to be more favourably evaluated than standard accented speakers with respect to personal integrity and social attractiveness; tendencies in this direction were also apparent in the traits of reliability and entertainingness. More specifically, the nonstandard speakers were perceived as less serious and more talkative, good natured and humorous than the RP speakers. In another study, to be cited in Chapter 6, Powesland and Giles (1975) found that listeners whose own accent was RP rated the regional guise of one of the same speakers as more sincere than his RP guise.

Looking at the results of the three U.K. studies as a whole in the light of Tajfel's (1959) explanation of the findings of Lambert et al. (1960), discussed in the previous chapter, we see that RP speakers were evaluated more favourably by both standard-accented and nonstandard-accented listeners on socioeconimocally-related traits. But this does not help us to explain why the high prestige group of listeners conceded superiority in certain affective traits to the "inferior" group.[2]

2. Such evaluative ambivalence has also been shown in a South American context. Wölck (1973) found, using the matched guise technique, that Peruvians rate speakers of their national language, Spanish, more favourably on traits related to socio-

Perhaps a clue to the explanation of this latter trend can be found in Mann's (1963) study of intergroup rivalry between Hindus and Whites in South Africa. Mann found results similar to those just mentioned in that both Whites and Hindus believed the White group to be superior on traits related to competence and socioeconomic success, whereas both groups considered the Indian group superior on traits of friendliness, popularity, sensitivity and "getting on with people". In other words, the Indian group excelled on traits of social attractiveness. Mann had hypothesized such results in his paper and argued for the superiority of the lower socioeconomic group on certain traits in the following terms:

> He (the Hindu) would not feel entirely crushed by the hierarchical system, however much of life is presumed to be under control . . . Indeed, since he himself does not have to rule and keep others in place, he might feel that he can get on more pleasantly with people than the power-brandishing white is able to. This comes about also, perhaps, because in subordination he has had to learn to accommodate himself with others.

It could be argued, therefore, that regional accented speakers, precisely because they maintain their nonstandard speech patterns, may be perceived by both groups (i.e. listeners from both the standard and the nonstandard accent groups) as being not at all concerned with a determination to improve their socioeconomic position. Accordingly they may be seen as more community-oriented, and more concerned with the development of interpersonal relations, personal integrity and social attractiveness. One might speculate further that to a nonstandard-accented regional listener, RP speech implies that the speaker has a need to camouflage his origins and perhaps even his true personality. This suspicion of a deliberate disguise in the form of pronunciation pattern may lead regional-accented people to question the genuineness of the RP speaker's nonlinguistic characteristics, such as his motivations and attitudes. Thus, for example, his apparent good nature, sincerity and reliability may, like his accent, be regarded as something of a "fake"—hence his relatively poor showing on traits of personal integrity

---

economic success than speakers of the nonstandard (native) language, Quechua. Nevertheless, speakers of this latter language are perceived more favourably on affective traits than speakers of the prestige code; they are considered for example as stronger, more sincere and less arrogant. See also the evaluative ambivalence among North American Jews as shown by Anisfeld, Bogo and Lambert (1962).

and social attractiveness. Moreover, it could be that RP speech is perceived as the voice of power and perhaps economic and social exploitation. In other words, an RP speaker may be perceived as having
attained his position of prestige largely through ambition and intelligence but also through sacrificing to some extent his integrity and trustworthiness. An emphasis on achievement in this sense might also make
him less concerned with interpersonal relations outside "business" and
involve sacrifices in terms of social attractiveness. This is all highly
speculative, of course, but some such attempted accommodation of
Tajfel's model is likely to be quite fruitful in generating research hypotheses.

It is interesting to note that according to Giles's (1971b) findings,
the correlates of nonstandard usage in Britain show some differences
from the French dialect situation in Quebec. But it would be naive to
rely too heavily upon the generality and finality of the findings so far
in either culture. The variables involved in this field of study are
numerous and complex. Giles (loc. cit.) paid some attention to the
listener variables of age and regional provenance and found some consistencies.

For example, on ten traits[3] the Somerset subject sample evaluated
all three stimulus accents less favourably than did the Welsh listeners.
The reason for this regional difference is an open question at the present
moment. Also, a significant age × voice interaction effect was found in
the analysis of variance of five traits (good looks, ambition, intelligence,
self-confidence and determination) in that 17 year olds rated RP more
favourably and the two regionals less favourably than did 12 year old
listeners. This trend is consonant with findings reported on the perception of status from voice in Chapter 3.

Perhaps a slightly more interesting listener variable is that of social
attitudes. In Chapter 3, it was mentioned that subjects scoring low on
an ethnocentrism scale rated the standard accent less highly and the
regional accents more highly in terms of prestige than did highly ethnocentric subjects. The results of the above study were analysed in terms
of the 17 year old subjects' scores on the British Ethnocentrism Scale
(Giles, 1972a). The hypothesis was that highly ethnocentric subjects
would evaluate the personalities of the South Welsh and Somerset
speakers less favourably and the personality of the RP speakers more

3. Generosity, good looks, seriousness, goodnaturedness, honesty, imagination,
ambition, intelligence, kindheartedness, and industriousness.

favourably across all traits than would subjects scoring low on ethno-centrism. However, the hypothesis was supported on only two competence traits—those of intelligence and determination. A trend of the same sort was evident with regard to ambition and industriousness. Rather surprisingly, on five traits concerned with social attractiveness and personal integrity (sociability, humorousness, popularity, entertainingness and kindheartedness), the low ethnocentrism sample rated all three stimulus voices more favourably than did the highly ethnocentric. Perhaps less ethnocentric people tend to be less socially cynical than the more ethnocentric in the sense of being more prepared to perceive favourable qualities in all speakers regardless of their status.

We shall now consider a study which supports the notion that non-standard accent usage is perceived more favourably in Britain than in Quebec.

## A Cross-National Study

In Chapter 3 it was reported that if a British speaker modified his regional accent to make it closer to the standard model, his perceived status increased, whereas if he broadened it his prestige declined. What effect would similar accent changes have upon perception of his personality? The previous study by Giles (1971b) would suggest that a speaker in Britain who standardized his accent in the course of social interaction would be perceived as more competent than a person who did not initiate such a speech shift. On the other hand, the speaker should be perceived as possessing more integrity and social attractiveness if he broadened his accent. The work conducted in Quebec leads to a different prediction. It would suggest that "standardizing" an FC accent would elicit a favourable personality impression across most traits whereas broadening it would have the reverse effect. A study in both cultures was designed by Bourhis, Giles and Lambert (1975) to examine possible differences in evaluative reactions to shifts in speech style towards and away from the standard accent.

The South Welsh accent was the regional variety of speech chosen for empirical attention in the British context since certain parallels could be drawn between the language situations in Quebec and Wales in that elements in both cultures are striving for language maintenance. Although few sociolinguistic data are available there seems to be a small but growing interest in language survival and nationalism in Wales over the last few years. And so, a broadening of the Welsh accent in English could be taken as a reflection of an individual's desire to emphasize his national identity.

For the Welsh part of the study subjects from South Wales were randomly divided into six experimental groups. They were all told that a Welsh athlete had recently been placed seventh in a Commonwealth Games diving competition and that they were to hear him in two consecutive radio interviews, purportedly taped after the competition. In one interview, the athlete's interviewer was an RP speaker while in the other the interviewer possessed a mild South Welsh accent. In this latter interview, the athlete always employed a mild South Welsh accent also —the baseline condition of the stimulus material—but with the RP interviewer his speech style (using the matched-guise technique) varied from condition to condition. Thus, in one condition he maintained his mild Welsh accent in conversation with the RP interviewer (the no-shift condition), in another he modified his accent towards that of the interviwer (i.e. towards standard speech) and in yet another condition he broadened his Welsh accent (i.e. away from that of his interviewer). These conditions are tabulated in Table 5 below. The interview order was balanced, thereby yielding the six experimental conditions. Since the two consecutive interviews were to be presented to each group of subjects, the dialogue differed slightly in order to make the interviews

TABLE 5

Stimulus presentation (Bourhis, Giles and Lambert, 1975)

| Conditions | Cultural contexts | Speech styles in Interview 1 | | Speech styles in Interview 2 | |
|---|---|---|---|---|---|
| | | Interviewer | Athelete | Interviewer | Athelete |
| 1 (No-shift) | Wales | m Welsh | m Welsh | RP | m Welsh |
| | Quebec | FC | FC | EF | FC |
| 2 (Shift to standard) | Wales | m Welsh | m Welsh | RP | RP |
| | Quebec | FC | FC | EF | EF |
| 3 (Shift away from standard) | Wales | m Welsh | m Welsh | RP | b Welsh |
| | Quebec | FC | FC | EF | $FC_{pop}$ |

m = mild;  b = broad;  EF = European French;  $FC_{pop}$ = popular FC interesting and plausible. The texts for the two interviews were matched as to duration, information content, vocabulary and grammar. After listening to the two interviews, subjects were required to rate the athlete's personality on a 21-item rating scale.

Few of the scales showed a significant voice effect but the three which did were in the directions hypothesized. The athlete was perceived as more intelligent when he shifted to RP than when he did not shift at all, and more intelligent in the latter case than when he broadened his Welsh accent. However, this accommodation to the RP interviewer also involved a decrease in perceived trustworthiness and kindheartedness relative to the no-shift condition. The shift to more Welsh-sounding speech with the RP interviewer (although associated with diminished estimates of intelligence) resulted in the athlete's being rated as more trustworthy and kindhearted than in any other stimulus condition.

The study was repeated in Quebec with appropriate modifications. In this context, FC subjects were told to listen to a tape-recording of a Quebecois athlete who had been placed seventh in a Pan American Games diving competition. They were to hear the athlete in two radio interviews said to have been taped in a Latin American studio after the competition. In one interview, a commentator from France would conduct the interview while the other, an FC commentator from Quebec would conduct the discussion. As in the previous context, the athlete spoke formal FC with the FC interviewer, but changed his style (using the matched-guise technique) with the European French (EF) interviewer (see Table 5 again). In one condition he maintained his formal FC style, in another he standardized it to a European-style French and in the last condition he broadened his accent to a more popular FC style. Again, subjects were asked to rate the athlete's personality on a large number of rating scales.

The results did not totally conform to expectation in this instance. The athlete was indeed perceived as more intelligent and educated when shifting to EF than in the no-shift condition, and as least intelligent and educated when shifting to a popular FC style. However, the athlete was rated equally sociable, likeable, trustworthy and so forth in all three conditions. Perhaps one reason for the fact that the results were not entirely as expected on the basis of the earlier work was that in this case the stimulus passage was a dialogue, whereas the previous studies in Quebec had used monologues. It may be recalled that Kramer (1964; reported earlier) stated that differences in evaluations of speakers were likely to occur as between the two types of stimulus material. Perhaps different evaluative dimensions become salient in interactive passages. It was unfortunate that the study by Bourhis *et al.* did not include the trait of toughness. On the basis of the findings of d'Anglejan and Tucker (1973) it might be expected that the speaker would be more favourably rated on this trait when he shifted to a more popular FC style rather than to an EF style. Nevertheless, this study shows that, irrespective of cultural context, the standard variety of the language still tends to evoke a stereotyped impression of competence. However, the authors stated:

> The reasons for these cross-national differences are difficult to explain at the present time and are worthy of further investigation. It could be that informal FC in Quebec is not considered the most favourable style of speech in which to emphasize one's Quebecois identity and perhaps formal FC is considered a more appropriate medium for communication. In Wales, on the other hand, a broad Welsh accent may be perfectly acceptable as a medium for expressing one's national identity.

Perhaps of equal interest to these cross-national differences (to which we shall return later) was the finding that 86% of the French Canadian subjects in the "shift-to-EF" condition asserted that they themselves would *not* have spoken to the EF interviewer in the standardized speech style, as had the stimulus speaker. Unfortunately, no data were available to indicate whether these subjects could have switched effectively anyway. Almost all of these subjects said that the reason for not changing their speech style was that they felt by so doing that they would be losing their Quebecois identity. Nevertheless, they credited the speakers who shifted to standard EF with more intelligence for having done so. These findings corroborate that of d'Anglejan and Tucker (1973) referred to in Chapter 4, which was that their French Canadian subjects showed no overt admiration of EF at the more conscious level (i.e. they denied its superiority to FC) but actually upgraded EF at the more unconscious level in the indirect phase of the study.

## The Welsh Language

Thus far, our discussion of the speech situation in the United Kingdom has been limited to the varieties of accented *English*. However, it would be wrong to consider Britain a homogeneous community in terms of language use as there are still many native speakers of Irish, Scottish Gaelic and Welsh residing in the islands. Nevertheless, it would not be unfair to suggest that only Welsh has to any reasonable degree effectively withstood the pressures of the English language. In considering the Welsh language situation, it is useful to note the following statement by Thomas (1971):

> It is the indigenous language of Wales spoken today by 26% of the population according to the 1961 census. This represents a steep drop in the present century from 54·4% of the population recorded in the 1891 census and more than 90% earlier in the same century. It is in fact a beleaguered language, and undoubtedly faces a stiff struggle for survival; indeed, the struggle is closely underway, and no observer of the contemporary scene can fail to be struck by the vigour and determination with which friends of the language have begun to marshal their resources on its behalf.

Although a study by Giles (1971b) included Welshmen's reactions to speakers of Welsh accented English, it did not investigate their judgements of Welsh *language* speakers. This would appear to be a most interesting question particularly in view of the tremendous revival of interest in the Welsh language recently. (The number of Welsh language evening classes for adults in South Wales has multiplied several fold since 1971. In addition, there has emerged a Welsh Language Society (*Cymdeithas yr Iaith*) which has militantly protested about the inferior role assigned to the language in the principality (see Thomas, 1973).) And so Bourhis, Giles and Tajfel (1973) designed a matched-guise study to determine how different groups of Welshmen perceive members of their own group who adopt various speech styles.

Three groups of Welshmen acted as listener-subjects: (1) Welsh-English bilinguals, (2) those who were learning the Welsh language and (3) Welshmen who neither could speak the language nor were learning it. These subjects were given a questionnaire tapping their social and language attitudes in order to validate the assignments to groups. As their reported ability in speaking and understanding Welsh declined significantly across the three groups, so also did their ability to speak English,[4] their use of Welsh at work and at home and their dissatisfaction with the government's handling of Welsh autonomy. In addition, the non-learners of Welsh thought it less useful for their

4. This is, of course, a surprising finding. It could be that bilingualism gives one such confidence in one's linguistic skills that one tends to over-evaluate facility in one's non-native language. Moreover, since the Welsh learners also rated their ability to speak and understand English higher than the non-learners did, it could even be that *learning* a second language allows one confidence in one's first language.

children to learn Welsh than did either the Welsh learners or the Welsh speakers and assessed themselves as feeling less Welsh than did the latter groups. Moreover, it was found that the learners of Welsh had significantly more of a Welsh accent in their English than either the Welsh bilinguals or the non-learners of Welsh. It could be suggested from this evidence that a Welshman is able to assert his Welsh identity by making an effort to learn his national tongue and uses the Welsh accent to emphasize this identity until such time as it can be replaced by the language itself. The three groups were thus distinct on a number of issues relating to the language.

All three groups of listeners were asked to evaluate the personalities of various Welshmen they would hear on tape. They were told that those speakers who were bilingual chose to read the standard passage of prose in Welsh while those who could speak only English would, naturally enough, read it in that language. Actually, the passages were read by the same two male bilinguals in each of the following guises: in Welsh, in English with an RP accent, and in English with a South Welsh accent. In view of the differences already reported between the three groups in their language attitudes, it was rather surprising to find no evaluative divergence between them in their rating of the various Welshmen speaking on tape. Whether subjects could speak Welsh or not, or how Welsh they felt themselves to be, did not seem to matter, in the sense that all groups upgraded the Welsh language speaker on most traits. Indeed, on many traits such as trustworthiness, friendliness and sociability, the mere possession of a Welsh *accent* appeared to secure for the speaker ratings as favourable as those accorded to speakers of the language itself. However, the Welsh language speakers on tape were rated the most nationalistic and patriotic of all. Moreover, on the scale "How much I'd like to be like that speaker", all groups of Welshmen preferred to attain the image of a Welsh speaker rather than to model themselves after the supposedly high prestige, RP speaker. Indeed, when the RP-accented Welshman was rated highly it was almost exclusively on dubiously-valued traits such as conservatism, snobbishness and arrogance. Nevertheless, the RP speaker was the most favourably rated of all on the trait of self-confidence, although no evaluative differences between the speakers emerged on the scale of perceived intelligence. Certainly, these results suggest that the Welsh have a favourable image of themselves as a group: they do not appear to seek the prestigious English, RP mode of speaking. Even those Welshmen who express doubts about the value of speaking Welsh nevertheless accede to this view.

The dependent measures chosen for this study were not those employed in traditional matched-guise studies. Prior to the voice evaluation study, a pilot investigation had been undertaken with a sample of Welsh adults. These subjects were asked to list as many words and phrases as they could which best described their idea of a typical Englishman, bilingual Welshman and so forth. In fact they were asked to describe the kinds of people who would be represented on the stimulus tapes. From their responses in this open-ended task a word order was tabulated according to word frequencies and the words most frequently used were retained for the matched-guise study proper. It was considered that these concepts would be the most salient dimensions for Welshmen when evaluating the voice samples. The salient traits turned out to be rather surprising, including such adjectives as romantic, sportloving and patriotic. As the scales based upon these traits were so unusual, having been to all intents and purposes chosen by the subjects themselves, it is a little difficult to compare the results of this study directly with those of the evaluative reactions to Welsh accented speech reported earlier by Giles (1971b) and Bourhis, Giles and Lambert (1975). Nevertheless, if this is done, an important discrepancy between the two sets of findings emerges. It may be recalled that in the latter studies, RP speakers and those who shift in the direction of this speech style were more favourably evaluated on traits of competence (e.g. intelligence and self-confidence) than Welsh accented speakers. Although the same trend for the trait of self-confidence was found in the Bourhis, Giles and Tajfel (loc. cit.) study, there was no such difference between the Welsh accented and RP speakers on the trait of intelligence. This evaluative discrepancy between the findings could be attributable simply to differences in the subjects sampled: the Welsh language study used adults as listeners whilst the other studies used adolescents from South Wales. On the other hand it may be of significance that the data for Giles (1971b) and for Bourhis et al. (1975) were gathered before 1972 whereas the data for Bourhis et al. (1973) were collected at the very end of that year. Now this was a year when considerably more attention was given in the mass media to issues relating to the Welsh language and Welsh political separatism and activism than perhaps ever before in recent times, and it is possible that within an extremely short period of time, Welshmen had come to view their

native speech styles very positively on dimensions that were important
to them, and that their speech had become symbolic of their Welsh
identity. Informal discussions with Welshmen, particularly in the south
east of the principality, confirm the notion that a dramatic re-evaluation of all things Welsh has recently occurred. But nobody really
understands what has brought about the change or why the process
apparently got under way in 1972. However, many ethnic groups in
the western world—and not only the American Blacks—are now re-
defining their identities. One could cite as examples the Basques, the
Catalans and the Bretons amongst others. Later we shall discuss how
these Welsh findings, and those obtained from matched-guise studies in
other cultural contexts, may be considered within a framework of
ethnic identity.

## The United States of America

Much of the work conducted in the United States on the perception of
personality from speech style has concentrated upon White standard
and Black nonstandard language varieties. In relation to this culture,
Buck (1968) comments that "although dialect variations have been
described in the literature, scant attention has been given to their effect
on the listeners' impressions and judgements of the speaker." However,
Semmel (1968) has attempted to show the importance of dialect
differences in judgements concerning White and Negro children. Negro
and White children were subjected to two structured interviews, the
tape-recordings of which were played to college students who were
required to rate the children on semantic differential scales. The racial
characteristics of these students were in fact not mentioned; it is therefore assumed that the majority were White. These semantic differential
ratings indicated distinct differences between the two groups of children,
particularly in terms of intellectual ability. Typescripts of the interviews were given to another group of judges who were required to
differentiate White from Negro children and were unable to do this.
The author then inferred that the distinct differences in the semantic
differential ratings were due to the children's dialect. Unfortunately,
Semmel did not ask this second group of judges to complete semantic
differential ratings from the typescripts alone; these may have revealed
similar trends to those of the first group. If this had indeed been found,
it would have suggested that the listeners in the first part of the

experiment were responding to content cues rather than vocal ones.

Tucker and Lambert (1969)[5] conducted a study with adults concerning personality evaluations from White and Negro accented speech. Taped samples of the speech of representatives of six American accent groups were played to three groups of college students—Northern White, Southern White and Southern Negro—who were asked to evaluate them. The most favourable profile of trait ratings was accorded to a style of speech known as "Network English". This is the typical mode of speaking used by national newscasters in the United States and is perhaps the nearest American equivalent to the British "RP" style. Apart from this general agreement as to the accent which evoked the most favourable impression, the subjects diverged on racial/regional lines in the ordering of various speech-styles. Both Northern White and Southern Negro judges rated an Educated Negro Southern accent in second place, for example, whereas Southern White subjects put Educated White Southern (the speech of their own peer group) in second place. Negro judges placed this same accent last in order of preference.

Once again listener characteristics were shown to be an important variable affecting judgements as they have been in relation to other cultures and at other levels of analysis. But also of interest here is the question raised in Chapter 3 as to whether or not there really is a regional stratification of speech styles in the United States as there is in Britain. This study surely suggests that there may be some kind of hierarchical structuring of regional dialects in the United States. Indeed, there must be areas of the United States where a larger number of less prestigious forms are included in the local speech than elsewhere; this would tend to stereotype local speakers as at least less competent than speakers from other areas. Perhaps a regional stratification could also be found amongst speakers of English in Canada. Kleiven (1974) has been looking at a similar question at a preliminary stage in Norway.[6]

Many of the studies reviewed thus far have utilized monologues of an emotionally-neutral nature. However, a study by Houck and Bowers (1969) using persuasive messages shows that the evaluation of Southern speakers in relation to Northern speakers with respect to perceived personality characteristics depends on the specific content of

5. See also Ryan (1969) and Fraser (1973).
6. For a discussion of the language situation in Scandinavia see Lind (1972).

what is being said. Groups of Northern college students were played passages arguing against government aid to needy students. Matched-guises of two male speakers were used, one speaking in a Northern dialect and the other in a Southern dialect,[7] and listeners were required to rate the competence (experienced/inexperienced; expert/ignorant; trained/untrained) and trustworthiness (just/unjust; admirable/contemptible; honest/dishonest) of the particular speaker they heard. On this passage, which was deemed to be irrelevant to regional norms, the Northern speakers received higher ratings on the two dimensions than did the Southern speakers.

However, when the passage was relevant to regional norms—in this case a moderately-toned speech opposing racial integration in Southern colleges on the grounds that this would tend to destroy Negro culture—the Southern speakers were credited with significantly greater competence than their Northern counterparts. No significant differences were found with respect to trustworthiness. It may be the case that, on matters relevant to regional norms and to the problems of a particular community, a speaker from the region concerned may be considered an expert and therefore perceived more favourably than a speaker from outside the region. (If the speaker also puts forward an argument which is unexpected, or thought to be uncharacteristic of his group, this may carry further conviction.) Pear (1971) gives an example of the significance of a regional accent in relation to subject-matter of regional relevance in the British context:

> It is doubtful if behaviourists of speech-study can deal adequately with attitudes and deeprooted sentiments towards certain types of speech. A person's attitude towards a variant of "his" language may be temporary, connected with a particular situation. I resented having to listen with unusual care to BBC world news telephoned from Central Europe in a strong Scottish accent, but when I heard similar speech from the disaster at Ibrox Football Ground, my sympathy with the speaker was intense.

Studies indicating interaction effects produced by the combination of vocal stimuli and message content should serve as a warning against over-enthusiastic generalization from experiments in which evaluations are based entirely upon hearing neutral passages of prose read by an anonymous voice. The number of possible variables under the heading of "message content" must be enormous. There are also, as we have

7. It would appear from the description of the stimulus material that in fact only *accent*, not dialect, was varied.

seen, important listener-variables. In addition, it is undoubtedly the case that in "real-life" situations judgements are affected by numerous other interconnected variables relating to the appearance and supposed identity of the speaker and general context in which the judgements are made.

A rather curious study by Buck (1968) suggests, according to the author herself, that whether a speaker possesses a standard or non-standard dialect is more important in terms of perceived personality than whether it is White or Negro. She tape-recorded a neutral passage of prose read by four speakers who were representative of (i) a Standard White dialect, (ii) a Nonstandard White dialect, (iii) a Standard Negro dialect and (iv) a Nonstandard Negro dialect and were identified as such by five speech teachers. A group of 25 women college students rated their impressions of these speakers on semantic differential scales. Results showed that they preferred standard to nonstandard dialect speakers, and for the most part did not express preferences as between White and Negro speakers when both used a standard dialect. Another group of judges rated the recordings with respect to competence and trustworthiness, and once again, standard dialect speakers irrespective of race were judged to be more competent than nonstandard users of the language.

> Only in ratings of trustworthiness of speakers did the subjects' consistent patterns of response give way. Negro and White speakers with standard dialect were perceived as more trustworthy than the White speaker using nonstandard dialect, yet the Negro speaker using nonstandard dialect was not judged less trustworthy than the White or Negro speakers with standard dialect. (Buck, loc. cit.)

However, although speech specialists were able to distinguish a Standard White from a Standard Negro dialect, it seems that non-specialists may be unable to do so since the vast majority of judges in the first evaluative task of Buck's labelled the Standard Negro speaker as "White". This may very easily account for the lack of differentiation in personality assessment between them. Furthermore, to make a distinction between Standard Negro and Standard White seems a little dubious as the mere presence of Negro features in standard speech should, by definition, one would have thought, make it nonstandard. Buck's criteria for "dialect differences" are defined in her paper with references to pronunciation variations, and it would appear that in this and other studies concerning the evaluation of American "dialects" (e.g. Markel, Eisler and Reese, 1967; Houck and Bowers, loc. cit.) there may be a misleading use of this term. Dialect differences according to Spencer (1958) refer to a "nonstandard form of language differing from the Standard, if one exists, in lexical, grammatical, phonological and phonetic respects", whereas accent is "synonymous with manner of pronouncing". The studies in this area seem to be referring only to the evaluation of personality from patterns of pronunciation and intonation, and do not take account of other linguistic levels.

In Buck's study, the more favourable ratings were fairly consistently given to standard speech styles. A finding indicating selectively favourable ratings of nonstandard speakers comes from a study by Labov, Cohen, Robins and Lewis (1968). In their study on the nonstandard English of Negro and Puerto Rican speakers in New York they found, as would be expected, that all social classes rated a middle-class speaker more favourably in terms of job acquisition than a working-class speaker. But in response to a question as to how well these speakers would fare in a fight situation (perhaps a measure of "toughness"?) all social classes indicated a preference for the working class speaker's chances. This result is similar to the finding by d'Anglejan and Tucker that nonstandard FC usage is perceived as related to toughness. There is thus rather limited evidence to support the finding from studies in Britain that nonstandard speech attracts some favourable evaluations.

There are, of course, numerous ethnic minority groups in the United States, many of them having "old country" languages which may be retained over several generations of residence in America. Although members of these ethnic minority groups theoretically have the opportunity to achieve any position in society, realistically their advancement is often severely limited, unless they conform to the norms of the dominant society. A variety of forces exist which exert pressure on the minority group member to neglect his traditional language in favour of English. It is necessary for him to become bilingual in order to be successful in American society. This process has important consequences in terms of identity, because achieving bilingualism often involves the adoption of the values, attitudes and motives associated with the new language (Lambert, 1967). For the minority group member, a positive orientation towards English is frequently accompanied by a negative orientation towards the "inferior" mother tongue. He is pushed by political, social and economic necessity to learn and use English and to neglect his mother tongue. On the other hand, he may be encouraged by personal and group identity to continue the use of his mother tongue, or he may be discouraged from using English by the difficulty of learning it or by the prejudiced reactions of others towards accented English. The problems of these conflicting positive and negative reinforcements for both English and the traditional language frequently place the adolescent, in particular, in an alienated state or give rise to a crisis of identity.

However, it would appear that some ethnic groups, despite this crisis situation at the present time, have a very positive view of their own ethnic speech styles. This is certainly the picture which emerges from data gathered in two studies of the Franco-Americans of Northern Maine. The first of these studies was conducted in the summer of 1971 in St. John's Valley (Lambert, Giles and Picard, 1975). The researchers asked 10, 13 and 17 year olds and college students to listen to and rate various speakers using different varieties of English and French. The results may be considered developmentally. At the age of 10 years, middle class American English and local-accented English were rated superior to any form of French including the European model. But by the adolescent years, a different pattern emerged. Admittedly, the 13 and 17 year olds still seemed to be aspiring towards the English model, but other factors came into play to modify this trend. For instance, the European French speakers were seen to be equally as competent and socially attractive as the English speakers. Moreover, the upper class variant of the local French dialect was also equivalent to the European French and English models in terms of social attractiveness. By college age, there appeared no difference between the European French dialect, the English models and the upper class variety of local French. Even non-Franco-Americans of college age from Maine showed this evaluative trend. This apparent lack of prejudice against the minority by the majority may to a limited degree help to explain why the Franco-Americans of Maine are less inclined to self-depreciation than other minority groups.

It is interesting to note that people in this Franco-American region, in contrast with the situation in Quebec, have an evaluative tolerance for their own form of French dialect, which was rated as favourably as European French. In addition, upper class local French speakers were rated more favourably than the upper class Canadian French speakers in terms of intelligence, friendliness and politeness. The European model does not appear to have superior status over the upper class local dialect form as in French Canada. Also of interest was the finding that sex of speaker, in contrast to the results found in Canada by Preston (1963), was not really an important variable.

In the summer of 1973, Lambert, Giles and Albert (1975) conducted a follow-up study of similar design in and around the small rural city of Caribou, some forty miles south of the St. John's Valley region. It was found that here too Franco-Americans had a very favourable attitude towards speakers of upper class local French. Indeed, this trend was even more marked in Caribou than further north as there was no downgrading of upper class local French by 10 year olds. Although this speech style was also rated very positively by an adult sample, its credibility as reflecting traits of competence suffered somewhat amongst adolescent respondents as it had with the St. John's Valley sample. Nevertheless, taking both studies in Northern Maine together, it would seem that the future of French there, and local French in particular, should be viewed optimistically.

Unfortunately, however, research conducted by Ellen Bouchard Ryan on Mexican-Americans' evaluative reactions to various forms of Spanish and English spoken in the Chicago area suggests that not all ethnic minorities in the United States have such a positive attitude towards their native language and ethnic speech styles. In a series of three voice-evaluation studies, Ryan took into account the context in which each speech style was used since it has been suggested that Mexican-Americans come to see Spanish as valuable in a familial setting, and English as valuable in more formal, public domains (Rubel, 1968). This she accomplished by having her stimulus speakers on tape read one passage relating to the home domain (a mother preparing breakfast in the kitchen for her family) and one passage concerned with the school domain (a teacher giving a history lesson to her class). In the first of these studies (Carranza and Ryan, 1975) the paragraphs were written in both English and Spanish with careful attention given to ensure that the content and grammar in both paragraphs were applicable to the subjects being tested. Hence, four types of passages were employed—English-Home, Spanish-Home, English-School and Spanish-School—and each of these was represented on tape by four speakers, making 16 different speakers in all. Anglo- and Mexican-American adolescents were required to evaluate the personalities of sixteen speakers representing the four "context × language" categories. The scales used for their assessment included semantic differential traits and four status-stressing scales (educated-uneducated; intelligent-ignorant; successful-unsuccessful; and wealthy-poor) and four solidarity-stressing scales (friendly-unfriendy; good-bad; kind-cruel and trustworthy-untrustworthy). The results showed that for both groups of listeners, there was a definite preference for English in the school context, and a slight preference for Spanish in the home context. In addition, while English was rated higher than Spanish on both status and solidarity scales, Spanish was rated higher on the solidarity scales than on the status scales. This important effect of the contextual domain on the listeners' reactions to these speakers suggests that the subject takes into account the appropriateness of the speaker's speech style as well as his ethnic identity.

Accentedness is particularly important for Mexican-Americans because as Ortego (1970) has argued, the vast majority of bilingual and even monolingual Mexican-Americans in the southwest speak English with an unmistakable influence from Spanish phonology. Indeed, Carter (1970) has suggested that such accented English can reduce chances for educational and occupational success. For this very reason, there are numerous references in the literature (e.g. Krear, 1969) to the attempts of some Mexican-Americans to eliminate any traces of accent from their own speech and that of their children, in the hope of obtaining broader opportunities. Yet at the same time, there are positive functions served by an accent, as maintaining one's accent may be associated with maintaining one's identity.

In the light of these negative and positive social and psychological attributes of accented speech, Ryan and Carranza (1975) explored the evaluative reactions of Anglo, Black and Mexican-American adolescents towards speakers of standard English and Mexican-American accented English. These three groups of listeners evaluated the personalities of twelve speakers representing four "context × accent" categories and using the same rating dimensions as in the previous study (Carranza and Ryan, 1975).

The results showed that although standard English speakers received more favourable ratings in every case, the differences were significantly greater in the school context than in the home context, and for the status ratings than for the solidarity ratings. Unexpectedly, Anglo and Black raters followed the pattern of Mexican Americans in their overall ratings of the four passages. Thus, even the adolescents who would not associate the accented speech with their own group were more tolerant of deviations from standard speech in a home context than a school context. It would seem that a wider range of speech styles is acceptable in an informal setting than in a formal setting. Also contrary to expectations was the finding that Mexican-Americans did not prefer accented English in the home context or on the solidarity scales. As the authors suggest, "it may be that Spanish, rather than accented English, is the language preferred in the home and used more commonly as a symbol of ethnic identity". Furthermore, in a third evaluative study, Ryan, Carranza and Moffie (1974) investigated the relationship between the amount of accentedness heard and the attributed characteristics of the speaker. They found high correlations between the accentedness ratings and each of the other ratings indicating that small increments in accentedness are associated with gradually less favourable impressions of the speaker.

These findings are of considerable interest in relation to the evaluative reaction process more generally. It would appear, as Ryan and Carranza (1974) have pointed out, that they are inconsistent with the accepted view that evaluative reactions to speakers involve a two-stage process of inference which consists in first identifying a speaker's group membership and then applying the associated stereotypes (Robinson, 1972). These studies, together with other previously cited in the course of the last three chapters, have established the effects of context and degree of accent on the evaluative reactions to speech styles, thus indicating that group membership is only one factor underlying the reactions. Obviously further research is needed to unravel the evaluative process before definite statements can be made.

## Speech style and group self-esteem

The findings discussed in this and earlier chapters indicate that some groups, such as the Franco-Americans and the Welsh, respond with favourable evaluations to voice-samples representing their own characteristic speech styles, whereas others, such as the French-Canadians, give mainly unfavourable ratings when presented with samples of speech similar to their own. Some British regional-accented speakers appear to be ambivalent about people with accents similar to theirs. The reasons for this variability are not yet understood. Neither is it clear what social or other circumstances might lead a group to change its responses to voice samples representing its own members. It is hoped that research in progress at the University of Bristol and other European centres, within a theoretical framework suggested by Tajfel (1974, 1974a), will help to elucidate these problems.

Lambert's original assumption that listeners' judgements of voice samples give an indication of their opinions and attitudes in respect of the social groups which the voices represent, has never been seriously questioned. The more particular assumption that when members of a class, community or ethnic or language group make evaluations in response to samples of speech-styles similar to their own they are actually providing evidence of the group's self-image, is also generally accepted. Perhaps we should remind ourselves that these are assumptions and seek to validate them. This presents a problem. To validate speech-sample ratings against conventional attitude scale scores would be inappropriate since, according to Lambert (1967), responses to voice guises provide a more accurate picture of a person's real feelings towards outgroups than can be found by the direct questionnaire approach. The value of speech-style evaluation studies, whether the stimulus material relates to an outgroup or to the subjects' own group, rests upon the presumption that they are capable of eliciting unconscious affective responses and attitudes. This being so, they have the status of a projective technique—a method of appraisal notoriously difficult to validate.

There is, however, some evidence that language and speech styles are closely bound up with feelings of group identity. For example, Taylor, Bassili and Aboud (1973) showed that French Canadians perceived English Canadians who spoke mainly French as more similar to themselves than those who spoke mainly English. Equivalent criteria of identity were found for bilingual Franco-Americans by Giles, Taylor, Lambert and Albert (in press) and for Welshmen by Giles, Taylor and Bourhis (1974). There are also indications that speech style is becoming an increasingly important dimension of ethnic identity for Black Americans. Kaplan (1969) believes that the Black minority "has sought to make the 'nonstandard' dialect . . . the focus of cultural and ethnic identity." Similarly McDavid and Davis (1972) say that "the new militancy of rising expectations following the recent civil rights legislation and court decisions has led to feelings of group identity and pride in all forms of social experience including language, so that the patronizing depreciation of nonstandard forms of speech . . . is deservedly rejected." Bourhis, Giles, Tajfel and Taylor (1974) have proposed that the more positively a group views its own identity, the greater will be the range of social situations in which it is acceptable for members of the group to use the speech style peculiar to it. In other words, a group with a very positive self-esteem will feel able to use its characteristic speech style in most social situations, however public. In contrast, a group with feelings of inferiority will restrict its own demotic speech style to very informal situations. In the more formal situations it will feel obliged to use the dominant group's language variety. For example, we have observed earlier (Ryan and Carranza, 1975) that both Anglo- and Mexican-Americans are prepared to tolerate the use of the low prestige Mexican-accented English in the domain of the home but are less inclined to do so in the more public context of school. Support for the proposed hypothesis may also be gained from another study discussed earlier. Bourhis, Giles and Lambert (1975) have shown that Welshmen, a group with a supposedly positive self-esteem, take a favourable view of the broadening of the Welsh accent in English by one of their own group in a public radio interview. French Canadians, however, a group thought to have low self-esteem, do not upgrade an ingroup speaker on affective dimensions when he emphasises his ethnic accent in a comparable situation. The interrelationship between language variety and ethnic identity is very complex[8] and more research is needed before an adequate theoretical framework can be constructed. However, the validity of the hypotheses suggested above could be tested in a number of different cultures.

Perhaps the most appropriate test of the voice-evaluation procedure as a means of obtaining measures of group self-esteem would be to determine its usefulness in the context of a theoretical formulation. We noted earlier that Tajfel (1959) was able to construct a coherent account of French Canadians' evaluations of their own group on the assumption that their responses to French Canadian voice-samples could be regarded as indications of their group self-esteem. This in itself goes some way towards vindicating the assumption. It would be possible to elaborate Tajfel's suggestion that group self-evaluation is related to socioeconomic success. It could be hypothesized, for example, that when there is socioeconomic disparity between two groups in the same culture,

  (1) the greater the socioeconomic disparity, the greater would be the
      disparity between the "deprived" group's evaluations of itself
      and its evaluations of the more successful group, and

8. In this respect see Kloss (1967), Fishman (1972) and Fellman (1973a; 1973b).

(2) the greater the objective socioeconomic disparity between the groups, the greater would be the disparity between
   (a) the successful group's evaluations of the unsuccessful group on socioeconomically related traits and
   (b) the unsuccessful groups' self-ratings on these traits.

Some support for this hypothesis might be found by comparing the situation of French Canadians in Quebec with that of Franco-Americans in Maine. It would be necessary to show that the French Canadians, who appear to have a poor opinion of their own group on traits related to socioeconomic success, are objectively less successful than English Canadians, and that Franco-Americans, who take a more positive view of themselves, do not suffer from socioeconomic inferiority to the same extent. One could also hypothesize that changes in the objective socioeconomic disparity between groups would be correlated with changes in ingroup and outgroup evaluations obtained from voice-samples.

# 6

# Speech Style and Attitudes

We have been considering the evidence with regard to the relation between speech style and listeners' evaluations of the speaker. Evidence concerning the relation between speech style and the impact of the speaker's message, in terms either of its effect upon listeners' attitudes or of judges' evaluations of its content quality is rather sparse. It is to this question that we shall now turn. Unfortunately, there has not been sufficient work on the problem to allow of cross-cultural comparison and we present instead a general review.

## Content quality

A study by Glasgow (1961) investigated the effects of manner of speech upon the appreciation of spoken literature. He employed four different speech variables (voice quality, pitch, speech rate and enunciation), and hypothesized that readings from literature presented in a "good" manner with regard to these variables would favourably influence audience appreciation of the material, whilst presenting them in a "poor" manner would adversely influence audience appreciation. Goodness and poorness were assessed by experienced university speech teachers in terms of whether the manner of speech was aesthetically pleasing, expressed suitable emotional states, sustained attention, gave appropriate intonation, emphasis, etc. His hypotheses were borne out in the results, and it was found that enunciation was the most critical variable: poor enunciation decreased appreciation more than any other variable.

An unpublished study by Stolinski and Thayer (1970) showed the effect of speech style on the perceived quality of a story. It was found that White college students rated taped readings more favourably when the speaker was White than when the speaker was Black.

More impressive results in the same culture were found by Crowl and MacGinitie (1970). Six White and six Negro fifteen year olds read answers to each of two questions: "Why do we celebrate thanksgiving?" and "What is the difference between discovery and invention?" Although race of speaker and passage were balanced so that the Negro and White students read exactly the same material, the White students were rated as having answered the question better than the Negroes by White judges.

Another finding relating pronunciation prestige with perceived quality of message content has been produced by Taylor and Gardner (1970). In this study, French- and English-Canadian subjects were required to select which of five photographs was being described in English on tape by either an English-Canadian or a French-Canadian accented speaker. Speakers not only gave their own spontaneous descriptions of the target pictures but also read each other's descriptions. After the task, subjects judged the performance of the speakers, and it was found that the speaker possessing the lower accent prestige (the French-Canadian) was rated significantly poorer in the quality of his description by both groups of listeners.

A small number of studies, then, have shown that the quality of a communication may be downgraded if it is spoken in a nonstandard accent. Does it follow that such a message will be less persuasive?

## Persuasiveness

Obviously it is quite beyond the scope of this monograph to include anything like an adequate synopsis of the large body of research concerned with persuasion and attitude-change. The interested reader is referred to reviews by Jones and Gerard (1967) and McGuire (1969) on the effects of communicator, communication and communicatee variables upon attitude-change, and to Fishbein (1967) for a comprehensive review of the nature of attitudes and their measurement. We are concerned here with a limited aspect of the whole problem. Hollander (1971) stated:

> Much of the research on the role of the communicator as a source of influence has centred on his *credibility*. This general characteristic em-

bodies several features which the recipient may perceive to give the source validity, including expertise and trustworthiness. There are also such factors as background, appearance, and other indentifiable features of the person which might determine his acceptability. Part of the content of his communication, therefore, is the impression he conveys to the audience in terms of these characteristics.

Several experiments have demonstrated the operation of a "prestige" factor in the persuasiveness of a communication. For example, Haiman (1949) presented to three groups of subjects a tape recorded speech variously attributed to the Surgeon-General of the United States, to the Secretary of the American Communist Party and to a "Northwestern University sophomore". Not only was the Surgeon-General rated significantly more competent than the other two speakers but also his speech was significantly more effective in changing attitudes than were the others. In a subsequent study, Paulson (1954) attributed a taped speech either to a political science professor or to a student. For female listeners there was no significant difference in the effects of the two speakers, but among male listeners the proportion of those shifting opinion was greater for the group which thought it had been addressed by the professor.

However, Miller and Hewgill (1964) claim that "while considerable emphasis has been placed on the 'who the source is' dimension, little consideration has been given to 'how the source says it'." It would seem reasonable to suppose that if nonlinguistic cues to a speaker's prestige (for example, knowledge of his occupation) can influence the persuasiveness of his message, linguistic cues to prestige or competence could have a similar effect.[1]

## British studies of persuasive speech

Although we have presented evidence to suggest that an argument is perceived as superior in quality when spoken in a standard accent rather than a nonstandard accent, there is little but conjecture to suggest that a standard accent is actually more effective than a nonstandard accent in bringing about a change of opinion on the part of

1. Studies by Pearce (1971) and Pearce and Brommel (1972) have not confirmed this assumption. They found that although speakers who delivered their persuasive messages in a conversational rather than a dynamic style were rated as having more credibility, they were not in fact any more persuasive.

the listener. However, a study by Giles (1973), in the context of British regional accent use, looks at the relative persuasiveness of standard and nonstandard accents. The question he considered was: would a standard-accented speaker, because of the prestige and competence with which his speech pattern is associated, possess greater credibility than a nonstandard speaker? It would seem likely that the subject-matter of the message would be of crucial importance. As mentioned in the previous chapter, there is evidence that a speaker from a particular region when presenting an argument related to regional norms is more persuasive than a speaker with a standard accent. It may be the case more generally that an impression of competence with regard to a particular topic does not necessarily go hand-in-hand with an impression of social status and prestige. The subject of the persuasive message in Giles's experiment was assumed to be unconnected with regional values and norms. It was capital punishment.

First, Giles (1973) tested whether the attitudes of 17 year olds towards capital punishment were stable over a period of seven days. When an acceptable level of reliability had been established in a pilot study, the investigation proper began. The attitudes of more than 500 17 year olds towards capital punishment were obtained and five groups of 50 subjects each matched for sex and their attitude on the topic, were eventually formed. All of these subjects were considered to be regional accented speakers. Seven days after the initial attitudes were elicited, each group was presented with the same argument against capital punishment but in a different form. The message was given in one of five forms, namely, a typescript which the subjects read and four recorded male matched-guises of RP, South Welsh, Somerset and Birmingham accented speech. These accents had previously been found to command different levels of prestige, decreasing, in the order given, from RP to the Birmingham accent (see Chapter 3). After attending to the stimulus material, members of each group of subjects were asked for their attitudes towards capital punishment. They were also asked to give a rating of the quality of the argument with which they had been presented. Although the content of the argument was exactly the same irrespective of its mode of presentation, the ratings of content quality were found to be a positive function of the communicator's accent prestige. This finding helps to substantiate the findings from research in North America reported earlier in this chapter. However, a different trend was found for the actual persuasiveness of the arguments. Only the regional voices were effective in producing a significant shift in subjects' attitudes; the typescript and RP guise did not.

Whittaker and Meade (1967), using college students in Brazil, Hong Kong, India, Rhodesia and Jordan found that a communication was perceived as being more credible in oral than in written presentations. However, it seems that the form the oral presentation takes is of the utmost importance. Indeed, it would appear that the persuasiveness of an RP speaker, at least with reference to this particular topic and in the case of these particular subjects, is no greater than that of the lifeless, printed word. This reference to topic specificity should not be taken lightly for Klapper (1960) contends that

> no mass medium can be assumed to be generally or always more persuasive than any other mass medium . . . Some topics furthermore may be susceptible to better presentation by visual than oral means, or by print rather than by film, while for other topics no such difference exists.

But how can we explain the fact that the perceived quality of the argument appears to be unrelated to the persuasive effect of the same argument? There are two possibilities here. The first of these relates to communicator credibility. Hovland, Janis and Kelley (1953) analyzed the factors leading to the perceived credibility of the communicator of a persuasive message under two headings:

(i) The extent to which a communicator is perceived to be a source of valid assertions (his *expertness*).

(ii) The degree of confidence in the communicator's intent to communicate the assertions he considers most valid (his *trustworthiness*).

Unfortunately, this study by Giles did not attempt to determine directly how the subjects perceived the communicator's credibility. However, the results of a previous study (Giles, 1971b, reported in Chapter 5) are pertinent to this question. It was found that RP speakers evoked a stereotype more favourably evaluated in terms of personality traits of competence in contrast to regional accented speakers who were more favourably evaluated in terms of personal integrity and social attractiveness. On the basis of these findings, it is reasonable to suppose that subjects stereotyped the competence (including the intelligence) of the anonymous communicators in the persuasion study in terms of their relative accent prestige values and hence we find the predicted results in the evaluation of argument quality. However, with regard to persuasiveness, the two aspects of communicator credibility seem to be in conflict in this instance. If it can be assumed that a communicator's perceived trustworthiness is comparable with his perceived integrity (reliability and sincerity, for example) then the following conflicting situations are apparent:

(a) RP communicators are high on expertness (competence) but low on trustworthiness (integrity), while

(b) Nonstandard communicators are low on expertness but high on trustworthiness.

Studies to be found in the literature have either compared the persuasiveness of a communicator high on perceived expertness and trustworthiness with a communicator low on both, or have presented communicators who were of unequal status on one credibility dimension but equal on the other. No study so far has manipulated both dimensions in different directions and so it cannot be claimed with any confidence which is the more salient of the two. From the results of this investigation it might appear that perceived trustworthiness is possibly of relatively more importance than perceived expertness. In any event, this hypothesis is worthy of empirical attention on a number of wide-ranging topics.

Giffin (1967) in his review of the factor analytic studies of source credibility suggested that *five* dimensions were operative, not merely the two mentioned by Hovland *et al.* These were the communicator's expertness, reliability, intentions, dynamism and personal attraction. In the preceding chapter it was speculated that the pronunciation patterns of an RP speaker may be perceived at least by some listeners as being something of an affectation or disguise. This perceptual tendency, it was suggested, may be generalized to a conception of the RP speaker as a person who strives for social advancement, modifying his behaviour (verbal and social) in pursuit of this end. Thus it may be proposed, on the basis of the previous findings and of this speculation that the regional accented speaker may be more favourably perceived in terms of his realiability and intentions relative to the RP speaker. It also seems likely from the findings of Giles (1971b) that the regional accented speaker may be high on personal attraction, being evaluated favourably in terms of sense of humour, talkativeness and kindheartedness. Moreover, it could be hypothesized, from the evidence that an RP speaker has been found to be less talkative, less humorous and more serious than a regional accented speaker, that the former would be stereotyped as staid, passive and perhaps even lacking in physical vitality. Therefore in terms of Giffin's theoretical framework, there is at least reason to suppose that regional accented communicators would be more favourably perceived on four out of five credibility dimensions in relation to an RP communicator, that is in terms of reliability, intentions, personal attraction and dynamism. It is likely then that this "credibility bias" in favour of nonstandard accented communicators may be the cause of the curious relationship shown in the above investigation between perceived quality of argument and its degree of persuasiveness. If one were to accept this possibility, since standard accented speakers typically concede integrity to nonstandard speakers, the same trends should have occurred with standard accented listeners in the capital punishment study also.

An alternative explanation of the findings however, can be proposed. At the present time, it may be supposed, moderately-expressed liberalism and evidence of a social conscience are culturally-valued characteristics of the individual. An argument attacking the use of the death penalty for murder could be regarded as an expression of such liberal-mindedness. It may be the case that when a communicator of perceived low status and competence (the regional accented speaker) adopts this culturally-valued orientation, there is a greater tendency to shift opinion in his direction than when the communicator is an RP speaker, for the following reason. The attitude of the low status person (although the actual quality of his argument is evaluated somewhat unfavourably) may be perceived as being at variance with that expected of the social class to which, according to accent stereotype, he should belong, and this may increase his perceived trustworthiness and the apparent sincerity of his viewpoint in relation to an RP communicator (cf. Walster, Aronson and Abrahams, 1966; Koeske and Crano, 1968). If this tentative explanation has any validity it would imply that the greater persuasiveness associated with regional speech in Giles's experiment was not an inherent feature of such speech but a consequence of contrast between expressed and expected attitudes. Although this explanation was offered as an alternative to the first, it is conceivable that they may operate in combination. The second explanation suggests that had the argument presented been more compatible with the expected attitudes of a regional accented speaker, the RP speaker might have been more persuasive.

Powesland and Giles (1975) decided to test this latter possibility by using *standard* accented listeners, and arguments that were more clearly related to perceived social status. Six days prior to the presentation of a persuasive message, a large group of medical undergraduates were asked the following question: "What is your attitude towards the recent Industrial Relations Act which governs the activities of trade unions and employers?" They were asked to express approval or disapproval of the Industrial Relations Act, using a seven-point rating scale. From those subjects who cooperated it was possible to obtain four groups of subjects matched for sex and attitude score.

Two stimulus passages each taking approximately five minutes to read, were prepared. One argued for and the other against the Act. The scripts were based upon debates in the House of Commons. It was assumed that support of the Act could be regarded as politically conservative (or Right) and opposition to the Act could be regarded as politically Left. (These had been the alignments during House of Commons debates on the issue.) It was further assumed that listeners would tend to associate RP speech with Right opinion and regional speech with Left opinion. Thus there were four possible combinations of opinion and speech-style as shown in Table 6. Two of the conditions

TABLE 6

The experimental design (Powesland and Giles, 1975): supposed compatibility of accent and argument

| | Arguments | |
| Speaker's Accent | In favour of Industrial Relations Act (Right) | Against Industrial Relations Act (Left) |
| --- | --- | --- |
| RP | Compatible | Incompatible |
| Bristol | Incompatible | Compatible |

were defined as "compatible" and two as "incompatible" in terms of the relation between expressed attitude and attitude presumed to be associated with speech style according to stereotype. The two arguments were presented on tape by the same male speaker, using the matched-guise technique, in both RP and Bristol regional accented guises. Each group heard only one version of the stimulus material and afterwards subjects were asked to rate the speaker on a number of personality traits and to indicate again their attitudes concerning the Industrial Relations Act. As expected, the RP speaker, irrespective of the argument presented, was rated superior in social class to the regional speaker but less favourably in terms of sincerity. Interestingly enough, the speaker reading the Right-wing passage was rated higher in social class than the speaker reading the Left-wing passage, irrespective of accent. Also of interest was a voice $\times$ argument interaction in that the "compatible" messages tended to be judged as more sincere than the "incompatible" ones. There was a non-significant trend indicating a tendency for the RP speaker to be more effective than the regional speaker in bringing about attitude change ($0.05 < p < 0.10$). However, the only condition which produced a statistically significant shift in attitude was the "incompatible" combination of RP speaker adopting the Left-wing argument. Thus, the hypothesis that accent-message incompatibility would have a persuasive function received some empirical support but the supposed link with sincerity was not confirmed by these subjects' judgements which suggest, if anything, that an impression of sincerity is fostered by compatibility between accent and opinion (cf. Argyle, Alkema and Gilmour, 1971).

If the present findings, in which RP-speaking listeners tended to be most influenced by the argument spoken in RP, are taken in conjunction with the capital punishment study, in which regional accented listeners were most persuaded by an argument spoken in a regional accent, a possible conclusion would be that the listeners' identification with the speaker is the most important factor. Conceivably the listener is most persuaded by a speaker who is perceived as "one of us" in terms of social class as indicated by accent. And so, to use Jones's and Gerard's (1967) terminology, there may be some need for people to be persuaded by those whom they consider to be co-oriented (cf. Weiss, 1957). As McGuire (1969) points out,

> there is a considerable body of evidence that a person is influenced by a persuasive message to the extent that he perceives it as coming from a source similar to himself. Presumably the receiver, to the extent that he perceives the source to be like himself in diverse characteristics, assumes that they also share common needs and goals. The receiver might therefore conclude that what the source is urging is good for "our kind of people" and thus changes his attitude accordingly.

In the kind of experiment described here, accent is one of the very few indications available to the listener as to the attributes of the message source. He probably uses accent as a clue to the speaker's social class, as shown in Chapter 3, education, and personality, as shown in Chapters 4 and 5, and is thus able to form a judgement concerning the similiarity between the source and himself.

The results of these two studies of the effect of accent upon opinion-change are explainable by the notion of co-orientation or identification between source and receiver. However, accent-message incompatibility has not, from these results, been ruled out as an unimportant variable, but it appears to need to be in combination with identification to be effective. It does not appear that incompatibility creates an impression of sincerity. Possibly a perceived discrepancy between what is expected of a communicator and the message he actually gives has the effect, as suggested by Taylor and Gardner (1970), of giving the message salience and making it more memorable. The effect of accent-message incompatibility upon such variables as recall of content should perhaps be investigated.

Thus, drawing the two persuasiveness studies together, one comes to the following tentative conclusion. The quality of an argument is more favourably perceived when presented in a standard accented voice—even regional accented listeners were prepared to concede this in the capital punishment study. But when it comes to attitudinal (and per-haps behavioural) consequences of an argument, listeners may be more convinced and persuaded by a speaker with whom they can identify—an ingroup member. Certainly further research needs to be conducted to verify this conclusion on a wide variety of topics in Britain. But similar studies need to be conducted in French Canada and the United States at least to test the cross-cultural nature of the phenomenon.

We have spent a great deal of space demonstrating that a nonstandard speaker is evaluated less favourably than his standard speaking counter-part along personality dimensions of competence. But what, if any, are the likely behavioural consequences of such a negative bias? It could easily be suggested that the regional accented speaker is very likely to be the recipient of a certain amount of social prejudice on a variety of levels. Hogan (1968) briefly discusses the social implications of prestige patterns of pronunciation (in relation to American speech) and claims that the nonstandard speaker exhibits speech characteristics "which can close off casual conversation among strangers, which terminate job interviews, which even on the faceless telephone evoke a statement that an apartment advertised as vacant was leased earlier that same day."

However, before proceding to consider some of the possible be-havioural implications of nonstandard linguistic usage, it is as well to be cautious about the relation between expressed attitude and actual behaviour. Fishbein's (1967) approach to attitudes and behaviour has been that "behaviour toward a given object is a function of many variables, of which attitude toward the object is only one."

Indeed, a number of empirical studies in the literature on attitude change have illustrated the lack of correspondence between reported attitude and later behaviour (e.g. Leventhal, Singer and Jones, 1963). We shall draw attention to certain potential social prejudices that could arise from nonstandard speech, some of which have as yet not been empirically explored. We approach this subject in full awareness of the dangers of generalizing from attitude to behaviour in this manner. The areas with which we shall be mainly concerned are: co-operation, employment and education.

## Co-operation

One possible consequence of the negative evaluations accorded to non-standard speakers of a language might be that people would be less willing to cooperate with a nonstandard than with a standard speaker. Limited evidence for this proposition stems from a study by Gaertner and Bickman (1971) using what they called the "wrong number technique". This study was concerned with the effect of racial attitudes on helping behaviour.[2] 540 Black and 569 White subjects received what was ostensibly a wrong number telephone call. The caller, identifiable by his voice characteristics as being Black or White (i.e. nonstandard or standard speaker) explained that he was attempting to call a mechanic from a telephone booth near a main road because his car had broken down. The caller also said that he had no more change with which to make another telephone call to the garage. The subject could help the caller by contacting the garage for him. The number provided to subjects was that of a confederate of the caller and so the responses could be checked. The result showed that Black subjects helped Blacks and Whites to approximately the same extent whereas White subjects helped Black callers somewhat less frequently than White callers. In another study, Gaertner (1972) found that the political viewpoints of the White subjects was an important variable: Black callers elicited less help from conservatives than from liberals.

2. See also Weitz (1972) for a study concerned with the relationships between Whites' attitudes towards Blacks and the nature of their behaviour (including voice tone) directed toward them. In addition, see Daniel (1970) for the types of verbal cues emitted by Whites which Blacks use to attribute insincerity to them.

Moreover, conservatives terminated the telephone conversation prior to a request for help more frequently for Blacks than Whites.

Clearly these results may more readily be interpreted in terms of prejudice against a particular ethnic group than as a reaction to non-standard speakers *per se*. But it would be interesting to use the technique to discover whether nonstandard White speakers in the United States elicit less help than is offered to standard speakers. Similarly, it would be interesting to determine whether White nonstandard speakers would discriminate in their helping behaviour between standard and non-standard callers. One might predict that in Canada, French Canadians would receive less help than English Canadians from English Canadian subjects. Predictions of results in Britain would need to take into account not only the generally high prestige of RP but also the apparent hierarchy of regional accents. There would probably be interaction effects as between characteristics of caller and subject. For instance, the use of a standard accent in a working class district in order to elicit help might not be as well received as a nonstandard variety. There might also be differences in terms of the latency of help, its quality and so forth, under certain conditions. This would seem a fruitful area of research. In the light of Fishbein's cautionary words, quoted above, regarding the prediction of behaviour from assessed attitudes, the "wrong number technique" is of special interest because it is a way of eliciting actual behaviour on the part of the subject: will he or will he not call the number requested? There remains the question as to how well behaviour elicited by this technique would correlate with equivalent responses in a face-to-face situation.

In a recent study conducted in Britain by Giles, Baker and Fielding (1975), the matched-guise technique was extended for use in a face-to-face situation to determine by means of a very simple behavioural index whether subjects would behave differently with standard and non-standard speakers. The investigation was also designed to take into account two serious methodological problems associated with the matched-guise technique. The first of these problems relates to the fact that the stimulus material in most studies concerned with speaker evaluation has consisted of tape-recordings. This has prompted many critics (e.g. Tajfel, 1962; Lee, 1971; Robinson, 1972) to suggest that providing subjects with vocal stimulus cues only, may be far too artificial and limiting a procedure to be meaningful in an evaluation task. It has been suggested that such an evaluation situation lacks social reality. The second problem was raised by Lee (loc. cit.)[3] who was concerned with the effect of repeated message content from stimulus speakers upon raters' evaluations. The fact that listeners continually heard the same message from a series of target speakers would, he suggests, make them place more emphasis on vocal variations in speech than would be the case in ordinary discourse. Evaluative biases educed by the method could be due in large measure to the evaluative set induced in the listeners.

In view of these methodological problems Giles et al. designed their study with three aims: (1) to use the matched-guise procedure with a stimulus speaker present face-to-face with listeners rather than using the more artificial taped stimulus material; (2) to provide listeners with no prior evaluative set and have subjects act upon the stimulus speaker's instructions without knowing they would be required to evaluate his personality subsequently; (3) to determine, using a simple index, whether subjects would behave differently towards standard and non-standard British accented speakers.

The behavioural index adopted was that of communication length. Mehrabian (1965), Weins, Jackson, Manaugh and Matarazzo (1969) found that subjects were prepared to write 25% longer letters about an imagined liked person than they were about an imagined disliked one. Similarly, Höweler and Vrolijk (1970) found that a subject's verbal output, shown by a "spoken letters" technique is increased by 40% when he is speaking to an imagined liked person rather than to an imagined disliked person. Giles et al. considered the possibility that factors other than likeability (for example, perceived status) might also be influential in determining communication length. Hence, their study was specifically designed to test whether subjects would provide more written information to and about an RP speaker than they would when the same speaker provided the same message but with a lower prestige accent (Birmingham).

The subjects of the experiment were two groups of 17 year old high school students from South Wales. It was found from post-experimental rating scales that these groups were matched for their self-reported knowledge of, and interest in, psychology. Two experimenters, one male and one female, were introduced to the two groups separately as members of a University psychology department. After the introduction, the male addressed the first group in an RP accent and said that he

3. For a critique of Lee's paper, see Giles and Bourhis (1973).

and his colleague were interested in how much the students knew about psychology. He told them that few students entering University to specialize in psychology actually knew what was involved in the subject. He said that a proportion of the new entrants became unsettled and disillusioned with University work when their expectations about the subject were not met, and to avoid this happening in future, the University had decided to find out exactly how much high school students knew about psychology. The subjects were each handed a sheet of paper and requested to write down what they thought psychology was all about in five minutes. After about a minute, the male experimenter left the room never to return. When the time allotted was up, the subjects were told to put their pens down and were addressed by the female experimenter (in RP). She told them that if, as was expected, it was found that young people did not have a realistic notion of the content of modern psychology, then the University would consider having a member of staff visit schools informing students of the true nature of the subject matter. They were told that the University was wondering whether the gentleman who had previously addressed them was the right person for that job, and that they could help in this decision. The subjects were then handed another sheet of paper and asked to write down their opinion of the male experimenter and his suitability for that kind of work; they were given five minutes for this task also. The subjects were afterwards provided with a questionnaire containing traditional rating scales and were asked to evaluate the speaker on them.

The same procedure was adopted for the second group of students except that this time the male experimenter spoke the same words in a Birmingham accented guise. The authors claimed that the speaker assumed both guises realistically, attempting the same speech rate and paralinguistic features in both situations. In addition, he was made fully aware of possible experimenter effects in his presentations and therefore attempted to reflect the same personality, mannerisms and interest in the proceedings on both occasions.

It was found that the subjects wrote 24% more to, and 82% more about the psychologist when he addressed them in a standard accent (RP) than when he used the nonstandard accent. In addition, he was rated significantly more intelligence in the former than in the latter guise. Interestingly enough, 13 out of 28 subjects in the RP condition mentioned in their description of the stimulus speaker that he was "well-spoken" but only two subjects out of 28 in the nonstandard accented condition focussed on voice characteristics in their descriptions at all. This avoidance by subjects of comments about voice characteristics when describing the Birmingham accented speaker may be related to an individual's general reluctance to communicate perceived unpleasant information (see Rosen and Tesser, 1970).

Despite the departures from the more traditional procedures, a perceived difference in the speaker's intelligence still emerged in the two conditions as in many previous studies. Another difference between this study and many of its predecessors, was that the stimulus person was assigned the same occupational status in both his roles. In previous studies, speakers on tape have usually been unidentified. But this study shows that, even when a person is assumed to possess relatively high social status (in this case, that of a member of the staff of a university), his speech style nevertheless appears to be a salient cue in attributing competence to him.[4] It would seem important in future studies in this area to determine the effect of assigning different occupations to a stimulus speaker when he adopts different speech styles. Certainly, it seems essential to procure more information as to how speech style interacts with other relevant personal characteristics such as occupational status, dress style[5] and so forth.

A follow-up study using the matched-guise technique has been conducted by Richard Bourhis at University College, Cardiff, with a live theatre audience. During the interval, those attending the performance were invited to help the theatre by cooperating in a short audience

4. Thus far, our discussion has been concerned with how a person's speech style can affect another's judgement of, and behaviour towards him. Professor R. J. Baker, University of Prince Edward Island, has, however, observed (personal communication) quite a different chain of events in an inter-personal judgement process. He believes that "frequently a judgement is made of an individual on other grounds and then comments about speech are made to rationalize that judgement". Professor Baker came to this conclusion on the basis of taperecording employers' interviews with job applicants having *similar speech styles* and asking the employers subsequently for their assessments of the applicants' speech. When the employer had decided not to hire a person, perhaps on the basis of academic record, general appearance, or some other factor, he usually found fault with the applicant's speech. However, when the decision had been to hire the applicant, the speech evaluation was favourable. The fact that people may often rationalize their somewhat arbitrary decisions about an individual at the level of speech is an interesting phenomenon, and one worthy of further empirical investigation.

5. In this connection, see Harris and Baudin (1973).

survey. This information was transmitted to them via the loudspeaker system—some nights in a standard accent and others in a nonstandard accent. Preliminary analyses show that more people completed the questionnaire and wrote more on their forms when the plea was made in the former rather than the latter guise. A speaker's speech style has thus been shown to be influential in affecting the quantity of his audience's information output and the willingness of other's to help him. Perhaps future studies in this and other cultures will determine whether the quality of information given to a standard accented speaker would be superior to that conveyed to a nonstandard speaker. It would be important in such studies to examine the role of setting, topic, the nature of the audience, etc. as these would significantly influence the effectiveness of standard accented speech.

## Employment

It may well be the case that the nonstandard speaker is at a disadvantage in terms of occupational opportunities and advancement as Hogan's statement quoted above implies. Indeed, Bellows and Estop (1954) have shown in a review of the literature that interviewers frequently base their decisions about whether or not to hire a man on some personal whim or mannerism of the applicant which is totally unrelated to his qualification for the position. Speech characteristics are a fairly salient feature of an applicant during an interview and are likely to be the basis of judgement or the stimulus to prejudice. More specifically, Ellis (1967) claims that the evidence "although not conclusive suggests that the student who comes from a lower class family is likely to be discriminated against at hiring time." Petrucci (1959) found that engineers from lower status backgrounds earn less than engineers from higher status background. This does not necessarily indicate bias against engineers with lower-class origins: there may be many other reasons why they make less money than their higher status colleagues. Nevertheless, a job applicant with a nonstandard accent is liable to attract whatever bias there may be against lower-class applicants and to be perceived as less competent than a similarly qualified applicant with a standard accent. A factor analytic study by Hopper and Williams (1973) demonstrated that "intelligence-competence" was the prime factor in employability as judged by employment interviewers. We have seen (Chapters 4 and 5) that nonstandard speakers in various different cultures tend to be rated lower on competence traits than standard speakers.

Subjects for the studies reported by Hopper and Williams were people who, as part of their regular job routines, conducted employment interviews and made hiring decisions. They heard a 90-second simulated employment interview on tape. The interviewee was variously a Black, a Mexican-American, a Southern White or a standard American speaker. A set of 40 semantic differential scales were then used (e.g. the speaker sounded sure-unsure, intelligent-unintelligent, relaxed-tense etc.). Each subject also assessed the probability that he would actually employ the person for a range of occupations. A factor analysis of these ratings revealed four factors. Factor 1 appeared to be concerned with the speaker's perceived intelligence and competence. Factor 2, comprising four scales, related to the speaker's agreeableness. Factor 3 was "self-assurance". Factor 4 consisted of the single scale, "Anglo-like—non Anglo-like".

The authors concluded from their study:

> Only the first of these factors, intelligent-competent, served as a consistent predictor of employment decisions. And its predictability was strongest in leadership occupations (executive, foreman). By contrast, speech seems unimportant as a predictor of success in job interviews for manual labor positions. This seems intuitively reasonable, since speaking the standard dialect may be irrelevant, or even ineffective in such positions. Between these two positions lie the categories of clerical and technical positions. Speech ratings appear to be a partial predictor of success in these interviews, but perhaps not a vital one.

If we add to these findings the possibility that in some occupations the possession of a regional or nonstandard accent may be a positive advantage, the situation does not look too bleak for the less prestigious speaker. For instance, such a person may be perceived as having personality characteristics important to the job requirements, such as personal integrity and social attractiveness. Nevertheless, it appears that the nonstandard speaker tends to be stereotyped as suitable only for relatively low-grade occupations. He might have difficulty in persuading interviewers of his suitability for jobs normally occupied by standard accented speakers. The problem may become more pressing in the future if competition for non-manual jobs increases, for as Lawton (1968) warns:

> There is the socioeconomic fact that traditional working class socialization processes are preparing its young members for a world which is disappear-

ing: in the near future, routine manual jobs are going to disappear and jobs will become available in industry or in bureaucratic, welfare and distributional spheres which require a much higher level of symbolic control.

## Education

A number of studies cited in the previous chapters suggests that a teacher in a classroom situation is likely to expect less of a child with a nonstandard accent than of one with a standard accent. For instance, Seligman, *et al.* (see Chapter 1) showed that a child's speech patterns were a more important determinant of his assessed ability than even some of his actual classwork. Another study by Crowl and MacGinitie (mentioned earlier in this chapter) also showed that possession of a nonstandard accent could have a detrimental effect upon assessments of one's work. The well-known research by Rosenthal (1966) has shown what effect poor expectations of a child's performance can have in terms of the child's subsequent achievements. A study by Frender, Brown and Lambert (1970) examined the relationship between speech characteristics and scholastic success. Lower class pupils who had received good grades in school were found to have a distinctly different speech style from others with poorer grades matched for age, verbal and nonverbal intelligence. These "better " students used intonation more appropriately and spoke in softer voices and their pitch was higher than the "poorer" lower class students. These authors concluded that "how a child presents himself through speech may very well influence teachers' opinions and evaluations of him".[6] This study was, however, correlational, and thus only suggestive of speech style as a possible determinant of teachers' attitudes. But, as Wilkinson (1965) has commented: "that accents should carry such social (and hence psychological) disadvantages in this way, is not a desirable state of affairs." It is interesting to note with regard to second language learning that Tataru (1969) suggested that foreign accents erect a social barrier between the speaker and members of the native speech community. He therefore recommended that foreign language teachers should make their students' pronunciation *socially acceptable* and not merely intelligible.

Turning to the more applied aspects of this problem, Brook (1963) claimed that

---

6. See also Frender and Lambert (1972).

the remedy would seem to be that those who are not prepared to adopt Standard English as their manner of speech on all occasions should be prepared to be bilingual: they should continue to understand and to use their native dialect, but in the world of today it is as well for a dialect speaker to be able to speak and understand Standard English or something near it when the occasion requires it.

Giles (1971c) also tentatively suggested, in a discussion of some of the factors involved,

> that at some initial stage in a child's educational career, the regional accented pupil might be oriented towards the standard code—without eliminating his original speech habits—for use in socially appropriate, verbal situations . . . It was emphasized that a programme of this type would facilitate accent *extension* not *conversion*.

Many workers in the United States have considered the value of such a programme in their own cultural context, particularly with respect to Black nonstandard-speaking children (Baratz, 1970; Johnson, 1971). Indeed, many such programmes have been in existence for a good number of years with varying degrees of reported success (e.g. Stewart, 1964; Lin, 1965; Feigenbaum, 1969; Gladney and Leaverton, 1968; Karnes, Teska, Hodgins and Badger, 1971).[7] But there are a number of difficulties associated with these programmes such as a need for real parental support (see discussion by Giles, 1971c). Perhaps the most important of these difficulties have been stated well by Sledd (1969) and O'Neil (1972). Sledd (1969) considers that,

> the psychological consequences of an extension programme are likely to be nervous affectation, self-distrust, dislike for everyone not equally afflicted with the itch to get ahead and eventual frustration by the discovery that the reward for so much suffering is intolerably small . . . enforced bi-dialectalism should not be tolerated even if it were possible. Predators can and do use dialect differences to exploit and oppress, because ordinary people can be made to doubt their own value and to accept subservience if

---

7. Recently, owing to the impetus derived from the "difference theorists" (see Chapter 2), there has been in some areas of the United States almost a reversal of educational programming policies. The emphasis in these programmes now seems to be on teaching Black children reading skills via their own native dialect and by means of Black English texts (see Taylor, 1971). In parallel with these educational innovations, has also come over 300 bilingual programmes in the United States designed to teach children from certain ethnic minorities via their own native language, e.g. French, Spanish (for a review, see Edwards, 1974). The rationale for these policies seems to be that the child will attain much higher degrees of scholastic success and maintain a healthier sense of cultural identity if he is taught by means of the home dialect or language rather than that of the majority.

they can be made to despise the speech of their fathers. Obligatory bi-dialectalism for minorities is only another mode of exploitation, another way of making Blacks behave as Whites would like them to.

It may at this juncture be worthwhile suggesting possible educational implications of a study conducted by Williams, Whitehead and Miller (1971a) that was reported in Chapter 3. It may be recalled that in one of the experimental conditions listeners were asked to evaluate the speech patterns of a Black child whom they saw and heard by means of a videotape recording. Despite the fact that standard White speech patterns were superimposed on the tape, the child was nevertheless perceived to be speaking less standardly than a White child voicing those same speech patterns. Thus, even if all the inherent problems involved in extending a child's speech style could be overcome so that the child was objectively able to speak the prestige code, he might still be perceived as speaking in a nonstandard way. Extending such a line of argument, Taylor (1971) has also commented that

> there is no reason to believe that economic and social discrimination against blacks will end in proportion to the blacks' ability to talk the white man's language. History reveals that when individual blacks have acquired an abundance of "Standard Speech" and "Standard Behavior" they have still been perceived as "niggers" by the so-called standard society and new reasons are often developed for denying equal opportunity. Black people are rejected and discriminated against because they are BLACK— not because they speak a form of BLACK English.

Although these comments are rather specifically directed to the Black-White cultures of North America, they are nevertheless pertinent to a language extension programme (whether it be in relation to language, dialect or accent) in any cultural context. Accordingly, the possibility of a programme of attitude change, in an attempt to eliminate prejudiced reactions against nonstandard speech, as an alternative to speech extension might be considered. At least its feasibility might be tested empirically. Indeed, Griffin (1970) has advocated the teaching of dialectology in schools, firstly to increase the children's linguistic sophistication but, more important in the present context, to induce them to become more tolerant of speech (and also cultural) variations.[8]

8. An extension of this notion has arisen in the St. Lambert bilingual immersion experiment in Montreal (Lambert and Tucker, 1972). In this programme, English Canadian children are taught their school curricula via a second language (French) from a very early age. Indeed, this venture was brought about as a direct response to parental demands for their children to be bilingual and bicultural. For a recent appraisal of its success, see Lambert, Tucker and d'Anglejan, 1973.

Johnson (1971a) and Burling (1971) have also suggested similar measures as part of teacher training. Certainly, there is no easy solution to this problem. Obviously, the ultimate ideal would be to educate people to tolerate nonstandard speech styles. Yet even if this process were undertaken—and its success could not at all be guaranteed—we should still have in the meantime children who are in the socially disadvantageous situation of not having facility in the prestige code. Perhaps the most reasonable stance to be taken is that proposed by Taylor (loc. cit.). He argued that the real decision as to whether a child should have its speech repertoire extended or not should be left to the parents and not to educators or social scientists.

## Speech style in medical and legal contexts

The consequences of nonstandard language use are likely to be as important in a clinical setting as in any other social situation. A broad question could be posed as to whether physicians react differently to patients, in terms of diagnosis, sympathy and treatment, according to the patient's speech characteristics. Certainly a number of studies have shown that the working class individual is assessed in a less favourable manner, all other factors being equal, than the middle class person (e.g. Hollingshead and Redlich, 1958; Levy, 1970; Levy and Kahn, 1970). For instance, the former are generally viewed as more maladjusted, have a poorer prognosis, and are less likely to receive individual psychotherapy than the latter. It is also possible that the doctor might place more reliance upon an account of symptoms related in a standard form of speech than upon similar descriptions given in a nonstandard style. This could have consequences in terms of decisions about further diagnostic tests and about treatment. As in other situations, such as the employment interview, whatever prejudices and stereotypes are attached to race or class would tend to be evoked by language variety. We do not know what stereotypes of patients doctors may tend to have. It would be interesting to find out.

Other questions arise concerning the effect of the doctor's speech style upon the patient. Does the patient feel more at ease and relaxed when the doctor's speech style matches his own? Are all doctors "expected" to have a standard accent as a guarantee of competence? Are there "special cases" with regard to regional or alien accents (e.g. in England, Scottish doctors seem to command unusual prestige and an

Austrian accent gives a psychiatrist a certain cachet, but a Pakistani doctor would probably be viewed with suspicion as to his skill, especially by working-class patients). In the absence of research findings we can only draw attention to these questions.

Almost certainly, nonstandard usage can also effect forensic situations such as police and courtroom decision-making. As in the case of the medical setting, a number of empirical questions can be posed. For example, when members of the public are stopped in the street or on the highway by the police for inquiries, do standard speakers undergo a less severe interrogation than nonstandard users of the language? Is evidence by standard speakers generally regarded by courts as more reliable and substantial than evidence given by nonstandard speaking witnesses? Are juries prejudiced by the speech style of accused persons? How does the speech style of a lawyer affect his advocacy? At present there are no answers to these questions.

*     *     *

We have been discussing the ways in which various speech-styles are evaluated by the listener. We shall now consider the ways in which a speaker may adapt his style of speaking according to the different circumstances in which he finds himself. Later we shall attempt to relate speech diversity to social evaluation.

# 7

# The Dynamics of Speech Style

Speech characteristics represent a fairly stable feature of the adult individual. Just as we can recognize someone from his physical appearance, so also, with only slightly less certainty, can we recognize someone familiar to us from his voice alone. Friends often have no need to identify themselves to each other by name when speaking on the telephone. It is not only the phonic characteristics of speech which give it the stamp of individuality. Gall, Hobby and Craik (1969) asked subjects to talk about nine visual displays placed in front of them and it was found that the amount of speech (in terms of a word count) showed a moderately high degree of stability across all nine situations. Another study by Levin and Silverman (1965) looked not only at verbal output in different situations but also at measures of hesitation and speech rate. In their study, the situations used were quite a severe test of the speech stability notion. Twelve year olds were asked to tell two stories under each of two conditions: addressing an audience of four adults, and speaking into a microphone while no-one was actually present. It was found that subjects were consistent in their fluency and hesitations from story to story both within a single session and between the two sessions. The number of words spoken was clearly the most stable variable and the rate of speaking more stable than measures of hesitation. A study by Cassotta, Feldstein and Jaffe (1967) shows that in two-person conversations individuals have characteristic modes of pairing their silence and speech. These workers looked at three speech-silence parameters: the pause (an uninterrupted silence between two vocalizations of the same speaker), the switching pause (the silence between the time one speaker finishes and the other starts) and vocalization length. Fifty females were interviewed on two occasions. On the first occasion they were interviewed by person A, and on the second occasion first by A again and then twice by person B. The first three interviews dealt with biographical details of the subjects while the final interview was a stress interview. These four interviews thus permitted comparison of subjects' vocal patterns with different interviewers, over time and across kinds of interview. Product-moment correlations for each of the six possible interview comparisons revealed relatively high stability for each vocal parameter. A study by Dinoff, Morris and Hannon (1963) has also shown stability of utterance duration and switching pause in the speech of schizophrenics in a standardized interview situation.

Despite these consistencies in the characteristics of speech, it is nevertheless the case that we are capable of modifying our speech patterns to suit particular occasions. John and Jack talk every day in the school playground and know each other's way of speaking very well. Yet each may derive a certain amount of amusement from hearing the other standardize his accent when reading aloud in class or when talking to the head of the school. Most people are probably aware that they are especially careful of their word-choice, syntax and pronunciation in situations such as job interviews when they feel it expedient to make a good impression upon the listener. Grimshaw (1967) has illustrated the phenomenon as follows:

> ... Suppose the janitor comes into the office while the academician is (1) alone, (2) with a senior member of the administration, (3) with a colleague of peer status, (4) with an undergraduate student, or (5) with another maintenance man. The ensuing patterns of interaction, including speech, could vary widely. Additional changes might be anticipated with the entrance of still other actors into the situation—the professor's wife, for example ... Before other audiences, say, the parents of students, other variations could be anticipated. Similarly, a shift from the academician's own office to another physical setting—elevator, classroom, coffee-shop etc. —would produce other changes.

Hymes (1972) has made the same point perhaps more forcefully:

> No normal person, and no normal community, is limited to a single way of speaking, to an unchanging monotony that would preclude indication of respect, insolence, mock seriousness, humor, role distance, and intimacy by switching from one mode of speech to another.

It is only fairly recently that this kind of "code-switching" has received any attention in the scientific literature. Gumperz (1967) commented on this omission:

Structural linguists, by the very nature of their attempts at formalization, have felt it necessary to operate with the assumption that languages are unitary, homogeneous wholes. Even with the recent expansion of the scope of linguistic analysis, this attitude has not changed. The concept of linguistic competence, so far, is applied only to those rather general aspects of grammar which apply to all individuals in a society; interpersonal and intergroup variation tend to be assigned to the level of performance and, by implication, are viewed as not subject to systematic analysis.

The recognition of this lacuna in the science of linguistics gave rise to the new subject of sociolinguistics for, as Hymes (loc. cit.) has pointed out, it "is this notion of code variation and speech diversity that has been singled out as the hallmark of sociolinguistics".

Let us now consider the various factors which lead to changes in individual speech patterns and, in doing so, try to devise a theoretical framework to explain not only what these factors are but how they operate.

Central to the idea that "linguistic diversity begins next door, at home and within one and the same man" (Martinet, 1953) is the notion that "a speaker in any language community who enters diverse social situations normally has a repertoire of speech alternatives which shift with situation" (Ervin-Tripp, 1964).[1] Gumperz (1964a) has noted the relevance of a concept of repertoires to the phenomenon of speech change and has described their characteristics and functions as follows:

> The structure of verbal repertoires ... differs from ordinary descriptive grammars. It includes a much greater number of alternants, reflecting contextual and social differences in speech. Linguistic interaction, as Bernstein (1962) has pointed out, can most fruitfully be viewed as a process of decision-making, in which speakers select from a range of possible expressions. The verbal repertoire then contains all the accepted

---

1. With respect to the preceding chapters, it is a methodological weakness of studies concerned with evaluative reactions to spoken languages and speech styles that the notion of speech diversity has rarely been considered. Indeed, as Agheyisi and Fishman (1970) point out, it has appeared as though the matched-guise technique "presupposes that each population or subpopulation is characterised or identifiable by a *single* language variety ... so questions of speech repertoire ... become very important and must be reckoned with rather than ruled out as does the matched-guise technique". A study by Silverman (1969) has in fact shown the importance of repertoire size in evaluative reactions to languages. He found that speakers of Spanish and English were evaluated differently according to whether they possessed narrow or wide ranges of linguistic styles. Those displaying a narrow range were considered as less educationally advanced that those whose repertoire displayed a wide range of styles.

ways of formulating messages. It provides the weapons of everyday communication. Speakers choose among this arsenal in accordance with the meanings they wish to convey. Ultimately it is the individual who makes the decision, but this freedom to select is always subject both to grammatical and social constraints. Grammatical constraints relate to the intelligibility of sentences; social restraints to their acceptability . . . restraints on language choice have one other important set of characteristics. This concerns the linguistic relationship among the constituents of a statement. An alternant once chosen sets limits to what can follow within the same utterance.

Obviously differences must exist between speakers in the structure of their linguistic repertoires. For instance, Bernstein (1962) claims that the working class are confined more or less to a "restricted" code of language usage which serves to maintain or change social role relationships and has structures appropriate to this function. The middle class, on the other hand, possess in addition to the restricted code, an "elaborated" code which is used for the conveyance of information about personal intentions and feelings. More important is the notion that the user of the elaborated code rather than the restricted code will "through verbal planning modify his speech in relation to the specific requirement of the listener". However, there is some evidence which suggests that the working class person can, under appropriate circumstances but to a lesser extent than the middle class individual, produce an elaborated code (Lawton, 1965; Robinson, 1965; Henderson, 1969). Bernstein's theory[2] would imply that the elaborated code-user is able to modify his grammatical constructions with greater ease and efficiency than the restricted code-user because of his more varied early verbal learning in meeting the demands of different social situations. Unfortunately, this assumption has not yet received direct experimental attention. To extend this argument further, it may be suggested that the working class may be restricted at the phonic levels as well, particularly with regard to accent use. Yet it could be argued also that the upper classes may in fact be just as "restricted". An upper class privately educated child may be so restricted in his exposure to nonstandard usage and accents that he is confined to one style of speech only.

2. See Lawton (1968) for a detailed review of Bernstein's earlier work, and also Coulthard (1969) and Rosen (1973) for a critical review of Bernstein's theoretical and empirical findings. For a more recent discussion of Bernstein's current theoretical position, see Bernstein (1970). For an interesting discussion of social class differences in language see Robinson (1972) and Bruck and Tucker (1972).

The results of a study conducted in Quebec recently by Clément and Taylor (1974) suggest that working class speakers may engage in code-switching to no less an extent than their middle class counterparts. Nevertheless, the investigation also shows that the structure of their speech repertoires may be quite different. In this study, French Canadian students were presented with stimulus tapes on which matched-guise speakers described their work (e.g. as a librarian) in three styles of Quebec French. These language varieties were termed, from the most to the least formal, the "standard", "familiar" and *Joual* speech styles. All subjects began by making judgements concerning the probability that they themselves would use each of these speech styles in six different social situations. Two of these situations were considered informal (with friends; in the street), two semi-formal (with parents; in the school cafeteria) and two formal (with a superior; in an official interview). Following this phase of the experiment, half the subjects repeated the procedure, this time judging the probability that middle class people would use the various styles in the six situations. The remaining subjects were asked to make judgements about the language use of lower class persons in these situations.

It was found that these students had well-established expectations with respect to code-switching. For example, subjects thought that both they and middle class persons would adopt the standard style in formal situations. In both semi-formal and informal situations, however, the familiar style seemed most likely to occur. Indeed in no case was *Joual* perceived as most probable. By comparison, when evaluating the probability of code-switching by lower class speakers, subjects thought that they were most likely to speak familiar French in formal situations and *Joual* in both semi-formal and informal situations. Thus, students perceived that middle and lower class speakers have different ranges of speech-codes available to them. The code restriction of middle class people is seen to be a lack of use of *Joual*, whereas for lower class people it is that standard French is not part of their productive repertoire.

According to the perceptions of these students, a familiar style of French is the only code common to both middle and lower class speakers. This does not, however, suggest that communication across class will necessarily involve the use of this code since middle class subjects are perceived as using this style for semi-formal and informal situations while the lower class use of familiar French is associated with formal situations. In this way, there is no social situation where members of different classes share the same code, and this fact could be a serious deterrent to cross-class communication. Clément and Taylor discuss the implications of their study thus:

> If the perceptions of the present subjects are correct, lower class people will indeed face problems in contexts such as schools, government agencies and Courts where the formality and middle class presence requires a standard variety of speech. Of equal concern, however, is the fact that subjects in the present studies report little or no use of very informal styles of French. Hence middle class people are also restricted in terms of the situations where they can operate appropriately in terms of language style. This would also seem to have serious consequences for it suggests that there exist important social domains where middle class people have little or no social experience or understanding.

Although the judgements of the subjects in this experiment suggest well-defined language norms it must be remembered that all the subjects tested were middle class college students. Clearly their perceptions may not be shared by members of different social classes or by people with different occupational roles. Moreover it would be useful to discover whether the language behaviour of the social classes in different situations does in fact reflect the above normative expectations. Nevertheless, it would seem that a speaker's social class membership may determine to a large extent the structure of his phonic repertoire.

In addition to social class background, personality may affect the nature of a person's linguistic repertoire. For instance, many studies[3] have shown that personality affects the type of speech patterns an individual produces. This suggests that the composition of his repertoire would also be affected. Age, sex and several other demographic factors could also affect the responses that an individual was capable of producing.

Probably one of the most easily recognizable examples of selection from a speech repertoire is that of language or dialect code-switching. In Chapter 2 this was mentioned in connection with "context-related standards". In many cultures, it may be recalled, it is expected that

3. For example, extraversion (Mann, 1959; Carment, Miles and Cervin, 1965; Stern and Grosz, 1966, 1966a; Ramsay, 1968; Jawande, 1970); ascendance (Cervin, 1957; Gall, Hobby and Craik, 1969); anxiety (Boomer and Goodrich, 1961; Mahl and Schulze, 1964; Eisenmann, 1966; Meisels, 1967); psychological health (Cope, 1969); MMPI (Grosz and Wagner, 1971; Markel, 1969); need for achievement (Smith, 1970); need for approval (Crowne and Strickland, 1961).

people will adopt a particular language or dialect in a particular social situation. Gumperz (1964) has stated that "whenever several languages or dialects appear regularly as weapons of language choice, they form a behavioural whole, regardless of grammatical distinctiveness, and must be considered constituent varieties of the same verbal repertoires." Furthermore, Hymes (1972) stated that "bilingualism par excellence (e.g. French and English in Canada, Welsh and English in North Wales, Russian and French among prerevolutionary Russian nobility) is a salient, special case of the general phenomenon of linguistic repertoire". However, Ervin-Tripp (1964) has commented on the fact that the focus of attention on speech change has been upon "relatively pure codes" and not towards what she calls "sociolinguistic variants", that is speech variations *within* the same basic language. However, this chapter and the succeeding one will testify that recently more attention has been devoted to such sociolinguistic variations. Ervin-Tripp (loc. cit.) and Hymes (1967; 1972) have attempted to describe speech change within a taxonomy of situational determinants such as topic, participants and setting. These workers have not discerned any theoretical distinction between interlingual code-switching and *intra*-lingual variations in their analysis of the causes of speech change. Indeed, as MacNamara (1967) points out, "Fishman, Hymes and Gumperz also stress the further point that both bilingualism and diglossia are best not considered in isolation, but rather as salient examples of a capacity for code variations which is also found among monolinguals".

If we take Ervin-Tripp's taxonomic approach, we can say that any factor, such as a given topic or person, which influences a speaker's code choice is a "situational determinant" of choice from a speech repertoire. Now the situational determinants of speech choice can be categorized primarily in terms of whether they are "endogenous" or "exogenous" factors. The sender's[4] physiological state or mood prior to social interaction may predispose him to choose certain patterns of speech from his repertoire. This kind of "internal" determinant may be termed an "endogenous" variable. The exogenous determinants of choice are those factors which are external to the sender but present in the immediate social situation. The remainder of this chapter will be concerned with

4. The "sender" in social interaction is the speaker (under study), who, consciously or unconsciously, selects from his speech repertoire certain linguistic variants to be directed towards a "receiver" or "receivers". The "receiver" is thus the person who interprets the sender's speech choices, but nevertheless, must be regarded as an *active participant* in the ongoing verbal interaction (see Hymes, 1962).

a review of the endogenous variables, and certain of the exogenous variables such as topic and context. The exogenous *interpersonal* variables will be reviewed separately in Chapter 8. The reason for this division of situational determinants will become much clearer later. Suffice it to say at present that the model to be proposed in Chapter 9 for explaining speech diversity emphasizes interpersonal aspects of social interaction.

## Endogenous factors

As we have said, the sender's physiological and emotional states at the time of interaction, which may predispose him to select certain patterns of speech from his repertoire, are termed the endogenous factors. Interestingly enough, neither Ervin-Tripp (1964; 1969) nor Hymes (1967; 1972) has paid any attention to these complex situational determinants in their descriptive analyses of speech change. However, changes in an individual's physiological or clinical state may induce language modifications as is shown in a study by Innes, Miller and Valentine (1959). These workers found that an increase in a patient's blood-pressure corresponded to a greater count of spoken syllables during ten-second periods.

Emotional states, such as high anxiety can influence a speaker's speech rate, vocal disturbances and pronunciation patterns. Anxiety may emanate from the topic of conversation as it may be stimulated by characteristics of the receiver. The mood or emotional set in which the speaker enters the interaction may also affect the pattern of his speech choices.

A somewhat extreme example of the effect of emotional set can be found with research on depressive patients. Pope, Blass, Siegman and Raher (1970) and Hinchcliffe, Lancashire and Roberts (1971) have found that depressed people show less verbal productivity than control subjects.[5] Hargreaves and Starkweather (1964) found that a change in mood in some patients (as evaluated by self-descriptions and interview

5. Verbal productivity is an interesting measure of repertoire selection since it does not depend on a choice between alternatives (like languages of a bilingual) or modifications (such as speech rate). Selection here simply involves the notion of *how much* a speaker is prepared to select from his repertoire. In some situations, it may be the case that we are concerned with how much effort a speaker is prepared to put into selecting from his repertoire in a given social situation.

ratings) corresponded with characteristic vocal patterns as measured on
a sound spectrograph. But this pattern was not found in all patients as
they became less depressed, and so it may be that speakers are idiosyncratic in their vocal responses to changes in mood and clinical states
and perhaps to situational determinants in general.

Another study by Hargreaves, Starkweather and Blacker (1965)
looked at 32 depressives over a period of five weeks and once again
there did not appear to exist a general pattern for all cases of acute
depression. Nevertheless, the most common pattern was a "depressed"
voice, low in overall loudness and often lacking in high overtones and
a very dull-sounding voice. But some depressed patients' speech patterns
were characterized, on the other hand, by louder as well as higher
pitched voices. And so, while individual A may react with modifications
in certain vocal aspects of his speech, individual B may react to the
same stimulus or internal state with changes in other vocal patterns or
even in verbal output. Indeed, a further study by Starkweather (1967)
found just such differences when he distinguished between *types* of depression, although the sample sizes are absolutely minute: he recorded
the speech patterns of three "retarded" and one "agitated" depressive.
Each of these four patients was individually interviewed on six occasions
and these sessions were divided by the therapist into three where the
patient appeared most depressed and three where he appeared least depressed. For the retarded depressives, the less depressed state as inde-
pendently assessed by clinicians was characterized by an increased
speech rate, and utterance length. In the case of the agitated patient,
mood was reflected not so much in vocal characteristics as in the content of his verbal utterances; for example, in less frequent references to
self and anxiety. To generalize, it is possible that some people demonstrate emotional change primarily by language *content* while others do
so by the *form* of their vocal behaviour. How valid this generalization is,
how consistent these individual differences are and what underlies them
remain at present a mystery. Extrapolating from these studies, it is
reasonable to suppose that everyday changes in mood or emotion may
also be reflected in linguistic choices from a speaker's repertoire. Hargreaves and Starkweather (1963) have noted changes in voice quality
when tape-recording the same speakers from day to day. Fairbanks and
Provonost (1939) and Fairbanks (1940) have described measurable
differences in pitch among five simulated emotions. A more recent
study by Costanzo, Markel and Costanzo (1969) extended this earlier

work and showed that high pitched voices were judged as portraying grief, loudness was interpreted as indicating anger or contempt, while fast speech was judged to be indicative of indifference. Other studies (Markel, Meisels and Houck, 1964; Saxman and Burke, 1968) have instanced language changes in relation to the onset of the schizophrenias. But such findings are very difficult to interpret reliably with reference to everday changes in mood, temperament and cognitive functioning, at least at the present stage of knowledge. Interestingly enough, a study by Starkweather and Hargreaves (1964), using the drug sodium phenobarbitone, failed to find any effect on vocal behaviour in subjects' responses.

Thus far, we have discussed endogenous factors purely in terms of intralingual variation. An interesting paper by del Castillo (1970) shows that a bilingual's mood or personal problems may be reflected in only one of his languages. The author describes several cases in which North American patients showed psychotic symptoms in psychiatric interviews held in their native language (Spanish), but not in those conducted in a foreign language (English). Del Castillo attempted to explain this phenomenon in terms of the patient's being more on his guard when using a second language, and thus perhaps being motivated to maintain a closer contact with reality. It would be interesting to determine whether the apparent lack of an emotional outlet in terms of semantic content when a bilingual uses a second language is compensated for by changes in the physical and temporal characteristics of his vocal behaviour that do not so readily occur when the patient uses his preferred language.

## Exogenous factors

As stated previously, the exogenous determinants of linguistic choice are those factors which are "external" to the sender yet present in the immediate social situation. It can be appreciated that often the dividing line between endogenous and exogenous factors may be a little indistinct since endogenous variables (particularly mood) are likely to be influenced by exogenous features of past or present situations.

Bearing this caveat in mind we shall discuss in the remainder of this chapter a number of situational determinants of linguistic choice and, in the following chapter, we shall examine interpersonal influences upon speech style.

(1) *Topic*

The topic of conversation in social interaction can be influential in determining speech modifications when the subject matter is high on one or more of the following dimensions: salience, emotionality, technicality, abstraction and humorousness. Let us take each in turn.

(a) *Salience* In a series of three studies, Matarazzo and his colleagues have gathered evidence which suggests that topic salience is an important situational determinant of speech choice. They found that undergraduates increased their mean utterance durations when discussing education and their college major subject, by comparison with durations for other topics—occupation, family and place of abode (Manaugh, Weins and Matarazzo, 1970; Matarazzo, Weins, Jackson and Manaugh, 1970). Also, job applicants in interview situations, when discussing these same topics increased their utterance durations when discussing the topic of occupation (Matarazzo, Weins, Jackson and Manaugh, 1970a). The authors conclude that individuals will speak more on topics which are important to them in a particular situation than topics which are less important to them. Unfortunately, they did not incorporate in their experimental design any independent measure of topic salience. However, Jackson, Manaugh, Weins and Matarazzo (1971) have devised a 45-item questionnaire technique (the Topic Importance Scale) which may enable workers to elicit individuals' ratings of topics important to them in given situations. A pilot study from Tanzania by Beardsley and Eastman (1971) has looked at topic salience in relation to bilingual code choice. They asked three people to rank eight topics in order of relevance to life in Tanzania, and asked one male-female couple to discuss these topics; the couple were Swahili-English bilinguals. It was found that the more relevant a topic was to Tazanian life, the lower the proportion of English and mixed words there was in their speech. So it appears that topic relevance affects not only the amount of speech but the type of words chosen too.

(b) *Emotionality* It has been found by Siegman and Pope (1965) that an anxiety-loaded topic is related to increased verbal productivity in conversation. However, most of the work on topic emotionality and speech patterns has been concerned with the levels of speech rate, speech disturbances and accent use. Kanfer (1958; 1958a; 1959; 1960) and Feldstein, Brenner and Jaffe (1963) have measured the variation in subjects' speech rate during experimental procedures and have re-lated a high rate of speaking to the discussion of topics, such as family and sex, on which subjects were rated as poorly adjusted, or in which they were highly emotionally involved. Siegman and Pope (1965) on the other hand, found that discussing an anxiety-provoking topic did not affect speech rate. Nevertheless, a study by Cook (1969) does point to the idiosyncratic nature of people's reactions to stress in their speech styles.

Using only ten students as subjects, Cook found that discussing topics which seemed to worry or embarrass them had no clear effect on speech rate, as four subjects' rates rose, three fell and three showed no changes. Thus, it is possible that some individuals react to momentary topic tension by speaking quickly, whilst others speak more slowly. It may be worthwhile pointing out that the interviewer's assessment as to whether a topic induced "transitory anxiety" in these subjects or not may have been based largely on his perception of their speech patterns anyway. Those who do not show changes at this level may indeed emit them at other speech levels. Once again, the underlying causal factors of such individual differences are as yet undiscovered. It may be the case that individuals interpret the anxiety quite differently, or that they have widely differing thresholds, but whatever the possibilities more research needs to be undertaken here.

Mahl (1956) produced evidence to the effect that individuals (irre-spective of age, sex, educational level and socioeconomic status) pro-duce speech disturbances at the average rate of 1 per 16 words (every 4·6 seconds). These speech disturbances may be classified as "ahs"[6] (this includes all filled-pauses such as "ers" and "umms" etc.) and "non-ahs". The non-ah speech disturbances (in order of decreasing fre-quency of occurrence in U.S. speech) include sentence changes, repeti-tions, stutters, omissions, sentence incompletions, incoherent sounds and tongue slips. Kasl and Mahl (1965) found that when an anxiety-arous-ing topic was introduced in an interview subjects would show an in-creased frequency of non-ah speech disturbances by 34%. A large number of studies, notably Dibner (1956), Zimbardo, Mahl and Barnard (1963), Krause and Pilisuk (1961), Pope and Siegman (1962) and Cook (1969) have also found that transitory anxiety leads to an increase in non-ah speech disturbances. However, Krause (1961) has

6. For a discussion of the possible functions of ah-type disturbances in speech, see Cook (1971).

claimed that different measures of vocal behaviour are important for different individuals in identifying anxiety.

Brook (1963), with regard to British speech, has also observed that "it is not uncommon to find that people who have been brought up as dialect speakers learn to speak a modified form of Standard English, but revert to their native dialect when tired or excited or in old age." Similarly, Bender and Mahl (1960) have shown with Southerners living in the northern states of America who have lost their southern brogue, that when they discuss a topic which is stressful to them, they are liable to regress to using their southern accent. It has been hypothesized by Labov (1970) that people adopt more prestigious pronunciation features in their speech when their *attention* is turned towards their speech, such as in formal interview situations and when reading aloud. Certainly in an excited moment or when a person is discussing an emotionally-involving topic, his attention is likely to be diverted from the vocal encoding aspects of speech; this would accord well with Labov's notion. An interesting experimental test would be to inhibit vocal feedback by applying noise to a subject via earphones and assessing the effect upon speech. With reduced self-monitoring by the speaker we should expect less standardized speech patterns than in normal conversation.[7] In this vein also Herman (1961) reports that Jewish immigrants to Israel often revert to their native tongue rather than Hebrew when excited or tired.

A study by Craig (1966) may suggest an interesting interaction between topic emotionality and topic salience. A week before the experimenter interviewed psychiatric patients, a personality questionnaire was administered to them. On the basis of their scores on this test, some patients in the interview were given true information about their personalities while others were given false information. This topic was assumed to have high salience and also, in the case of patients for whom the information was incongruent with their own self-evaluations, high emotionality. These patients responded with shorter utterances than were made by patients who had been given congruent personality information. A somewhat similar study was conducted by Pope, Blass, Cheek and Siegman (1970) where subjects were given accurate information about the content of the first interview they were about to take, but were given less accurate information before the second. Prior to this

7. For studies investigating the effects of white noise masking on spoken thought, see Holzman and Rousey (1970; 1971).

second interview, they were told that the interviewer would tell them about their personality, an assessment of which had been obtained from the first interview. However, in the experimental condition, the interviewer did not do this but merely asked for more information from subjects. As compared with the control group, whose expectancies were confirmed, verbal productivity was decreased in the experimental group. Unfortunately, the design of the experiment permits more than one interpretation but salience and emotionality may have interacted to affect the speaker's linguistic behaviour.

(c) *Technicality* The factor of topic technicality is also a situational determinant very important in linguistic selection, whether the topic is scientifically complex or is esoteric in any other way. For instance, Moscovici (1967) found a greater variety of words used when a person discussed the parts of a car with a specialist than when the same topic was discussed with a non-technical friend, and that more technical words were used. Ratner and Rice (1963) also found that speaking was affected by the amount of information the listener had about the subject matter. Speakers with poorly-informed listeners on a topic used more words, more repetitions, and gave more complete descriptions of things talked about than speakers with moderately well-informed listeners. Another study by Loewenthal (1968) has also shown that a speaker's description of objects differs according to how well he thinks the audience is comprehending him. The more information he gets that his audience understands him, the more his message length will decline as will the percentage of function words (e.g. prepositions, conjunctions and articles). These experimental results do not, unfortunately, accord very well with the experience of everyday life. We often find that specialists seem totally incapable of disembedding themselves from technical jargon when discussing their subject with a layman.[8] Studies have shown that this ability to appreciate and identify with the role of another person in an encounter is a function of maturation and does not normally develop until adolescence, (Flavell, Botkin, Fry, Wright and Jarvis, 1968; Krauss and Glucksberg, 1969). As can be seen from the nature of the studies cited above, technicality of topic is not a pure topic dimension; the interpersonal aspects of interaction need to be

8. Interestingly enough, Walker and Chalmers (1971) have shown that the communication of simple, familiar ideas is accomplished more effectively by technical language whereas clear and simple language appears more effective for difficult concepts. See also Grace (1952) and Rosen (1973a).

taken into account as well. In contrast, a topic's salience and emotional value to a speaker can to a great extent operate without reference to the receiver.

(d) *Abstraction* The effect of the level of abstraction of the topic upon speech choice is well-exemplified in a study by Lawton (1965). Using the individual interview, Lawton found that when subjects turn from purely descriptive dialogue to a topic of a more abstract nature (such as ethics and morals) they are able, with varying degrees of success, to switch to relatively more complex grammatical structures. Such complexities find expression in a higher incidence of uncommon adjectives and a higher clause subordination ratio. If it is accepted that an ambiguous stimulus represents a higher level of abstraction than an unambiguous stimulus, there is evidence that this topic dimension can affect the vocal characteristics of a speaker's repertoire selection as well. Siegman and Pope (1966) were able to classify TAT cards (Murray, 1943) into low, medium and high ambiguity on the basis of the variability of themes evoked by a given card. It was found that, when subjects were asked to create a story in response to the cards, the more ambiguous stimuli evoked the more hesitant and disrupted speech.

Another study relevant to the dimension of abstractness is that of Levin, Silverman and Ford (1967) who compared the speech of children under two task conditions, one calling for a *description* and the other an *explanation* of various events demonstrated to them. It was found that explanation was characterized by more words, pauses and hesitations, longer pauses and a slower rate of speaking than occurred in the case of descriptions. Using adults, Goldman-Eisler (1968) also reported that the spontaneous interpretations of cartoons produced longer pauses than the descriptions of the same cartoons, but she found no differences in articulation rate.

(e) *Humorousness* The final topic dimension to be discussed here (although doubtless there are others) is that of humorousness. Giles, Bourhis, Gadfield, Davies and Davies (in press) asked subjects to relate standard stories of equal length, interest and recall difficulty into a tape-recorder. There were two serious stories and one joke. In a post-experimental questionnaire, subjects claimed that they had changed their speech styles appreciably when reading a humorous, as opposed to a serious story. Moreover, they attempted to specify the linguistic levels at which such modifications had occurred. In addition, when

subjects were asked to describe the qualities of a good joke-teller, 39%
of the characteristics mentioned referred to a flexibility of speech style.
Evaluations on a number of linguistic dimensions by phonetically-
unsophisticated listeners (see Chapter 9, p. 180f) indicated that the
speakers had consistently changed their speech styles on only one of the
dependent measures—fluency. They were more hesitant on a serious
than a humorous topic. In order to eliminate possible audience effects,
speakers were required to perform their stories in social isolation. Had
the tales been related to a person physically present and unfamiliar
with the material, changes might have occurred on more linguistic
dimensions. For instance, anecdotal evidence from televised comedy
would suggest that humorous speech tends to be more nonstandard in
accent, less precise in enunciation and to have more variety in tempo
and pitch than serious speech. Further research will enable us to verify
these notions. It may well be that the nature of a topic, such as its
humorousness or even its abstraction, has little effect in the absence of
a listener. Indeed, in Chapter 8 we shall argue that perhaps the attributes of the person addressed are, in many social situations, more important than those of topic or social setting. Nevertheless, the study by
Giles *et al.* has shown that even without a "live" receiver, the humorousness of a topic can influence an individual's speech style to some extent.

## (2) *General context*

There are many instances where the nature of the setting in which two
people interact may have an influence upon their speech patterns. In
some cases the physical characteristics of the setting may themselves
have some consequences but, for the most part, considerations of occasion and role are likely to be more important. Since differences of
occasion are sometimes marked by differences in physical setting there
is a danger of confounding the two sources of influence. A reasonably
clear example of a physical determinant is spatial distance between
sender and receiver. If two window cleaners, for example, are trying
to communicate with each other, when one is working two storeys
higher than the other, then the message passed between them is likely
to be louder, and more abbreviated in content and simplified in grammatical structure than would be the case had they been working on
adjacent windows. In an experimental study, Jourard and Friedman
(1970) found that the reduction of physical distance between a stooge
and subject resulted in an increase of self-references in speech. Albert

and Dabbs (1970) have also shown this variable to be important in judging a communicator's expertise and his persuasiveness.

A special type of physical setting which may affect linguistic choices by interlocutors is the telephone link. The ways in which speech in a telephone conversation is likely to differ from speech in a face-to-face encounter may be inferred from studies of the effects of the absence of visual cues upon communication. These suggest that, in comparison with ordinary speech, telephone conversations are likely to involve longer pauses, with more questions repeated (Cook and Lalljee, 1967; Feldstein, Jaffe and Cassotta, 1967); an increase of 40% in "ah"-type speech disruptions (Kasl and Mahl, 1965); an increase of 40% in speech durations for males and a decrease to the same extent in females (Cook, Argyle and Lalljee, 1967); an increase in the number of affective self-references (Janofsky, 1971); and the speech itself is likely to be much more formal (Moscovici and Plon, 1966).[9]

At the more macrolinguistic level of language and dialect, we have already mentioned in Chapter 2 how the nature of the setting or the occasion can influence code choice. For instance, it may be recalled that in the contexts of the Philippines and Paraguay, courting couples are expected to use the standard language and to switch to the native language (Tagalog and Guarani respectively) only after the marriage ceremony (Sechrest, Flores and Arellano, 1968; Rubin, 1962). Another study by Edelman, Cooper and Fishman (1968), using Puerto Rican children, found that children reported using more Spanish than English when talking to other bilingual Puerto Ricans in the contexts of the family and neighbourhood settings but were more likely to use English in church and in school.[10] Similar determinants of language choice have been found in St. Lucia by Midgett (1970), in Tanzania by O'Barr (1971) and in Ceylon by Thananjayarajasingham (1973) and in the United States by Hasselmo (1961), Barker (1947) and Sawyer (1965). At the level of dialect, it was found by Opler and Hoijer (1940) that the Chiricahua Apache switched to a special dialect when on a raid or on the war-path, while Hymes (1967) reported that the Subanun of the Philippines also use different dialect forms on festive occasions. Again, as mentioned in Chapter 2, the dialect code-switching observed

9. Research into this problem is being conducted by Dr. Geoffrey Stephenson, University of Nottingham.

10. See also Cooper and Greenfield, 1969; Fertig and Fishman, 1969; Greenfield and Fishman, 1970 and Brennan and Ryan, 1973.

in the Arab States known as "diglossia" (Ferguson, 1959) refers to the fact that the standard dialect is used only at formal speeches and festive occasions.

The rather complex relation between physical setting and occasion may be appreciated by reference to common experience. It is likely, for example, that an individual will modify his language and speech style when entering a church after a football match, or when he goes into a concert hall from a bar, but these speech modifications are not determined by the physical surroundings alone but principally by the social expectations with which they are associated. Thus, the patterns of verbal behaviour appropriate to the precincts of a church will be evident in some degree if a religious service were conducted in a barn or a football stadium. On the other hand, physical surroundings can have considerable effects upon mood and frame of mind. A great cathedral has an "atmosphere" conducive to religious feelings. The appropriateness of its design to its purpose is not entirely a matter of functional convenience, nor, probably, is our awareness of that appropriateness simply a matter of custom and association. Except for rather trivial instances, such as distance between speaker and listener or amplitude of ambient noise, purely physical environmental determinants of language are hard to find. But determinants arising from role expectancies and social situations are frequently keyed to physical surroundings.

Soskin and John (1963) studied the effects of change in physical surroundings on language with respect to a married couple on vacation. The authors found that explicit directive utterances were most frequent by the wife in the cabin and by the husband when the couple were out rowing. Here again, it may be suggested that it is the context of the husband's and wife's social roles which determine speech modifications rather than the locations themselves. In other words, if the wife were an Olympic oarswoman and the husband were a professor of food technology it is likely that their relative frequencies of directive utterances would have been reversed in the two situations. Another study by Gump, Schogger and Redl (1963) has shown systematic changes in verbal content with a 9 year old when addressing adults first at home and then in a vacation camp. These changes included a higher proportion of "sharing behaviour" (asking opinions etc.) at camp with a higher proportion of "submissive-appeal" behaviour towards adults at home. However, these changes cannot simply be related to differences in location. Different adults were involved in the two settings, and so it is possible that personality differences may have elicited different behaviour from the child. Nevertheless had the child been on vacation with his own parents the "holiday atmosphere" or the change of location or both may still have evoked comparable speech modifications. Thus it is necessary to be cautious in attributing particular speech modifications either to physical settings or to social and role determinants in the general context of the situation or occasion.

Much of this chapter so far has argued that aspects of the topic and context of conversation can constrain the speaker to adapt his speech patterns to the prevailing needs of the situation. These variables may be viewed as interacting with each other and with attributes of the receiver in a social encounter to provide constraints on speech along a dimension of formality-informality. In other words, a serious topic, a solemn occasion or a high status receiver may each, or in combination, provide a formal context for the discourse. The following section will look at some of the work related to this construct of contextual formality-informality.

## (3) *Formality-informality*

Situational determinants, singly or in combination, can provide contexts of interaction varying in degrees of formality-informality which may best be considered as points along a continuum. Joos (1962) has given concrete examples of such degrees of formality in terms of a speaker's request to be told the time of day. Examples from (a) to (e) are intended to reflect situational contexts decreasing in formality:

  (a) "I should be glad to be informed of the correct time".
  (b) "I should like to know the time please".
  (c) "Do you have the time on you, please?"
  (d) "What's the time?"
  (e) "Time?"

Gumperz (1970) has shown that the ability to select in terms of formality the appropriate style of speaking in the context of a particular interaction is very important. He showed that when speakers substituted a formal style, with explicit verbalization of shared background information, for the normally elliptical private style used in talking with their families, they were accused of "acting like strangers". One wife even asked her husband, "Don't you love me any more?"

The pioneer work of Joos was concerned with the grammatical-syntactical level of speech analysis but empirical work relating formality-informality to linguistic choice has also been carried out at the vocal level in relation to pronunciation changes.[11] Labov (1966) recorded interviews of about one-and-a-half hours' duration in the homes of 81 informants from the Lower East Side of New York. The interviews were conducted to determine whether changes in context would affect pronunciation patterns. He hypothesized that formal contexts of social interaction would require a greater reliance on prestigious variants of pronunciation by the speaker than less formal contexts of the discourse. A substantial proportion of these formal interviews were considered as eliciting a "careful" style of speech from the interviewees. However, for purposes of comparison, Labov required less and more formal contexts of interaction to test his hypothesis.

In order to elicit speech patterns in less formal contexts, Labov introduced two specific topics into the interviews. Interviewees were requested (a) to recite certain nursery rhymes and (b) to relate a personal experience of being near to death. Both topics were considered by Labov as being incongruent with formal expression. Labov was also able to gain access to speech data from three other informal contexts. These were:

(i) speech directed to the interviewer by the interviewee outside the formal interview situation
(ii) discussions in the home with people other than the interviewer
(iii) remarks or monologues not in direct response to the interviewer's questions.

Speech in these five (including his informal topics) contexts was considered as "casual" only if it was also accompanied by specific modifications from "careful speech" in one of the following five respects—more variety in pitch, tempo, volume and breathing and the occurrence of laughter. Unfortunately, Labov does not provide any information as to what proportion of the speech in the five contexts failed to meet the strict criteria for a concomitant change in one of the five channel cues in order to constitute casual speech. Thus it will be appreciated that any changes in pronunciation patterns found between careful and

11. See also Mbaga and Whiteley (1961) and Leginski and Izzett (1973).

casual speech are somewhat difficult to interpret owing to his curiously restrictive criteria for casual speech.

In order to elicit speech patterns in contexts more formal than the interview, Labov required his informants to read a passage of prose. To obtain an even more formal context than this he also required his subjects to read lists of isolated words.

Thus, Labov, however artificially, was able to abstract four styles representing four degrees of formality, namely, "casual" and "careful" speech and speech used in reading and in reciting word lists. He assessed pronunciation changes across these four contexts and related these changes to the social class of the speaker. Pronunciation changes were assessed in terms of the occurrence of standard and non-standard variants of pronunciation with reference to three consonant

TABLE 7

Percentage occurrence of the prestige form of the phonological variant /r/ over four situational settings for three individuals of three distinct social strata (from Labov, 1964)

| Three speakers from three social classes | Contextual styles | | | |
|---|---|---|---|---|
| | Casual | Careful | Reading | Word lists |
| Upper middle class | 69 | 85 | 96 | 100 |
| Middle class | 0 | 19 | 24 | 53 |
| Working class | 0 | 5 | 14 | 29 |

and two vowel sounds in his speech data. There are certain methodological problems associated with this type of analysis (as will be mentioned in Chapter 9) but the results indicate that all five phonological variables gave a "fine stratification" in that consistent shifts towards standard pronunciation occurred as formality of context increased and consistent social class differences emerged. The sharpest stratification came with the /r/ variant[12] and Labov (1964) cites three individuals as characteristic of his findings, and these are tabulated in Table 7, which represents the changes in the use of /r/ over the four stylistic settings.

12. In New York speech, the presence of the postvocalic /r/ in pronouncing, e.g., the word "guard", holds prestige value for the speaker; its absence would reflect non-standard usage and, for this word, pronunciation would be identical to that of "god". The presence of /r/ is also one of the main pronunciation features of prestige speech in South Carolina (McDavid, 1948).

It would thus seem that the more formal a social or verbal setting is perceived to be by the sender, the more he will adjust his speech to approximate to prestige forms. Labov, however, was not concerned with discussing along what dimensions his formal and informal contexts differed,[13] nor with the problems of to what extent his informal contexts were similar to each other. In Chapter 9 (p.170f) we shall see, by examining Labov's interaction situation more closely, that interpersonal factors were possibly the intervening variables between his context change and the speech modifications that followed.

In subsequent research, similar patterns of stylistic stratification have been shown among speakers of Puerto Rican Spanish and English (Ma and Herasimchuk, 1968; Fishman and Herasimchuk, 1969), among speakers of American Black English in Detroit, North Carolina and Texas (Wolfram, 1968; Anshen, 1969; McDowell and McRae, 1972, respectively) and among speakers of Canadian French (Deshaies-Lafontaine, 1974; Clément and Taylor, 1974) and British English (Trudgill, 1974a).[14] Also, Levine and Crockett (1967) have shown social and stylistic stratification with the postvocalic /r/ variant in the North Carolina Piedmont community by comparing sentence-list pronunciations with word-list pronunciations. Out of 265 respondents, 188 showed an increase in the use of the prestigious /r/ variant in reading word-lists as compared with the sentence lists (the less formal context), while 68 showed a decrease in pronouncing /r/, with nine respondents remaining constant between tasks. Demographic variables were shown to be important in determining the magnitude of pronunciation change. Women, young men, short-term residents and lower-paid white collar workers appear to be more susceptible to the demands of contextual style than men, longer term residents (more than 10 years),[15] older men (over 40 years) and professional and working class people. Another study by Iannuci, Liben and Anisfeld (1969) has studied variation in pronunciation at the formal pole of the continuum. The authors required subjects to read aloud words from cards as part of an ostensible learning task, and then read through the same list of words under

13. For an examination of the characteristics of formal and informal situations, see Clément and Taylor (1974).

14. In this respect see also the observations of Kučera (1961) on the use of common and literary Czech in the speech of 19 exiles on French radio stations, and the study by Rainey (1969) on teachers' speech in a Headstart classroom situation.

15. For a discussion on the effects of length of residence in a community on an individual's speech style, see Giles (1972).

instructions to pronounce the words "clearly and accurately". A significant number of more formal pronunciations were evident in the second
task as compared with the initial presentation of the words.

Evidence from the above studies clearly shows that contextual constraints are apparent in changing pronunciation patterns of a speaker.
Nevertheless, the generality of these findings and the validity of relating
word list pronunciation to speech patterns in ongoing interactions is
doubtful. When the speaker is required to pronounce a single word in
isolation from any other verbal context, it is quite likely that he may
allow himself the freedom to use more "affected", and to him somewhat more "foreign" pronunciations.

## (4) *Privacy, purpose and familiarity*

Finally, we shall look at three aspects of the context which have received little attention—its privacy, purpose and familiarity. An aspect
of the general context of a social interaction which appears to be important is the private-public dimension. This dimension relates to the
number and the characteristics of participants in a given verbal situation. Herman (1961) has described how Jewish immigrants in Israel
choose a language according to whether the context is public or private.
He claims that Jews normally use their native language with each other
when in private but switch to Hebrew in public situations. This dimension has received little empirical attention in the monolingual literature
except for Paivio's (1966) review of the verbally and vocally disruptive
effect of an audience on language behaviour.

The purpose or goal of an interactive setting can well be important,
although once again very little work has been conducted on this aspect
of context as it relates to speech patterns. For instance, a bilingual
aware that the function of a situation he is participating in is to reach
a speedy decision on a vital issue will use the language in which he can
best communicate on this particular topic. Moscovici (1967) found
that repetitious statements were more frequent in speakers when there
exist social pressures to reach a definite conclusion on a topic than when
there are not these pressures (see also Hargreaves, 1960).

Some consideration ought also to be paid to the notion of familiarity.
In other words, does the fact that we are familiar with a person, setting,
topic or a mood affect the way in which we select speech patterns from
our repertoire range? A study by Goldman-Eisler (1968) at first sight
appears to show that topic familiarity is an important determinant of

speech patterns. Familiarity in her study was manipulated by asking subjects to repeat their description or interpretation of cartoons over a series of six trials. In a study by Siegman and Pope (1966) the effect of familiarity was examined by comparing subjects' later TAT creations with their earlier ones. Both studies reported familiarity to be associated with fewer pauses and quicker articulation rates. Nevertheless, there is a problem of interpretation as to whether these studies (particularly the latter) are examples of topic or of setting familiarity. It could be argued that the subjects were more influenced by familiarity with the testing situation than by familiarity with the topic itself. Perhaps a clearer example of setting familiarity can be found in a study by Hartford, Blane and Chafetz (1970). They obtained two 55-word samples of speech, initial and terminal, extracted from each of 18 interview transcripts in a psychiatric outpatient clinic. It was found, using the Cloze procedure (see Taylor, 1959), that the lexical items used at the end of an interview were less predictable than those obtained at the beginning of the session. The authors suggested that, in this context, as the session progressed there was an attempt on the part of the subjects to put into words, "inner states" for which no ready vocabulary exists. Thus familiarity with a setting can often, it would seem, allow the speaker sufficient confidence to become himself in terms of producing his idiolect, and to try to express ideas to the full extent of his potential. One would expect that familiarity of both context and topic would lead the speaker to pay less attention to his speech patterns (see Labov, 1970), and so, as familiarity with a setting increases, less prestigious speech patterns at the phonological levels might ensue.

*     *     *

To summarize then, it has been suggested that we each possess a speech repertoire, and that its range for any given linguistic level will vary as between individuals. With this concept in mind, this chapter has shown that an individual tends to modify his language, dialect, utterance length, speech rate and so forth, according to the topic he is speaking about, the context in which speaks and the mood in which he finds himself. The next chapter adds to this notion of speech diversity by reviewing the research conducted at the interpersonal level.

# 8

# The Influence of the Receiver

We have seen that a speaker may adapt his speech style according to aspects of the topic, the context and his internal motivational state. Let us now consider the ways in which he may adapt to the behaviour and the characteristics, real or supposed, of the person he is addressing. We do not yet know enough about this process of adaptation to be able to classify and describe the various effects adequately or to present a unifying theoretical framework.

In this chapter we give an account of research findings related to various personal characteristics of the receiver, namely, sex, age, race and social status. This list is probably not exhaustive of the receiver characteristics which influence the speaker. Although we discuss them separately, it is also unlikely that these influences operate in isolation from each other or from other variables. Secondly we discuss the well-known phenomenon usually referred to as "verbal reinforcement" or "verbal conditioning" which represents one of the ways in which speech may be influenced by the reactions of the person addressed. Thirdly we draw attention to the more recently introduced concept of "response matching" as a feature of verbal exchanges.

## Personal attributes of receiver

Both research findings and common experience suggest that most people's style of speech is not a uniform product offered to all and sundry regardless of who or what they may be. Some people are less adaptable than others but most of us are "respecters of persons" so far as style and content of speech are concerned. We probably use less formal grammatical structures when talking to intimate friends than when addressing strangers, for example. Anyone who spoke in a similar manner to a two year old and to his employer would probably be regarded as eccentric.

When we speak to someone unknown to us we take cognizance of that person's sex, age, race, social class and other characteristics which we may believe to be relevant to how we should conduct the conversation. One of the first clues to these attributes is physical appearance. Some aspects of appearance are basically constitutional in origin whilst others are of a more superficial nature. Some are more readily controlled by the individual than others. Thus appearance represents a somewhat indeterminate mixture of signs, some indelibly indicating what the person is and others showing what he would wish to seem to be. Judgements based upon physical appearance alone are therefore subject to considerable error and we normally make use of other evidence derived from the style and content of his speech and from the whole context of the encounter and modify our judgements and our speech as the interaction proceeds.

SEX

Most speakers would regard it as important to know the sex of the person they are addressing, although the actual need for this information may be exaggerated. The effect of knowledge of a receiver's sex upon speech patterns has not been very thoroughly investigated. However, it has been suggested by Conklin (1962) that it is an important determinant of the selection by male speakers of synonyms for bodily functions. Benney, Reisman and Star (1956) found that references to "mental health" and "sex habits" were least for male speakers in the presence of female listeners and greatest for female speakers in the presence of female listeners.

A more recent study by Shinedling and Pedersen (1970) has shown that 10 year old boys in the United States perform worse with female teachers on oral tests (e.g. of reading) than with male teachers. Harris and Masling (1970) have also shown that the sexes of tester and subject can affect Rorschach productivity.

There is clearly a need for more systematic research on the effect of this particular receiver attribute.

AGE

With regard to age, Ferguson (1964) claims that in many cultures, including Arab, Commanche, Spanish and English societies, there are styles of speech peculiar to the situation in which an adult addresses an infant (see also Berko-Gleason, 1973). The formal features of this style may include a change in lexicon, simplification of grammar, formation of words by reduplication, simplification of consonant clusters and general labialization. Sapir (1915) found that in Nootka, Canada, there were special linguistic forms used in speech to or about children (as well as fat people, dwarfs and hunchbacks).

More recently, Granowsky and Krossner (1970) conducted a comparative analysis of kindergarten teachers' speech with each other and with their children in the classroom and demonstrated significant differences on several measures of speech complexity. It was found that adult-to-children speech involved shorter sentences, a greater number of simple sentences and fragments, and fewer compound and complex sentences than in the case of teacher-to-teacher speech. On vocabulary measures, adult-to-children speech showed a lower Type-Token Ratio (a measure of vocabulary flexibility, introduced by Johnson, 1944), and a greater proportion of words from the first thousand most frequently used in the language, than were found in adult-to-adult interactions. Spradlin and Rosenberg (1964) found that adults had a lower Type-Token Ratio when talking to children of low verbal ability than when addressing children of higher verbal ability.

If these speech changes by teachers represent attempts to adapt to the children's behaviour, one would expect the contrast with adult-to-adult speech to become less or qualitatively different as the child develops. As yet there is little evidence about this, but a study by Kean (1968) found that, on many grammatical indices, teachers did not appear to differentiate between 8 and 11 year olds. This piece of research does not enable us to draw firm conclusions as to adults' abilities to discriminate in their speech between children of different ages. Indeed, contrary evidence comes from a study by Fraser and Roberts (1974) in which it was found that middle-class mothers' speech styles became grammatically more complex as their children progressed through the ages of $1\frac{1}{2}$, $2\frac{1}{2}$, 4 and 6.[1]

Many of the studies of adult-to-child speech have been concerned with mother-child interactions, and the majority have studied, as Fraser and Roberts did, the interactions of mothers with their own children. However, a study of maternal speech behaviour by Halverson

1. For a discussion of the ways in which a mother's speech style can affect her child's cognitive behaviour, see Olim (1970).

and Waldrop (1970) looked at the differences between speech addressed by mothers to their own offspring and that addressed to other children. Using a structured interaction session with $2\frac{1}{2}$ year olds they found that mothers used significantly more positive, encouraging remarks with other people's children and significantly more negative admonitions with their own offspring. Therefore, studies using mother-to-own-child interactions should not be too readily taken as representative of adult-to-child speech in general.

A number of variables have been shown to affect the types of adaptations mothers make in their speech to children. For instance, the mother's verbal behaviour towards her child has been shown to vary with social class. Lower class mothers are more likely than middle class mothers to instruct a child in a task by means of physical demonstrations and to use negative feedback of information (Bee *et al.*, 1969; Brophy, 1970). Another variable affecting a mother's speech style appears to be whether she is addressing her first or later born child. Rothbart (1971) has shown with 5 year olds that mothers give far more complex technical explanations to their firstborn children and exhibit greater verbal pressure for achievement than in the case of later children. These tendencies were found to be accentuated when the firstborn child was female.

Studies of father-to-child interactions are rare. However, a study by Rebelsky and Hanks (1971) found that fathers talk infrequently and for very short periods of time to children in the first three months of life. Moss (1967) found that fathers of females verbalize far more than fathers of males when the child is about three weeks old whereas mothers of males verbalize more than mothers of females at this time. This pattern reverses, however, at 12 weeks. What the functions of such differential patterns of talking to children may be are quite obscure, but they are presumably related in some way to the differing roles of mother and father during these periods.

A number of recent studies have been concerned with variation in children's speech (see Weeks, 1971). As soon as a child begins to speak he varies his mode of expression according to the person to whom he is talking, the situation he is in and the things he wants to say. The different varieties of speech which he uses tend to be systematically patterned and, increasingly as he grows up, they conform to the patterns of diversity in the speech of adults around him. Indeed, Bodine (1971) has shown that even a five year old mongoloid boy whom she studied had at least three styles of speech. In a small-scale observational study, Berko-Gleason (1973) concluded that:

> Children talk in different ways to different people . . . Infants are selective about whom they talk to at all. Four-year-olds may whine at their mothers, engage in intricate verbal play with their peers, and reserve their narrative, discursive tales for their grown-up friends. By the time they are 8, children have added to the foregoing some of the politeness routines of formal adult speech, baby-talk style, and the ability to talk to younger children in the language of socialization.

Further research is needed to determine by what means a child learns this social competence: we need to map out developmentally the extent of a child's sophistication in being able to take into account the subtle characteristics, needs and intentions of others.

Hahn (1948) produced the unexpected finding that six year olds construct a greater number of elaborated and compound sentences when speaking to other children in the classroom than when speaking to a teacher. Moreover, Houston (1969) reported that eleven year old children use a special "school" register for talking to teachers and others in authority. Characteristics of this style of speaking, in contrast to a "nonschool" register, are foreshortened utterances, simplified syntax and hypercorrection of phonology. Whereas the simplification of adult-to-child speech is easily explained as an attempt on the part of the adult to adapt to the child's presumed lack of sophistication, the tendency for children to speak more simply to teachers than to peers is less readily understood. Possibly the child responds to the teacher's power and status rather than his age as such, and perhaps his laconic style of utterance represents a self-protective withdrawal and unwillingness to become involved in dialogue—such as is shown by the stereotyped British soldier who responds to anything an officer may say to him with the one word "Sir!".

RACE

Sattler (1970) and Ledvinka (1972) have provided reviews of the "racial experimenter-effect" with regard to Blacks and Whites in the United States. The research suggests that interactions between people of different skin colours, particularly in situations with a specific purpose, such as employment interviews, lead to anxiety and discomfort for the participants. Studies by Ledvinka have shown that Blacks are likely to use different language styles according to whether they are addressing a White person or someone of their own colour and to indulge in more self-disclosures when talking to other Blacks. He also found (Ledvinka, 1971) that Black interviewers elicited grammatically more complex speech from Black job-seekers than did White interviewers. It is possible in the case of the White interviewer, as was suggested above with regard to child-to-teacher speech, that the respondent ascribes status and power to his interlocutor and that his linguistic behaviour reflects a cautious, withdrawn attitude. It could be argued that an employment interviewer, regardless of race, is always in a position of power in relation to a job-seeker; but when the interviewer is a member of the majority group and the candidate a member of the minority group this superiority/inferiority relationship is likely to be accentuated.

In a recent analysis of the same data, Ledvinka (1973) found that Black candidates for employment were more likely, when the interviewer was also Black, to cite as reasons for being out of work their own rejection of a previous job or dismissal by an employer. He accounts for such selective self-disclosure in terms of a set of "rules" for interracial behaviour:

> One of the rules is that blacks should not express interracial conflict or hostility to whites . . . If the world of work is considered a white institution, then the rule suggests that a black job-seeker should not imply to a white interviewer that *he* rejected a job or that *an employer rejected him.*

Race seems therefore to be an important receiver attribute affecting a sender's choice of patterns of speech in terms of grammatical construction and message content. More work is needed on the effect of race in contexts other than Black-White interactions in the United States. It would be interesting to investigate the linguistic aspects of interaction between members of other ethnic groups and members of a majority culture.[2]

A rather quaint racial-linguistic phenomenon is reported in an interesting study by Haas (1951). She found that when Creek Indian and Thai students were speaking their native tongues in the presence of English-speaking listeners they tended to avoid the use of certain words that bore a phonetic resemblance to obscene words in English. The extreme delicacy of feeling thus evidenced can be appreciated when

2. For work on intergroup communication see Brein and David (1971), Taylor and Gardner (1970; 1970a), Taylor and Simard (1972), Simard and Taylor (1973), d'Anglejan and Tucker (1973a) and Reinstein and Hoffman (1972).

one realizes the improbability of the listeners' being able to detect such embedded items when produced at normal rates of speech.

## SOCIAL STATUS

Before we discuss research concerning the effect upon speech of differences in status between the speaker and the receiver it may be useful to consider briefly the concept of status and the ambiguity which surrounds it.

It is clear that by a person's "status" is meant his social position or rank in relation to others, the importance he has in the eyes of others and the degree of respect he commands. When a society has a generally-accepted status-system there is little difficulty in specifying a particular individual's status in that society. Status might be determined by wealth, by education, by hereditary caste or by some other agreed criterion or, with less certainty, by some combination of criteria. But in many modern societies there is no universally acknowledged status-system applicable in all circumstances. Various individuals or groups may adopt different criteria for deciding who should be regarded as important and worthy of respect. A parish priest may have high status in the eyes of church members but fairly low status in the eyes of other members of the community. Young people may accord high status to a pop-singer who is virtually unknown to their elders. Accordingly we should perhaps regard status as relative to some particular reference-group.

Status is presumably attributed to an individual or to a category of people to the extent that those persons possess characteristics which are highly significant for the reference-group. The characteristics which may serve as criteria for the attribution of status can vary indefinitely among reference-groups—the ability to sing a certain kind of song, prowess in battle, commercial achievement, the possession of power over others, and so on. (According to cynics, the mass media now make it possible for a person to achieve status simply by becoming famous for being well-known.)

Difficulties regarding the concept of status arise when it is not clear (a) what reference-group is assumed to attribute status to the person or category of persons concerned and (b) what criteria are employed by that reference-group. When no particular reference-group or context is specified, the terms "status" usually but not always relates to assumed conventional or consensus criteria. Thus, by conventional standards, bishops, professors, dukes, army generals, millionaires and prime ministers may be regarded as having high status in our society. But any or all of these may have low status in the estimation of members of a particular reference-group or subculture.

With regard to the research studies we are about to discuss, it is in most cases clear that we are concerned with a particular context and a particular status-system which is accepted as valid by both the speaker and the receiver. We should not be justified in assuming, however, that findings in respect of a particular status-system are applicable to the conventional status-system or to any other. There may well be important differences as to criteria adopted and the salient emotions and attitudes associated with those criteria. A system based upon a criterion of power, for example, might be permeated by fear, whereas a system based upon respect for knowledge would probably involve more tranquil feelings.

The effect of the relative social status of sender and receiver has in fact attracted very little research attention. Interest has generally been confined to the study of forms of address. Brown and Gilman (1960) found that the use of pronouns in French, Italian and German is dependent upon the social relationships between the people conversing. In surveying the use of the respectful *vous* and the more familiar *tu* in French conversation (and the corresponding terms in Italian and German), they distinguish between reciprocal and nonreciprocal usage. In non-reciprocal usage, one person in a dyad (the socially superior individual) addresses the other with *tu* and in return is addressed with *vous*. In reciprocal usage, both members of a dyad use the same pronoun. Mutual use of the *tu* form expresses intimacy and solidarity; mutual use of the *vous* form indicates a degree of formality or lack of intimacy. A follow-up study by Brown and Ford (1961) investigated the use of first name alone and title-plus-last-name in American speech. It was found that the same variables of relative status and intimacy were important. More recently, Slobin, Miller and Porter (1968) have studied the use of these forms amongst employees of an insurance firm and their findings represent an extension of the earlier work. Interview data from the employees yielded the finding, consonant with those of Brown and Ford (loc. cit.) that mode of address is related to organizational structure. First name only was used between equals but in interactions between people of unequal status in the firm the person of higher status was addressed by title-plus-last-name and the subordinate was addressed by his first name. Age, length of service in the firm, levels of aspiration and self-assurance were less important determinants of modes of address than formal status in the organization.

It may be noted that conventions about forms of address are subject to change over time. In English universities, for example, the very wide reciprocal use of surname alone, which was the practice thirty or forty years ago, has been largely displaced by a general reciprocal use of first name alone. Elderly academics continue to address colleagues of long standing as Brown, Despard-Smith etc. but younger staff members and students use first names (or even contractions of first names) on very short acquaintance. The use of "Sir" has almost entirely disappeared except as a formal mode of addressing the chairman in a committee meeting.[3]

A further finding by Slobin *et al.* (loc. cit.) was that informants indicated greater willingness to make self-disclosures to fellow workers at the same level and to immediate superiors than to immediate subordinates. This encouraged the authors to modify the suggestion by Brown and Gilman that it is always the higher status person who initiates steps towards increased intimacy and to propose that self-disclosure may be employed as a strategy for intimacy acquisition.

Many subsequent studies in other cultures have demonstrated the effect of receiver-status upon selection of forms of address: for example, Rubin (1962) with Spanish and Guarani; Slobin (1963) with Yiddish; Martin (1964) with Japanese and Korean; Link and Ishii (1966) with Japanese; Foster (1964) with Spanish; Howell (1967) with Korean; Kocher (1967) with Serbo-Croatian; Lambert (1967a) with French Canadian; Geohegan (1971) with Bisayan. A very odd and extreme case, quoted by Hymes (1967), is that of the remote Abipon tribe of Argentina who have the custom that the morpheme /-in/ must be added to the end of every word addressed to members of the warrior class.

It was pointed out earlier that different status-systems may involve different criteria and it was suggested that findings regarding "the effect of status" are not generalizable from one context to another. One might go further and suggest that the use of the concept of "status" is misleading or at least unhelpful in certain areas of sociolinguistic research because it may obscure or distract attention from more useful and meaningful variables related to the cognitions and feelings of the people being studied.

3. For a discussion of forms of address in an academic setting, see McIntire (1972).

Let us take as examples two experiments, both concerned with status but using quite different criteria. Siegman, Pope and Blass (1969) studied the effect of interviewer status upon interviewees' verbal productivity. Status was assessed in terms of the amount of knowledge the participants possessed on a given topic. They found that interviewees were more talkative with high than with low status interviewers. In a study by Alkire, Collum, Kaswan and Love (1968) status was related to the distinction between full members and "pledges" (probationary members) of an American college sorority. The authors specifically associate status with the idea of power, although it is not clear that the higher status students exercised any real power over those said to have lower status. In a task consisting of the transmission of descriptions of abstract drawings by a "sender" to a "receiver" it was found that low status subjects, whether acting as senders or receivers, behaved in a much more passive, submissive way than the higher status subjects. When higher status subjects were acting as receivers they tended to interrupt the sender frequently in order to ask clarifying questions. Lower status receivers were less inclined to do this. As a result, transmission of information from high status to low status participants tended to be faster but less effective than transmission in the opposite direction.

The differences in the conception and the design of these two studies is such that there is probably little point in trying to reconcile the two sets of results. The fact that they are both nominally concerned with "status" may be deceptive. It might be more worthwhile to try to identify some of the variables which are operating in interactions said to involve status differences.

Although the concept of "level of arousal" (see Duffy, 1957) is not as precise as one would wish in terms of its physiological indices, it may be of some value in interpreting the results of studies of social interaction and in generating hypotheses about some aspects of speech diversity. It is intuitively plausible that, in many instances, confrontation between people who are aware that they differ in status should result in the raising of the level of arousal of the lower status person. There is some support for this idea in reports by Mehrabian (1969; 1971) that lower status members of a dyad are less relaxed than higher status members. This increase in arousal is particularly likely when the higher status person has some degree of power over the person of lower status, i.e. when he exercises control over outcomes in matters which are significant to the lower status person. Awareness of the power of the higher status person is likely to produce emotional/motivational states in the lower status person ranging from abject fear to a mild feeling of tension. An intermediate condition would be represented by an anxious desire to please, such as is stylized by cartoonists (notably Charles Schultz) in the form of a wide grin with clenched teeth.

If we cast arousal as an intermediate variable with regard to speech changes in social interaction, a large number of independent and dependent variables suggest themselves. Independent variables would include aspects of the topic of conversation and the context of the interaction as well as relations between the participants, such as relative social status. Dependent variables would include speech rate and pauses, grammatical complexity, accent and other aspects of speech repertoire.

Producing specific hypotheses is no easy matter since individual differences are almost certain to affect the relation between the independent variables and level of arousal and between level of arousal and the dependent variables. Furthermore, it is necessary to take into account the inverted-U model of arousal which suggests that increases in arousal improve the effectiveness of behaviour up to a certain optimum arousal level after which further increases cause progressive impairment of performance. However, despite the complications, this concept might help to elucidate not only those speech changes associated with status differences but also some of those attributed to other interpersonal variables such as sex, age and race differences. There is some danger in using the concept in *ex post facto* explanations of research findings because the interplay of variables which is theoretically possible is such that almost any result could be "explained", given suitable assumptions. It is preferable to use the concept of arousal mainly to generate hypotheses and to suggest the design of new experiments.

## Reinforcement of verbal behaviour

A large number of similar studies, the earliest of which seems to be that of Ball (1952), have established that the content of a speaker's conversation can be modified by the use of a simple process of operant conditioning or reinforcement. The terms "verbal conditioning" and "verbal reinforcement", often used in this connection, are ambiguous since they do not make clear whether it is the stimulus or the response that is designated as verbal. The fact is that verbal behaviour can be conditioned by either verbal or non-verbal reinforcing stimuli.

The experimental technique consists in selecting arbitrarily some feature of a speaker's verbal behaviour and applying the reinforcing stimulus whenever the appropriate behaviour occurs. Ball (op. cit.), for example, by uttering the sound "mmmm-hmm" whenever a subject mentioned animals, elicited more animal references from members of his experimental group than were made by control-group subjects whose verbal behaviour was not selectively reinforced in this way. He found that using a buzzer as a reinforcer had no effect. Greenspoon (1954), however, successfully used a buzzer and also a light stimulus as reinforcers to produce increases in the utterance of plural nouns. He had similar results with "mmmm-hmm", but "huh-uh" reduced the production of plural nouns (*idem*, 1955).

In general, subjects in such experiments behave as if certain stimuli were positive reinforcers or rewards or encouragements ("mmmm-hmm", "yes", "good", "right", "fine", a smile, a nod of the head) and others negative reinforcers or punishment or discouragements ("huh-uh", "no", a shake of the head). They usually claim to be unaware that their speech has been influenced by these stimuli. Among the numerous aspects of speech which have been found to respond to reinforcement are: various grammatical categories of words, specific topic references, rate of speech, quantity of speech, pauses, expressions of opinion, self-reference and non-delusional versus delusional speech (see reviews by Krasner, 1958, Williams, 1964 and Hersen, 1970).

The implications of these findings for everyday situations and, more especially, interviews and psychotherapy, are clear. It seems highly probable that the course taken by a conversation, and the views expressed by the participants, may be biased through the operation of selective reinforcement. An interviewer, for example, may be unaware that, through subtle cues of verbal, vocal or facial expression, he is encouraging a respondent to give certain opinions rather than others. A psychiatrist may unwittingly influence what a patient says so that it tends to conform with his particular theoretical viewpoint and confirm his provisional diagnosis. The likelihood of bias would remain even if a respondent were astute enough to realize that his interlocutor was transmitting feedback information: he might wish to please the interviewer or say what the doctor wanted to hear. These possibilities have considerable practical importance with regard to opinion research, selection interviews, psychiatry and many other situations.

Indirect evidence suggesting that reinforcement by means of unintentional vocal nuances is at least a possibility comes from two studies. Milmoe, Rosenthal, Blane, Chafetz and Wolf (1967) recorded the voices of nine physicians during interviews in the course of which the question "What has been your experience with alcoholics?" was asked. For one part of the study speech signals were recorded through a low-pass filter which had the effect of rendering the words spoken unintelligible. Subjects listening to these content-filtered tapes were able, with a reasonable degree of agreement, to assess the speaker's tone of voice for such characteristics as anger, anxiety and sympathy. A significant positive correlation was found between ratings of anxiety and the doctors' success in persuading patients to accept treatment for alcoholism: the more anxious they sounded when talking about alcoholism, the more successful they were. In another part of the study subjects judged unfiltered speech, so that they were able to attend to the content as well as the tone of voice. In this condition judgements of anger were found to have a significant negative correlation with success in referral: the more angry the doctors seemed the less success they had in dealing with alcoholics. Thus physicians' voice characteristics appear to be related to patients' behaviour. We cannot of course be sure of the causal relationship here, but it is not impossible that the doctor's attitude to alcoholism was conveyed to the patient by his tone of voice and that the patient's attitude to treatment was affected by this knowledge.

A somewhat similar study was carried out by Duncan, Rice and Butler (1968). They asked nine experienced psychotherapists each to submit two tape-recordings of therapy sessions: one was to be a "peak" hour, when the therapist considered that the session was proceeding successfully, and the other a "poor" hour, when the therapist felt that the interaction with the client was going badly. Paralinguistic analysis showed differences between peak and poor hours with regard to characteristics of the therapist's speech such as pitch, intensity, tempo and the occurrence of nonfluences. In peak hours "the therapists' voice would give the impression of being serious, warm and relaxed. In those moments when open voice was present the therapist would sound especially close, concerned and warm." For poor hours it was found that "the therapist's voice would sound dull and flat, and rather uninvolved. When his voice took on more energy, he would seem to be speaking for effect, editorializing." Again we cannot be sure of the causal connection between tone of voice and the success of the therapy session, but it is possible that feedback of information carried by the therapist's tone of voice could affect the client's responsiveness, making good sessions better and poor sessions worse. There is support for this idea in the findings of Pope and Siegman (1968), Hamilton and Robertson (1966) and Johnson (1971) which indicate that people talk more freely to interviewers perceived as "warm" than to those whom they perceive to be "cold".

## Response matching

Various aspects of the receiver's characteristics, personal and linguistic, have been discussed in terms of how they might affect the sender's speech. A special case of the dependence of a person's speech behaviour upon behaviour exhibited by another person is the phenomenon of "response matching". This term was introduced by Argyle (1969) to refer to the apparent tendency of some speakers to model their speech upon some aspect of the speech of the person with whom they are conversing. Although the term "response matching" occurs in only a limited number of research reports there is reason to suppose that this process may be a very common feature of verbal interaction. Examples can be found on a wide range of linguistic levels from content to loudness and indeed it has been observed also in the interchange of visual signals. Charney (1966), Condon and Ogston (1966; 1967) and Kendon (1970) have shown that the postures of client and therapist become progressively more similar during the course of a therapy session.

Probably more research attention has been paid to the modelling of utterance durations than to any other aspect of response matching. Matarazzo and his associates have found in a number of studies (reported in Matarazzo et al., 1968) that a doubling of the average duration of an interviewer's utterances induces an approximate doubling in the duration of utterances by the interviewee. Fielding (1972) claimed, however, that these results might possibly be explained in terms of reinforcement. He points out that the investigators "did not report the frequency of such behaviours as head nodding, smiling and frowning, nor of such verbal behaviours as mmhmms, uhhuhs etc." and continues: "Both they and others have shown these actions to be effective reinforcers of verbal behaviour, including such behaviour as utterance duration. This ommision appears to me to be particularly crucial because the interviewer in all these studies was one of the experimenters, namely Matarazzo himself."

Nevertheless, Fielding's own results confirm the general finding of Matarazzo and his associates. In a study designed to avoid possible experimenter effects 48 subjects were presented with 12 open-ended questions concerned with matters of general interest. Each question was constructed in two forms, differing in length but not in essential content. Half the subjects were asked the questions in face-to-face interview by people uninformed of the experimental hypotheses. The remaining subjects heard prerecorded questions and themselves controlled their presentation. The results showed that subjects tended to increase the length of their replies when the questions were longer. Replies to the longer forms of questions were of greater duration than replies to shorter forms of the same questions.

A real-life study of the matching of utterance length is reported by Ray and Webb (1966). They studied 61 press conferences given by President John F. Kennedy during the years 1961 to 1963 and found a positive correlation between the length of the reporters' questions (1628 of them) and the length of the President's answers. It should be recognized, however, that this correlation, and possibly some other examples of utterance-length matching, could be accounted for, at least in part, by the fact that a complex and therefore long question often requires a long and complex answer.

Matching of the rate of speech has been found by Lightfoot (1949), Lightfoot and Black (1949) and Ruesch and Prestwood (1949). Goldman-Eisler (1954) found that, although within a given conversation subjects tended to maintain a constant verbal rate, unusually high verbal rates by one speaker either preceded or followed high rates by the other. Webb (1969) also confirmed the tendency of speakers to match each other's rate of speaking. He found that the rate at which interviewers spoke in standardized or nonstandardized interviews influenced the respondents' speech rates. However, Webb (1970) thought that previous studies of speech rate modelling might have been confounded by the effects of the experimenters' gestures or facial expressions, so he presented his subjects with tape-recorded questions on an impersonal topic—the world situation. Once again it was found that a subject's speech rate was influenced by the questioner's speed of talking.

Response matching has been demonstrated on a number of other vocal levels. These include precision of articulation (Tolhurst, 1955), loudness (Black, 1949), the frequency of interruptions (Argyle and Kendon, 1967) and the frequency of pauses in speech (Jaffe and Feldstein, 1970). Ruesch and Prestwood (1949) suggest that vocal expressions of emotions may also be "infectious".

A numbers of workers have investigated matching of the content of speech. Bales (1950), for example, showed that jokes made by one speaker in a small group tended to elicit jokes from others and that there was similar response matching in terms of showing solidarity, giving opinions and orientation and in voicing disagreement. Matching of self-disclosure has been shown by Taylor (1965), Tognoli (1969) and Ehrlich and Graeven (1971). Intimate self-disclosure by one speaker in a dyad often results in similar self-disclosure by the other.[4] This tendency is utilized in O. H. Mowrer's system of "integrity therapy": the therapist sets an example of frankness by making disclosures about himself in the hope that the client will be encouraged to be equally frank about his own problems (see Drakeford, 1967).

Another finding which could be considered as an example of response matching is that of Mosher, Mortimer and Grebel (1968) from their study of verbal aggression. Eight delinquent boys were divided into pairs and the members of each pair competed with each other in assembling form-boards. In certain of the pairs one member was instructed to distract the others with either mild or intense verbal abuse. It was found that boys who were thus verbally attacked showed significantly more verbal aggression than was shown by control subjects and that the intensity of their retaliation reflected the intensity of the verbal aggression they had themselves received. In a second study, however, the groups were arranged so that physically weak boys were competing against either strong and aggressive boys or strong but nonaggressive boys. In this case the weak boys were found to be less aggressive against the strong aggressive opponents than against strong nonaggressive boys. From a common-sense point of view this result seems to indicate a prudent weighing of the situation by the weaker boys and suggests that response matching is not a simple and automatic process of imitation but is just one of the possible ways of adapting to the behaviour of another person.

4. For other studies of self-disclosure response matching, see Jourard and Richman (1963), Chittick and Himmelstein (1967), Spiritas and Holmes (1971), Janofsky (1971) and Davis and Skinner (1974).

So far we have discussed response matching as if it were a one-way process, citing for the most part experiments in which subjects modify their speech to conform to a pattern to which they have been exposed by the experimenter. However, it is reasonable to suppose that two people interacting in a real-life situation would respond to each other's behaviour and might exhibit mutual response matching perhaps progressively over time. Studies by Lennard and Bernstein (1960) and Welkowitz and Feldstein (1969) provide evidence which suggests that response matching becomes closer each time the members of a dyad meet: their speech patterns progressively converge. The latter study showed, however, that matching tended to decrease within the course of any particular interaction. This finding is not consistent with the studies mentioned above which showed that posture becomes more similar in the course of an encounter.

A number of situational factors could determine the extent to which one individual matches another's behaviour. We shall pursue this matter further in the next chapter but for the moment we may note that Welkowitz and Feldstein (1970) found that individuals in a dyad show response matching to a greater extent when they think that they have similar personalities than when they do not. Perceived similarity seems to be more important than objective similarity.

Argyle (1969) considers that response matching might be explained in terms either of imitation or of reciprocity. Imitation refers to behaviour which is simply a copy of the behaviour of some other person in the same or a similar situation. Argyle summarizes the main conditions under which it is known to occur as:

> (a) when the follower is rewarded for his behaviour, especially (b) if he is rewarded by the model, (c) if the model is of higher power or status, (d) if the model is seen to be rewarded for the behaviour in question, (e) if the follower is similar to the model, and (f) if there are no clear guides to the follower's behaviour.

Of the various theories which have been put forward to explain imitation, Argyle says:

> It is not very clear how any of them apply to the interaction situation. In any case imitation during interaction might be something of a special case governed by different processes, in that the following behaviour is both visible to and directed towards the model.

Reciprocity implies an exchange transacted between two people such that one person confers a benefit of some kind upon the other and receives recompense from him. Argyle characterizes reciprocity thus:

> (1) The reciprocity act is not necessarily similar to the original, but is equivalent in reward value; (2) reciprocity is not an immediate, unthinking response, but is carefully calculated and follows after an appropriate interval of time; (3) conscious awareness of what is happening inhibits imitation, but makes reciprocity more probable; (4) reciprocation is *less* likely when the other is of high status, not more likely as with imitation.

Neither imitation nor reciprocity appears to be an entirely satisfactory explanation of response matching. "Imitation" seems to be little more than an alternative label for response matching and itself requires explanation. Reciprocity may apply to some forms of response matching, such as the exchange of self-disclosures, but leaves most of them unexplained unless one uses the question-begging device of assuming that, for example, a long utterance somehow "compensates" the other speaker for his long utterance.

Giles (1971) proposed two forms of response matching, positive and negative. "Negative response matching" refers to retaliatory speech acts such as those described by Mosher *et al.* (1968), in the case of verbal aggression, and Argyle and Kendon (1967) in the case of mutual interruption. By "positive response matching" he means forms of linguistic matching calculated to improve the relationship between members of a dyad. Earlier in this chapter we cited a number of examples of the tendency for a speaker to adapt his speech style according to the characteristics of the receiver. Some of these adaptations could be regarded as instances of positive response matching. When an adult, in addressing a child, simplifies his vocabulary and grammar, he could be said to be matching the child's own speech behaviour. Similarly, the use of more elaborate syntax and a more standard accent in speech to a high status person could be regarded as an attempt to match that person's typical or expected speech style.

Consideration of adaptive, integrative matching of speech characteristics forms the main theme of the following chapter.

# 9

# A Social Psychological Model of Speech Diversity

Fischer (1958) found in a linguistic survey in New England, when he interviewed 24 children, that the "choice between the participle ending /ing/ and the /in/ variant, appear to be related to sex, class, personality and mood of the speaker, to the formality of the conversation and to the specific verb spoken . . . (and doubtless of the person spoken to, although this was not investigated)". But more importantly, Fischer advocated a series of studies involving the interaction of different dialect speakers which he proposed to term "comparative idiolectology" where

> one might concentrate on a single informant . . . and note changes in his speech in different settings and situations and with different conversants. Moreover, since language is phenomenologically as much listening as speaking one would be led to analyse what was said comprehensibly to him by others, as well as what he said himself.

The present chapter is in fact an attempt to provide a starting point for the construction of a theoretical framework for such a comparative idiolectology.

Since 1958 much research has accrued which demonstrates that an individual's speech patterns are in part dependent on the person to whom he is talking, the topic of the discourse and the setting in which it takes place, as we have seen in the previous two chapters. The bilingual's and bidialectal's choice of language and dialect respectively have been shown to be a function of these three factors as has the monolingual's choice of speech style. Indeed it is, according to Hymes (1972), this notion of code variation and speech diversity that has been singled out as the hallmark of sociolinguistics. The models of speech dynamics that have emerged (e.g. those of Ervin-Tripp, 1964; Hymes, 1967;

Sankoff, 1971) have relied, as has already been stated, on a descriptive approach in terms of presenting a taxonomy of factors influencing code variations, such as topic, setting and so forth. This initial work has been extremely important since "the work of taxonomy is a necessary part of progress towards models (structural and generative) of sociolinguistic description, formulation of universal sets of features and relations, and explanatory theories" (Hymes, 1972). However, owing to the fact that our taxonomies have changed little over the past few years, Giles, Taylor and Bourhis (1973) felt the need to develop a tentative, explanatory sociolonguistic theory to account for at least specific types of speech diversities. The strategy at this initial stage was to formulate a theory which focussed on one taxonomic level, in this case, the interpersonal aspects of speech diversity. And it is an elaboration of this theory that this chapter is about together with a discussion of its usefulness in describing shifts at one particular linguistic level—accent usage. It is hoped that through the elaboration of this theory the two areas of speaker evaluation and speech diversity can be conceptually linked.

Before launching into a discussion of the theory, let us see whether we can categorize different types of speech shift at the interpersonal level. Most of the research at this level in multi- and bilingual societies (as was noted in Chapter 2) has been concerned with suggesting that social norms are operative in the choice of a language or code depending on the characteristics of the participants such as sex and status. Some studies of monolinguistic code variation (cited in Chapter 8) can also be understood within a framework of normative behaviour related to the listener's social status, sex and age. Therefore, certain shifts in speech styles can be the result of complying with social norms. In other words, it is expected that we speak in a particular manner to a certain type of person. The theoretical model advocated by Herman (1961) and discussed by Hunt (1967)—both discussed in Chapter 2—in terms of the personal needs system and background and immediate situations, would seem a useful starting point for explaining these types of shifts.

However, a great deal of work on monolingual speech diversity at the interpersonal level has been more concerned with demonstrating that often speakers adapt or accommodate their speech towards that of their interlocutors when social norms are in all probability not operative. How, theoretically, can we describe these? Such accommodative behaviour has been termed "positive response matching" (see Chapter 8) and may be a subtler, and perhaps more unconscious speech shift than those just mentioned. This phenomenon has been demonstrated in a number of studies indicating that at least one member of an interactive dyad tends to adopt the speech patterns of the person to whom he is talking. It may be recalled that it has been studied on a wide range of linguistic levels, and a recent investigations by Giles, Taylor and Bourhis (1973) has found evidence for accommodation as between members of entirely different ethnolinguistic groups.

Giles (1973a) has termed such accommodative changes in social interaction "convergent" behaviour in the case of accent changes. However, he has hypothesized that convergence, whether symmetrical or asymmetrical in a dyad, may be only one aspect of a wider phenomenon of speech change. He suggests that in certain social interactions there may exist *dissociative* motivational tendencies on the part of one or both of the members of a dyad such that speech is modified so as to become less similar—divergence rather than convergence. A sender might attempt to dissociate himself from any identification with the receiver or, more broadly, from the group which the individual represents. If the sender and receiver are similarly motivated then they may be symmetrical in their efforts towards progressive divergence. Speech convergence and divergence may both be seen as representing strategies of conformity or identification. Speech convergence is a strategy of identification with the speech patterns of an individual *internal* to the social interaction, whereas speech divergence may be regarded as a strategy of identification with regard to the linguistic norms of some reference group *external* to the immediate situation. This external reference group may not always be readily definable, and therefore may simply and loosely be described as those people who are different from the receiver (probably in terms of values and attitudes), and who do not share his regular use of certain linguistic items. It is quite likely that the strategy of speech divergence is more available to conscious awareness than that of speech convergence. In this sense, divergence is a strategy aimed at accentuating interpersonal differences (cf. Tajfel and Wilkes, 1963). For instance, suppose that a retired brigadier's wife in Britain, renowned in the district for her snobbishness, returns her Daimler to the local garage because of inadequate servicing, voicing her complaint in elaborately-phrased, yet mechanically-unsophisticated language with a high-pitched tone. Her superior manner and attitude may induce the mechanic to respond with a flood of almost incomprehensible technicalities in a louder, more deeply pitched voice than usual—speech divergence at both verbal and vocal levels. This speech divergence would represent an attempt to fabricate a *persona* which distinguishes the sender from the receiver more sharply and definitely than his normal speech pattern would—a kind of deliberate "dis-identification" or dissimilation. Admittedly, there is little empirical work so far which demonstrates such divergent speech patterns either in a bilingual or in a monolingual context (cf. Bourhis, Giles and Lambert, 1975) and the idea has to be left, for the moment, in the realm of supposition.[1] Nevertheless, work on language and code loyalty and cases where a minority group retains its code as an expression of group or national identity in the face of the majority culture's language could be regarded as demonstrating forms of divergent behaviour (e.g. Gumperz, 1964a; Fishman *et al.*, 1966).

Thus one may identify at least three forms of speech modification in interpersonal situations, namely, normative, accommodative and divergent code variations. These may cover too broad an area to permit effective model-building at this stage, and so our emphasis will be on one of these—accommodation. Later, we shall discuss the problems of identifying certain speech shifts as clearly normative or accommodative.

## The accommodation model

The essence of the theory of accommodation lies in the social psychological research on similarity-attraction (see reviews by Byrne, 1969; Simons, Berkowitz and Moyer, 1970). This work suggests that an individual can induce another to evaluate him more favourably by reducing dissimilarities between them. The process of speech accommodation operates on this principle and as such may be a reflection of an individual's desire for social approval. In exchange theory terms (Homans, 1961), it seems likely that the accommodative act may involve certain costs for the speaker, in terms of identity-change and expended effort, and so such behaviour may be initiated only if poten-

1. The phenomenon has however, been used often in literature. Consider the following extract from one of D. H. Lawrence's short stories, *A Modern Lover*:

The conversation went haltingly ... Then there grew an acute, fine feeling of discord. Mersham, particularly sensitive, reacted. He became extremely attentive to the others at table, and to his own manner of eating. He used English that was exquisitely accurate, pronounced with the Southern accent, very different from the heavily-sounded speech of the home folk. His nicety contrasted the more with their rough, country habit. They became shy and awkward, fumbling for something to say ... It was evident to him; without forming the idea, he felt how irrevocably he was removing them from him, though he had loved them.

tial rewards are available. If one can accept the notion that people find social approval from others rewarding, it would not seem unreasonable to suppose that there may be a general set to accommodate to others in most social situations. Indeed, this idea may be close to what Fielding (1972) termed a conversation rule for response matching, in that if a speaker desires a gratifying interaction he finds it advantageous to accommodate his speech style towards that of the person with whom he is interacting.[2] This accommodative set is, however, not unresponsive to possible contrary demands of the specific situation, as can be inferred from the reference to speech divergence earlier. It has been suggested that the accommodative act provides the sender with rewards referred to in general terms as the receiver's approval. What specifically these rewards may be in more concrete terms (e.g. increased perceived status) would depend upon the situation itself and the particular linguistic level upon which accommodation occurred. We shall discuss the nature of these rewards shortly when we concentrate upon one particular linguistic level. It is important to note that the receiver's approval does not necessarily imply liking for the sender—just as an employer's approval of a man as suitable for employment, does not necessarily imply liking for him.

Accommodation through speech can be regarded as an attempt on the part of a speaker to modify or disguise his persona in order to make it more acceptable to the person addressed. The speaker's rationale, of which he is not necessarily consciously aware, is represented in the following schema:

> There is a dyad consisting of speakers A and B
> Assume that A wishes to gain B's approval
> A then
> (1) Samples B's speech and
>     (i) draws inferences as to the personality characteristics of B (or at least the characteristics which B wishes to project as being his)
>     (ii) assumes that B values and approves of such characteristics
>     (iii) assumes that B will approve of him (A) to the extent that he (A) displays similar characteristics
> (2) Chooses from his speech-repertoire patterns of speech which project characteristics of which B is assumed to approve.

2. For a discussion of conversational rules, see McGuire and Lorch (1968; 1968a).

The effect of this decision process is that A produces speech similar—or at least more similar than his normal speech would be—to the speech of B. There is therefore speech convergence. If B at the same times goes through a similar process there is mutual convergence. One effect of the convergence of speech patterns is that it allows the sender to be perceived as more similar to the receiver than would have been the case had he not accommodated his style of speaking in this manner. But in addition, speech accommodation may be a device by the speaker to make himself better understood. The more the sender reflects the receiver's own mode of communication, the more easily will his message be understood. However, Triandis (1960) claims that increased communicative effectiveness between members of a dyad increases interpersonal attraction anyway. It could be suggested that in certain interaction situations the emphasis with regard to accommodation is on increasing comprehensibility whilst in others it may be on causing the sender to be perceived more favourably. But since both processes produce interpersonal attraction, it may not be worthwhile at this point to attempt to disentangle them.

What is the empirical evidence for such a model? Since the desire for social approval is assumed to be at the heart of accommodation, it could be hypothesized that people high on a scale of need for social approval would accommodate more than those having a low need in this regard. Although this has not been tested directly, some encouragement can be derived from the study by Mehrabian (1971) in which he found that subjects highest on a measure of affiliative needs showed the greatest tendency to reciprocate positive verbal and nonverbal signals provided by their dyad partners. With regard to the idea that a person who accommodates would be perceived more favourably than one who does not, the evidence is more substantial. Dabbs (1969) found that a person who exhibited response-matching in respect of the gestures and postures of the person with whom he was interacting was liked more than someone who did not behave in this manner. Moreover, the person who matched responses was considered to have better ideas and be more persuasive than the person who did not. Although this example is outside the field of speech it does appear to be an instance of accommodation.

With regard to bilingual accommodation in Quebec, Giles et al. (1973) had a taped French Canadian (FC) stimulus speaker provide a message to bilingual English Canadians (EC) in either French (no accommodation), a mixture of French and English (partial accommodation) or English (full accommodation). It was found that the FC was perceived more favourably in terms of considerateness and of his effort to bridge the cultural gap the more he accommodated to the EC listeners. Moreover, when the subjects were given the opportunity to return a communication to their FC partner, subjects who were spoken to in English accommodated the most (i.e. spoke French). Subjects in the mixed language condition showed less accommodation and those who were spoken to in French showed least. The results clearly support the theoretical model thus far formulated. A follow-up study by Simard, Taylor and Giles (in press) has shown that such patterns are in evidence when the roles of the two ethnolinguistic groups are reversed. These findings complement those of Feldman (1968) who found that certain cultural groups are more favourably disposed toward assisting foreigners who accommodate to their language than those who do not.[3]

The study by Giles *et al.* (1973) showed some interesting levels of bilingual accommodation in the Quebec context. In all, 14 categories of accommodation were identified which could be thought of as occupying positions along a continuum of accommodation-nonaccommodation. On the basis of their findings they suggested a number of theoretical possibilities with regard to language choice in interactions between bilingual FCs and ECs in Quebec. First they considered the case of two bilinguals, each equally proficient in both French and English, but one being a member of the French-speaking community and the other a member of the English-speaking community. Notwithstanding their equal facility in both languages, the FC would regard French as his first language and English as his second, and the opposite would be the case with the FC. If both were set to accommodate, each would use his second language, the FC speaking English and the EC speaking French. After an initial demonstration of their equal willingness to accommodate, they would presumably realize how inefficient it would be for them to continue such patterns of accommodation. As Homans (1961) stated, "the profits from exchange decrease with the number of exchanges". It could be that the participants would then agree to adopt the first language of the one who first accommodated, as a kind of re-

3. Similarly, Harris and Baudin (1973) showed a nonsignificant tendency for Spanish-Americans to comply with a request for assistance from a member of their own ethnic group when the plea was voiced in Spanish as opposed to English.

ward for his willingness to adjust to the other. Thus there may be some advantage for the individual who initiates bilingual accommodation.

The situation would perhaps become more complex with bilinguals who were more proficient in the one language than in the other. Certain clues can be provided from the study by Giles *et al.* (op. cit.). In the event of such bilinguals interacting, it might be that they would both use an alternating mixture of languages. Should a bilingual with equal language proficiency from the one group interact with a bilingual with unequal proficiency from the other, the latter may still attract the former's approval simply by expressing his regret for not being able to match his ability to accommodate. The interaction could then continue comfortably in the second language of the one with equal proficiency in both. Both speakers would have accommodated to each other in some way but on distinctly different levels. According to reciprocity theory (Gouldner, 1960), things to be exchanged may be different in kind but equal in value. Here, expressed regret for not being able to accommodate through speaking the other's language may be accepted as an equivalent concession.

Cross-cultural interaction in a realistic context, however, suggests the need for further elaborations of the accommodation model. In the experiment by Giles *et al.* the EC listeners were fully aware that the stimulus speaker was bilingual and had voluntarily chosen to speak the language he adopted. However, in everyday life, we are very often unaware of the background information surrounding an accommodative or nonaccommodative act. For instance, we sometimes do not know whether or not a speaker who failed to accommodate to us had the necessary language skills to do so. Even when a person does accommodate we can often not be sure whether he was under pressure to do so, or whether he voluntarily made the effort to reduce the dissimilarities. The accommodation model thus far described does not take into account such attributed motives underlying accommodative behaviour and implicitly assumes that the perception of all linguistic adjustments *per se*, regardless of the motives attributed to them, will be equally effective. Similarly, different attributed motives underlying nonaccommodative behaviour have not been taken into account and the model has simply regarded the maintenance of regular speech habits as being unfavourably perceived by the listener.

Simard, Taylor and Giles (in press) suggested that recent developments in causal attribution theory (Kelley, 1973; Jones and Davis, 1965; Heider, 1958) could provide useful guidelines for an extension of the accommodation model. Heider (1958), for example, suggests that we understand a person's behaviour, and hence evaluate the person himself, in terms of the motives and intentions that we attribute as the cause of his actions. He proposes that a perceiver considers three factors when attributing motives to an act, namely, the other's *ability*, his *effort* and the *external pressures* impelling him to perform in the manner in which he did. In order to illustrate these factors in operation, Heider gives the example of someone rowing a boat across a stream where the perceiver's evaluation of the actor will depend upon the perception of the actor's *ability* to row, the amount of *effort* exerted and *external* factors such as wind and current prevailing at that time. Analyzing the study by Giles *et al.* (1973) in causal attribution terms provides a clear understanding of the subjects behaviour. The EC subjects knew that the FC speaker was capable of speaking English (ability) and that there were no external pressures on him to select one language rather than the other. Thus, subjects were likely to have assessed the FC's accommodative or nonaccommodative behaviour solely in terms of the perceived effort he was prepared to make for them. The greater the amount of effort perceived in accommodation when there were no external pressures, the more effective this behaviour was shown to be.

The implication of attribution theory for the present context therefore is that a listener can make a variety of attributions regarding accommodation and nonaccommodation. For example, since a person who accommodates clearly has the linguistic ability to do so, the listener can attribute this behaviour either to the speaker's being forced to converge by some external pressures or to his voluntarily making an effort to reduce dissimilarities between them.

Simard, Taylor and Giles (loc. cit.) designed a study primarily to determine whether accommodation was differentially perceived and could be classified according to the motives attributed to it by the listener. Specifically, the study examined whether the attribution factors of ability, effort and external pressure influenced listeners' reactions to accommodative and nonaccommodative speech acts. For example, how would the occurrence of nonaccommodation be attributed when listeners had little knowledge about the speaker's motives —to a lack of ability, to a lack of effort or to the existence of external pressures? Would voluntary accommodation be more effective than forced accommodation in terms of evaluation of the speaker and reciprocated accommodation?

The experiment had three major conditions, the first of which was designed to replicate the findings of Giles *et al.* (1973) using FC listeners with an EC speaker—the reverse of the original study. In this condition, the listener knew that the EC speaker was capable of speaking both English and French and was not under any external pressure to use one language or the other. For the second condition, the "no information" condition, the listener was not aware of the speaker's linguistic abilities or of any external pressure. For the final condition, the listener knew that the speaker did not choose the language of communication but that external pressure was placed on him to use one language rather than the other. In each of these three conditions, different FC subjects heard the EC stimulus speaker either accommodate to them in French or not accommodate to them by using his native tongue, English.

The tape-recorded message from the EC speaker was a three-minute description of a route to be followed on a city map. The FC listeners were required to trace the route on a blank map in front of them as the description was being given by the speaker. However, each of these descriptions was preceded by one of three different taped instructions apparently being given to the stimulus speaker; these instructions corresponded to the major manipulations in the study. The listeners were told that they would hear their speaker being given his instructions to ensure that they understood completely the nature of the task. In each introduction, it was made clear to the speaker that his listening partner would be a FC. After the description was completed and the subject had traced the route, he or she was presented with a map similar to the one used earlier. This map had a new route traced on it and subjects were asked to describe this route on tape to the EC who had just given them their description and to describe it in the language of their choice. The dependent measures used in the study included: perceptions of the stimulus speaker's language abilities and of his efforts to bridge the cultural gap; the number of errors made in interpreting the message; and the choice of language for the returned communication.

On the basis of their findings, Simard, Taylor and Giles (in press) proposed a revision of the accommodation model, a schematic representation of which appears in Fig. 1. It suggests that the perception of accommodation is effective in terms of speaker evaluation and reciprocal accommodation. However, a qualification needs to be considered

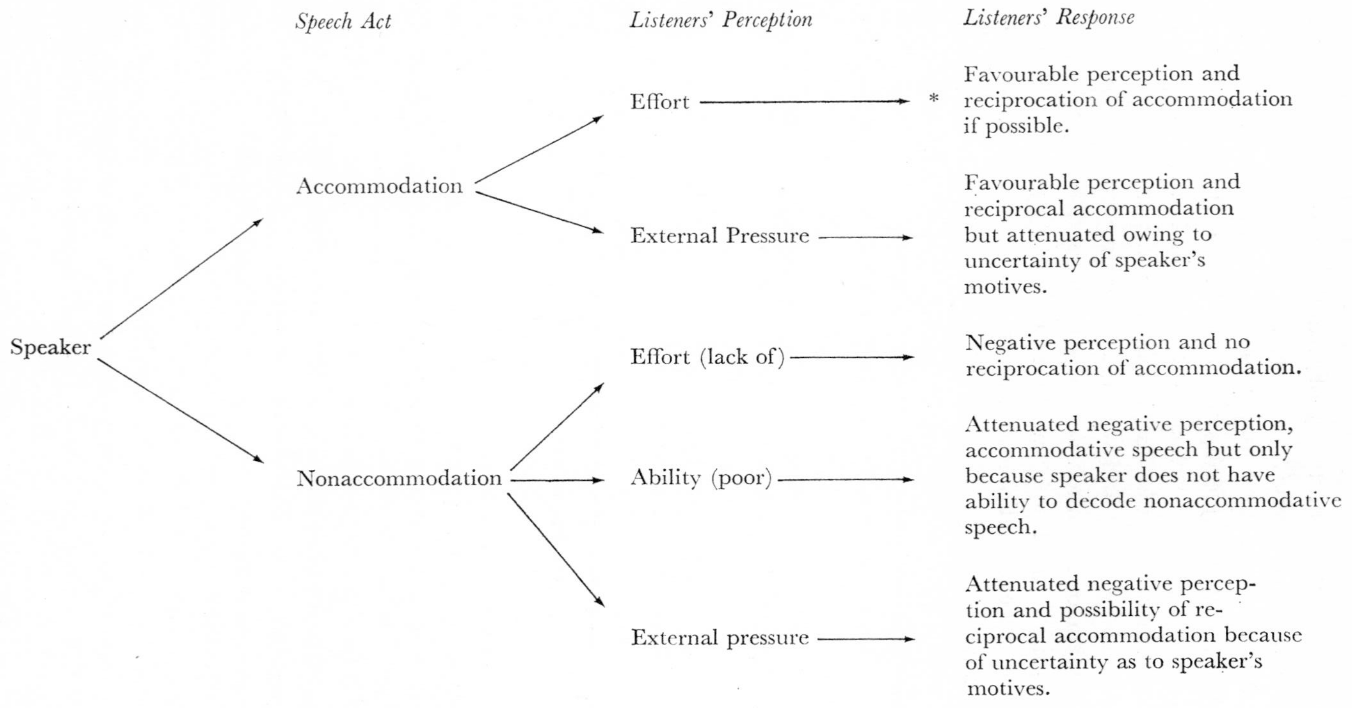
Speech Act
Listeners' Perception
Listeners' Response
Speaker
Accommodation
Nonaccommodation
Effort
External Pressure
Effort (lack of)
Ability (poor)
External pressure
*
Favourable perception and reciprocation of accommodation if possible.
Favourable perception and reciprocal accommodation but attenuated owing to uncertainty of speaker's motives.
Negative perception and no reciprocation of accommodation.
Attenuated negative perception, accommodative speech but only because speaker does not have ability to decode nonaccommodative speech.
Attenuated negative perception and possibility of reciprocal accommodation because of uncertainty as to speaker's motives.

* These responses were also obtained by Giles, Taylor and Bourhis (1973).

***Fig.* 1. A revised version of the accommodation model (after Simard, Taylor and Giles, in press).**

in that if accommodation is attributed to external pressures rather than voluntary effort, then it is likely to be less effective. More specifically, the results of the study by Simard *et al.* showed that listeners decoded an accommodating message attributed to external pressures less effectively (that is, made more errors), and were less prepared to return an accommodating communication than when the convergence was attributed to effort.

The elaborated model suggests that nonaccommodation is likely to foster a relatively unfavourable speaker evaluation and induce the listener to maintain his regular speech style. However, when this behaviour is attributed to a lack of language ability or to external pressures rather than to a lack of effort on the part of the speaker, then qualifications again have to be made in that the act may not be perceived or reacted to quite so negatively. For instance, the results showed that a nonaccommodating message attributed to external pressures was decoded better than the same message otherwise attributed. Also, listeners appeared more prepared to return an accommodating message attributed in this manner and still more when attributed to a lack of ability than to a lack of effort (see Fig. 1).

Future research may point to still further elaborations that need to be incorporated into this model using an attribution analysis. For instance, it would seem reasonable to subcategorize the factor of effort in the model in the following way. If a listener attributes accommodation to a voluntary effort, is the effort viewed as integrative, i.e. "because the speaker likes me"—or instrumental, i.e. "because the speaker needs me"? Does the effectiveness of accommodation depend upon such a distinction? Similarly, lack of effort indicated by nonaccommodation could be attributed perhaps to an attempt to increase social distance or to a need to emphasize language loyalty. Once again, listeners may react quite differently according to their attribution of intention. There is no specification of the speaker's motives in the schema shown in Fig. 1 nor any indication of the problems likely to arise should a speaker's actual motive for accommodation be different from that attributed to him by the listener.

Inconsistencies of the kind just mentioned (between real and attributed motives) may arise in situations of intergroup rivalry or competition. A number of studies have shown that people attribute the underlying intentions of another's act differently, depending on their own needs, and in such a way as to ensure consistency among their cognitions (e.g. Johnson *et al.*, 1964). Taylor and Jaggi (1974) have shown how certain behaviours may be perceived quite differently according to the characteristics of the actor. They showed that when a benevolent act was performed by an ingroup member it was attributed to an underlying (positive) disposition, but when performed by an outgroup member it was attributed to external pressures in the situation. On the other hand, when a malicious act was performed by an ingroup member it was attributed to external pressures in the situation, whereas it was attributed to an underlying (negative) disposition when performed by an outgroup member. Thus, in situations of intergroup tension, attribution errors may arise owing to sterotypes that are held of the other cultural group: we may be more prepared to attribute accommodation by an outgroup member to unknown pressures in the situation than to his desire for social integration. In the same way, we may be more ready to attribute his nonaccommodation to a lack of effort rather than consider that he has a lack of the appropriate language ability or that there were pressures in the situation forcing him to use his native speech style. Such misunderstandings are likely to be as resistent to correction as any other forms of prejudice.

However, it was also suggested by the authors that there may be a general tendency for people to attribute nonaccommodation to the speaker's limited repertoire, particularly in situations where no intergroup tension is apparent. The rationale for this may be that people appreciate the function of accommodation and recognize that attribution of nonaccommodation to a lack of effort implies that the speaker does not value the listener's approval. This implication would of course be harmful to the listener's self-image. One tactic of avoiding this tension is to attribute to the speaker a lack of ability, thereby eliminating any negative intent. Indeed, it could be hypothesized that those with high self-esteem would adopt this attribution strategy more frequently than those with low self-esteem. In any case, further research needs to be undertaken in different cultural contexts to determine the factors which influence the types of attribution an individual will make with regard to accommodative and nonaccommodative behaviours.

## Limitations of the accommodation model

The accommodation model represents an attempt to explain certain kinds of speech diversity which occur in interpersonal encounters. It attempts in particular to account for those speech changes which appear to be instigated by the speaker's motivation to gain the approval of, or dissociate himself from, the listener. We have seen that there is some empirical support for the model and for the suggested relationship between it and attribution theory. But we should not lose sight of the model's limitations. A full account of speech diversity must indicate the place of accommodation in a more comprehensive schema of the choices, constraints and decisions which determine the characteristics of the speech which a person emits. Even in the case of approval-seeking, the model presents some difficulties in its application to real-life situations.

Hymes (personal communication) has provided an example which illustrates one such difficulty. He cites the case of an English-speaking European addressing an East African official. In order to accommodate, the European begins speaking in Swahili. According to the accommodation model this should show a desire for solidarity and should earn the official's approval. However, in this particular context, such accommodation would probably be interpreted by the official as condescension and as implying that the European thought him incapable of understanding English. It would therefore be regarded as insulting. Hymes suggests that the "correct" procedure would be for the European to use English first, allowing the official to demonstrate his linguistic competence by replying in English, and then continue in Swahili.

This example suggests that the speaker does not automatically gain approval by adopting or approximating to the speech style of his interlocutor. A further example might be that of a tough, masculine, rugby-football playing young man seeking the favour of an exceptionally feminine and coy young lady. One might suppose that he would not advance his courtship by modelling his manner on hers but would be wiser to maintain or even exaggerate his own virile and masterful style of speech and behaviour. This is not to say that no accommodation is likely to take place in heterosexual encounters. Indeed the vogue of "unisex" indicates the opposite. The point is that there may be a conflict between accommodative tendencies and constraints to behave according to sexual norms and stereotypes. These norms may be acknowledged and subscribed to by both parties. The outcome so far as speech is concerned is not easy to predict.

Another example of how normative and accommodative tendencies may operate simultaneously is where a professional relationship exists between the members of a dyad, one being the client and the other a doctor, lawyer, priest or other such person having a well-defined public role. The latter would be constrained by his professional code to behave in a particular way towards the client regardless of his feelings towards him as a person. But he may have feelings about him as a person and there could be a degree of motivational conflict in the determination of his speech style.

Further research is needed to investigate the interplay of normative, accommodative and other endogenous and exogenous determinants of speech style.

A presupposition with regard to speech shifts in general is the obvious one that the speaker possesses the appropriate response repertoire. The speech repertoire can be thought of as having several different dimensions or levels. One level is that of the availability to the speaker, with varying degrees of facility, of more than one distinct language. The speaker's capabilities in respect of any one particular language can be subdivided into an indefinite number of different aspects or levels. Among the levels which it has been found useful to study are lexical style, in the sense of richness of vocabulary, grammatical complexity, use of pauses, speech rate and accent. The extent of a person's repertoire at a given level is in some cases determined by the upper limit of his knowledge and ability in that respect. For example, a person who possesses a large vocabulary has a choice between making full use of it or, as when speaking to a child, conveying his meaning (perhaps less precisely) by fewer and simpler words. But a person who has only a poor vocabulary would have a much narrower range within which he could vary his lexical style. Likewise a person well versed in the grammar of a language would presumably be able, should the occasion arise, to speak with a simplified grammar (e.g. using one tense only) or ungrammatically. A person not so sophisticated would be less able to vary grammatical complexity. It would be reasonable to assume that a person who habitually speaks quickly would be capable of speaking more slowly; but the converse is not necessarily true. Inferences about accent repertoire are less certain: it would not be safe to assume that a person who normally uses a standard accent would be capable of encompassing a nonstandard variant or that a nonstandard speaker would be incapable of producing a standard accent.

Consideration of speech levels and repertoires suggests a number of questions which may repay attention in future research. For example:

> Does accommodation typically take place on several speech levels simultaneously?
>
> Is accommodation at some levels more effective in influencing the listener's opinions than accommodation at other levels?
>
> What are the consequences of accommodating at one level and failing to accommodate (or even diverging) at another (e.g. suppose that the speaker switches from his own to the listener's preferred language but speaks it more correctly and fluently than the listener does)?
>
> How is accommodation through speech style related to accommodation in other ways—such as by speech content (e.g. agreeing), gesture, facial expression, posture?
>
> Might the speaker accommodate so much on so many levels that the listener becomes suspicious as to his sincerity?
>
> Are there analogues at other speech levels of the finding by Simard *et al.* (in press) (discussed above) that the listener's response to accommodative or nonaccommodative language choice is affected by his beliefs about the circumstances of the choice?

The last two questions both relate to the listener's awareness of accommodative acts. In this regard, it seems intuitively reasonable that a distinction should be made between *overt* and *covert* accommodation.

Some kinds of accommodation appear to depend for their effectiveness in influencing his attitude upon the receiver's being aware that accommodation has taken place—that he has received some sort of concession from the speaker. This category of "overt" accommodation would include switching from one language to another in a bilingual or multilingual setting (e.g. from English to French in Quebec). Perhaps accommodative self-disclosure should also be included. Ehrlich and Graeven (1971) report that "persons are directly aware of the magnitude and intimacy of their self-disclosing behaviour in dyadic encounter's" but do not tell us how well people can evaluate the extent of self-disclosure made to them by others.

Accommodation in other cases seems to depend for its effectiveness upon its *not* being recognized as such by the receiver. Such "covert" accommodation, of which the speaker himself may have little or no consciousness, would probably include changes in speech rate, pauses, grammatical complexity, accent etc. made by way of convergence towards the speech characteristics of the receiver. Detection by the listener of accommodation in this category would possibly tend to discredit the speaker. In the case of accent convergence, for example, the listener might feel that he was being mimicked or patronized and this would not enhance his approval of the speaker.

Even in the case of overt accommodation there may be an optimum degree of accommodation so that it is not seen as a too-obvious act of ingratiation. Jones and Jones (1964) have shown that there is an optimum level of agreement with another whose esteem one values, and Jones (1964) points out that part of the ingratiation tactic is that we do not agree with another indiscriminately lest we be too obvious.[4] So it would seem important to determine in different contexts and with different participants what constitutes optimal speech accommodation.

## Accommodation through accent

Perhaps the single most influential work on pronunciation or accent change was the study by Labov (1966) cited in Chapter 7. It may be recalled that as speakers moved from more formal contexts (the standard interview) to less formal contexts their speech became less standardized. In order to elicit speech patterns in less formal contexts, Labov introduced two specific topics of discourse into the interviews. These topics were requests for the interviewees (a) to recite certain nursery rhymes, and (b) to relate a personal experience of being near to death. Both topics were considered by Labov to be incongruent with formal expression. Labov was also able to gain access to speech data evoked in three other less formal contexts. These were: (i) speech by the interviewees outside the formal interview situation; (ii) discussions with people other than the interviewer in the home; and (iii) remarks or monologues not in direct response to the interviewer's questions.

Giles (1973a) suggests that these pronunciation shifts may be specifically attributed to aspects of the interpersonal situation rather than ex-

---

4. In Evelyn Waugh's *Scoop*, Mr. Salter, the foreign editor of "The Beast" ingratiates himself with the newspaper's owner, Lord Copper: "Mr. Salter's side of the conversation was limited to expressions of assent. When Lord Copper was right he said, 'Definitely, Lord Copper'; when he was wrong, 'Up to a point'."

plained in terms of a notion of "context". He suggests that an experimenter effect may have been operating in the context of Labov's interview itself. Labov claims that every stratum of society is involved in shifts in pronunciation patterns depending on the contextual situation. However, Labov does not discuss the nature of his *own* or that of his co-interviewer's accent usage during their interview sessions. Are we justified in assuming that they were constant throughout? Speech addressed to the experimenter outside the formal interview session, and during those parts of the session regarded as less formal, may well have reflected changes in the interviewer's own speech patterns and thus represent convergence. Speech in the home to people other than the interviewer would presumably be addressed to members of the respondent's family or close friends. Since they would be likely to speak to him in a more familiar and less formal style than that of the interviewer, the respondent's less standardized accent in their presence could be at least partly explained in terms of convergence. Giles goes on to provide a descriptive model for pronunciation and accent shift which could incorporate interpersonal aspects of the situation, topic and setting in line with the general accommodation model formulated. This model we will now put forward.

As was noted earlier, many workers have assumed that every individual possesses a speech repertoire from which he selects speech forms according to the nature of the situational constraints. We may suppose that a part of this repertoire relates to variations in accent, i.e. there is an accent repertoire. This accent repertoire may be thought of as having two components. The more important component with regard to accent mobility relates to a continuum of accent usage of which one extreme represents the standard pattern of pronunciation and the other represents the broadest local, regional or ethnic accent. Most people's changes of accent correspond to shifts along this one standard-broad pronunciation continuum, but there may be exceptions. It is possible, in the case of an individual who lives near an "accent border" (a somewhat arbitrary geographical boundary between regions with identifiable accents) for a speaker to possess more than one regional "branch" as in Fig. 2. This may also occur where a city or town has an accent which is distinct from that of the surrounding region. Examples in the United Kingdom are provided by Cardiff and Liverpool. In these cases the town-dwellers probably become familiar with both the urban and the regional accent. There is also the possibility, particularly in Britain, of an extension of the continuum at the opposite end in the form of various degrees of exaggerated or "affected" standard pronunciation. We assume that each individual has his own habitual accent (or idiolect) which could be located somewhere within this schema, and that most are able to modify their pronunciation so as to render it closer to, or further removed from, the standard accent (or acrolect). The extent of a person's repertoire would depend upon his early linguistic experience. For instance, it could be hypothesized that people reared in ghetto-like circumstances would have little flexibility in accent through

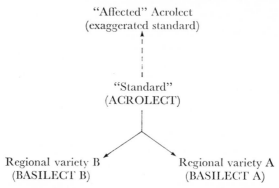

*Fig.* 2. The accent repertoire.

being exposed to a severely limited range of phonological styles. Hockett (1958) considers that a person's range of accent flexibility is almost complete by 17 years of age. It has also been suggested that it is impossible to acquire authentic native pronunciation in a second language after the age of 12 years (Asher and Garcia, 1969; Scovel, 1969). Phonological inflexibility is not necessarily characteristic of lower socioeconomic classes (cf. Clément and Taylor, 1974). As suggested in Chapter 7, it is quite likely that a child reared in a middle or upper class atmosphere, and educated in private schools, would, particularly in Britain, be so saturated with standardized speech forms that he could no longer produce any other for normal conversational purposes. However, with regard to flexibility, we should note Ervin-Tripp's (1971) assertion that

everyone who has collected considerable samples of speech of dialect speakers has found that the full range of most standard forms will appear *sometime* in their speech. That is, the problem of acquiring standard speech is in most cases not that the form is outside the repertoire but that the speaker *cannot maintain a consistent choice* of standard alternatives.

A second component of accent repertoire relates to accents which an individual can effectively mimic, but commonly uses only for entertainment and amusement. This may perhaps be regarded as a less important aspect of a person's repertoire, but his aptitude as an impersonator could affect the facility with which he accommodates to the speech of others or adapts his accent according to changes in geographical location. (One may notice that some Englishmen develop an American accent after a week's holiday in the United States whereas others may spend years there and yet sound as though they had never left Leamington Spa.)

It was proposed by Giles (1973a) that accent change may be in either of two directions, depending upon the motivation of the sender. In accord with the general accommodation model already advanced, if the sender in a dyadic situation wishes to gain the receiver's approval he may adapt his accent pattern so as to reduce phonic dissimilarities as between himself and the listener. This would be "accent convergence". On the other hand, if the sender wishes to dissociate himself from the receiver, then there may be a tendency to emphasize phonic dissimilarities—accent divergence.

Theoretically, accent convergence itself may be in one of two directions. This can best be understood in terms of the assumption that the standard-broad pronunciation continuum also reflects social prestige values. In Chapter 3 we reviewed evidence from three cultures in support of this assumption. We assume that, in general, standard patterns of pronunciation possess the highest prestige values while the broader, nonstandard varieties have lower prestige values. Stewart (1964a) has referred to the most prestigious speech form in a given cultural context as "acrolect" and the least prestigious form as "basilect" (see Fig. 2). The value of (or excuse for) these Hellenic neologisms is that they can be applied to standard-nonstandard usage in many cultures. In Britain, for example, the acrolect-basilect distinction would correspond to the distinction between RP and broad regional dialect speech. In Canada the distinction would be between European French and Joual and in the United States between middle class White and lower class Black speech. Between the extremes of standard and nonstandard pronunciation there exist not only intermediate levels of pronunciation mildness-broadness but also intermediate values of social prestige.

Thus, if a speaker in the course of social interaction perceives the listener's pronunciation pattern to be higher in accent prestige than his own idiolect, and if he is motivated towards integration and gaining the listener's approval, he may modify his accent so as to make it more similar to that of the listener. This would be called "upward accent convergence" (see Fig. 3) and would accord with the general accommodation model as a means of gaining the receiver's approval by reducing dissimilarities between them. But there should be additional gains for the speaker. The work reviewed in Chapters 3–6 suggests that in Britain, the United States and French Canada, speech changes away from the basilect and towards the acrolect improve perceived status, perceived competence, the perceived quality of the message and its persuasiveness, in the presence of a receiver who has higher accent prestige. Upward accent convergence can thus be thought of as tactic, whether the speaker uses it consciously or not, which has the effect not only of reducing linguistic dissimilarities between sender and receiver but also of presenting the sender and what he says in a generally more favourable light. In Chapter 6 it was suggested that the use of a standard accent might induce others to *behave* more favourably towards the speaker and so this may be another reward which the upward convergent strategy holds.

The other possible direction of accent convergence is "downwards". This implies that the sender perceives the receiver as possessing lower accent prestige than himself and in a move to gain approval may modify his pronunciation towards these less prestigious patterns. The effect of this speech shift would be to lower the speaker's prestige in the listener's estimation. By "prestige" we refer here to a notional consensus scale of prestige akin to the conventional status-system discussed on p. 142f (Chapter 8). By losing prestige in this generalized sense the speaker might well gain in terms of the listener's approval within the dyadic situation because of increased similarity. Since accent prestige is popularly associated with socioeconomic status, part of the difference-reduction would probably be in terms of perceived socioeconomic status. This should lead to a reduction in tension on the part of the person with lower accent prestige and a generally easier and more relaxed interaction. There may be other gains for the speaker who engages in "downward accent convergence" in terms of the way in which

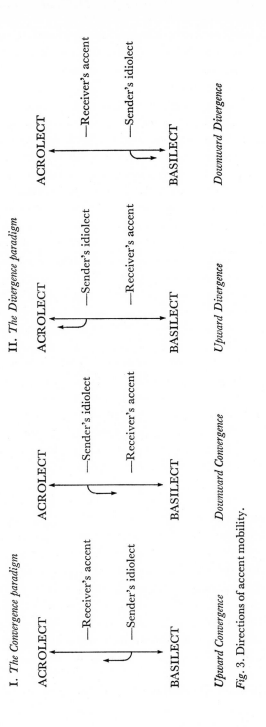

I. *The Convergence paradigm*

II. *The Divergence paradigm*

*Upward Convergence*      *Downward Convergence*

*Upward Divergence*      *Downward Divergence*

*Fig.* 3. Directions of accent mobility.

he would be perceived by the listener. In Chapter 5 we reviewed work on speaker evaluation and found that the use of a nonstandard code leads to different evaluations in different cultural contexts. The indications are that in Britain a shift towards a nonstandard accent would increase the speaker's perceived integrity and social attractiveness. In French Canada and the United States there would be an increase in perceived toughness but a reduction in perceived competence.

So far in this discussion accent convergence-divergence has been treated as if it were asymmetrical, in the sense that the receiver's accent has been regarded as immobile. This has been done for the sake of simplicity of exposition, but an asymmetrical relationship between members of a dyad may, in fact, be characteristic of many real-life encounters. Take, for example, the employment interview. The job seeker needs the interviewer's approval and whatever costs are involved in accent convergence (or other forms of accommodation) can be offset against his appearing to the interviewer in a more favourable light. The interviewer, on the other hand, does not normally need to gain the candidate's approval and there would be little or no pay-off involved in his doing so. One would predict in this case convergence on the part of the job seeker but none by the interviewer. Similarly, an industrial manager negotiating with a strikers' leader during a pay dispute might feel himself to be in a weak position and use accent convergence as a tactic of ingratiation. The strikers' leader, on the other hand, believing himself to be in a strong position, might feel no pressure to accommodate in any way. (Strength or weakness of position here relates to the question of which member of the dyad has the greater need of a concession from the other.)

But symmetrical convergence is also possible in real-life interactions, upward convergence on the part of one member of a dyad being accompanied by downward convergence on the part of the other. This would be most likely to occur when both stood to gain from the interaction. An example might be in the negotiation of a business deal of potentially equal advantage to both parties. Mutual convergence could result from the motivation of both participants to give and receive friendship, to gain and show approval, to facilitate communication, to engender mutual confidence and, in general, to foster a good relationship. Mutual convergence may also occur when no particular outcome of the interaction is expected, apart from the social support and satisfaction provided by the relationship itself. One might suggest as an example an occasion when two people, previously unknown to each other, find that they are to be workmates and are both new to the job. In fact any instance in which two people are "thrown together" by circumstances in a strange or hostile social environment would be conducive to mutual convergence for the sake of mutual solidarity and support.

Thus far it has been implied that in cases of upward convergence the receiver not only has higher accent prestige than the sender but also higher status within the particular social context. Similarly the idea of downward convergence carries with it the suggestion that the person addressed is of lower social status than the speaker. These conditions may often in fact apply or be assumed by the persons interacting to apply. But exceptions should be considered. For example, an occasion might arise whereby a speaker is motivated to gain the approval of a person who possesses higher social status within a particular context but who has *lower* accent prestige. Such a situation might come about either because the receiver possesses high regional and accent loyalty or because, having originated from a low socioeconomic background, he has attained his social position relatively recently.[5] In this situation the sender might experience some conflict between a tendency to change his speech patterns in the "upward" direction because of the receiver's high status and an impulse to change in a "downward" direction to match the receiver's own low-prestige accent. The resolution of this conflict would depend upon the precise circumstances but in many cases the speaker would probably maintain his own idiolect.[6] The converse situation might also occur in that the person whose approval the sender wishes to gain might possess a lower social status

5. The late Ernest Bevin, who left school at the age of thirteen to work as a delivery boy for a soft drinks firm and who rose to occupy with great distinction the high office of His Britannic Majesty's Principal Secretary of State for Foreign Affairs, maintained throughout his political career a broad Somerset accent, with concomitant grammatical imperfections. It is alleged that when he once said during a Cabinet meeting something which sounded like "That can best be left to you and I, Prime Minister", no-one was quite sure whether he was saying "you and I" (meaning "you and me"), Hugh and Nye (meaning Hugh Gaitskell and Aneurin Bevan), "Hugh and I" or "you and Nye". His idiolect did not differentiate these four possibilities.

6. It should perhaps be acknowledged here that the term "idiolect", although a useful one to refer to an individual's characteristic style of speech, is a little difficult to define operationally. Given the thesis that people modify their speech according to circumstances how can we identify a person's "characteristic" style? Probably the best solution is a statistical one: a person's idiolect consists of those speech forms which he uses most frequently.

but a higher accent prestige. In this case the result would presumably be "upward" accent convergence.

Accent divergence is probably a rarer form of accent mobility than convergence. It would mean that the sender changes his pronunciation so as to render it less like that of the receiver. It may occur when the sender wishes to dissociate himself from the receiver's real or apparent attitudes and characteristics. As with convergence, accent divergence could mean either upward or downward movement. Divergence would be "upward" when the sender's accent prestige is already higher than that of the receiver and "downward" when the opposite is true. Upward divergence can be interpreted as indicating the sender's desire to appear superior to the receiver in social status and competence. Downward divergence would emphasize his down-to-earthness, toughness or perhaps his ethnic identity.

As with accent convergence, so also divergence could theoretically be either symmetrical or asymmetrical. It would be symmetrical (or mutual) where both parties to the interaction were motivated to dissociate themselves from each other. It might be supposed that in these circumstances they would also both be motivated to terminate the encounter as soon as possible. But external pressures might force them to continue their mutually hostile conversation. An example might be a confrontation between a management representative and an employees' representative during an industrial dispute, with each equally confident of the strength of his position and the moral superiority of his case.

Asymmetrical accent divergence would occur when only one member of a dyad was motivated to reject or dissociate himself from the other. In such a case the receiver might well become aware, from the content of the sender's speech and from other cues, of the negative feeling towards him. His response to this awareness might be to use accent divergence too, thereby changing the relationship from an asymmetrical to a symmetrical one.

A final possibility involves both convergence and divergence in what might be called a "pursuit" manoeuvre. Imagine a very snobbish diner in a high class restaurant in conversation with an equally snobbish head waiter and suppose that the diner possesses a somewhat more prestigious accent than the waiter's. The diner might change his accent in the upward direction in order to assert his social superiority over the waiter. This would represent accent divergence by the diner. The head waiter, unwilling to acknowledge himself to be inferior, might also shift his accent in the upward direction. This would represent accent convergence on his part. Pursuit in a downward direction is also theoretically possible, although convincing examples are not easy to find: one might suggest, perhaps a conversation between two staunch Yorkshiremen, each trying to excel the other in a display of down-to-earth, shrewd, blunt-speaking Yorkshireness.

The limitations of the general accommodation model apply equally to the convergence-divergence model of accent change. It is unlikely that motivation tending to bring about convergence or divergence will operate in total isolation from the other determinants of speech style discussed in earlier chapters. The extent to which a speaker accommodates through accent change will almost certainly be influenced by the whole context of the interaction. For example, formality of setting would probably favour "upward" change of accent, whether convergent or divergent, but reduce the likelihood or extent of "downward" accent change.

The implications of the accommodation model include the probability of upward accent convergence by a speaker in the presence of a higher status person with higher accent prestige. It was proposed in Chapter 8 that the presence of a higher status person would raise the speaker's general level of arousal. Taken together, these two suppositions lead to the hypothesis that in certain circumstances the speaker will experience conflict. Zajonc (1966) suggests that raised level of arousal favours dominant responses but impairs performance in less well learned tasks. This would imply that in the presence of a higher status listener a speaker would find it easy to maintain his normal idiolect, in which he is presumably highly practised, but might have difficulty in producing an accent of higher prestige. The outcome of his attempt at convergence might therefore be a rather poor performance of the required accent, or perhaps impairment of skill in other aspects of speech, shown by hesitation, grammatical slips and corrections etc.

We have discussed accent convergence-divergence, and indeed the accommodation model in general, entirely in the context of dyadic interaction. Since, in real life, conversation frequently takes place within a group of more than two people, the model needs to be elaborated to account for such interactions. From the speaker's point of view a group can be conceived of as a single addressee plus an audience, as several addressees plus an audience or as a plurality of addressees. The presence of more than one listener, whether as persons directly addressed or as non-participating auditors, seems likely to give rise to conflict for the speaker. He may, for example, be motivated to engage in accent convergence by the presence of some of his listeners but embarrassed and inhibited from doing so by the presence of others. Diversity of listeners presents the problem for the speaker that convergence towards some necessitates divergence from others.

The principle of accommodation implies that people show different facets of themselves to different acquaintances but maintain fairly consistent behaviour towards each of them. If this is true, then occasional conflict of intention in the presence of more than one person is almost bound to occur. One would suppose, however, that for most people the range of accommodative behaviours is not very great and that consequently an appropriate compromise can be achieved without much difficulty. Extreme variability of behaviour on the part of an individual over different interpersonal encounters might indicate a pathological condition.

These problems and many others raised by the ideas we have discussed require further thought and investigation.

Testing the hypotheses we have put forward, and others which may be derived from what we have proposed, will involve techniques of assessing changes in speech style. Methods of doing this are not yet entirely satisfactory. There are two basic problems: what to measure and how to measure it.

With regard to the first problem, it may be questioned whether the parameters used by professional linguists and phonologists are necessarily the most appropriate indices of speech change in these sociolinguistic experiments. The accommodation model postulates that one speaker is capable of detecting and responding to the characteristics of the speech of another. As we mentioned in Chapter 1 with regard to the work of Wolff (1959), subjective views of language do not always correspond with objective assessments. Buck (1968) has shown that nuances of pronunciation differentiated by specialists may not be detected by the lay listener.[7]

This suggests the advisability of using lay judges for at least a part of the assessment procedure. Giles (1973a) describes what he calls the "gestalt-comparison" technique whereby naive subjects are asked to

7. For other criticisms of phonological analysis see Fasold (1970) and Pellowe, Nixon, Strang and McNeany (1972).

give a number of overall ratings of extracts of speech without knowing the source of the samples or the purpose of the experiment.[8]

Giles's technique ensures not only that assessments are of a kind which are meaningful to the layman but also that they are made "blind", i.e. without the assessor's being aware of the hypotheses being tested. Assessments in this field of study seem often to have been carried out by the experimenters themselves (e.g. Labov, 1966) without precautions to avoid bias in the interpretation of the data. Ma and Herasimchuk (1968) took the precaution of using two independent assessors and found a median reliability of +0·90, but again it is not clear that the assessors were unaware of the expected results.

The need for care in the use of assessors, whether professional or lay, is indicated by the work of Levine and Crockett (1967) and Giles (1972; 1973a). Levine and Crockett found that differences in phonological analyses made by two transcribers were related to their linguistic backgrounds. Giles presented evidence from two separate communities suggesting that people who reside in a particular area are less sensitive to variations in pronunciation of their local accent than people from another region.

Malcah Yaeger, one of Labov's graduate students at the University of Montreal, is currently working on acoustic-spectrographic analysis of speech. This sort of development gives hope that eventually it will be possible to make objective measurements of those speech characteristics which are of psychological significance to speakers and listeners.

*　*　*　*　*

Our main purpose in presenting this monograph has been to collate various studies of personal evaluation based upon speech characteristics, drawing attention in particular to the flexible nature of speech style and its adaptability according to circumstances. We have suggested that an important part of a person's motivation to alter his style of speech is the desire to modify the way in which he is evaluated by others. We have indicated frequently throughout the book that many of the ideas expressed are tentative and we have repeatedly pointed out that "much work remains to be done". We hope that readers will be stimulated to give further thought to the matters discussed and that some will be moved to carry out the experimental work that is needed.

8. Recent studies by Clément and Taylor (1974) and Giles, Bourhis, Gadfield, Davies and Davies (in press) have also used phonetically unsophisticated judges for their linguistic analyses.

# References

Abercrombie, D. (1953). English accents. *English Language Teaching*, **7**, 113–123.
Aboud, F. E. and Taylor, D. M. (1972), "Evaluative and Information seeking Consequences of Discrepancy in Ethnic Perception". Mimeo, McGill University.
Aboud, F. E. and Taylor, D. M. (1973). "Ethnic Interpersonal Attraction: Do We Ever Prefer Dissimilarity?". Mimeo, McGill University.
Aboud, F. E., Clément, R. and Taylor, D. M. (1974). Evaluational reactions to discrepancies between social class and language. *Sociometry*, **37**, 239–250.
Addington, D. W. (1968). The relationship of selected vocal characteristics to personality perception. *Speech Monographs*, **25**, 492–503.
Addington, D. W. (1971). The effect of vocal variations on ratings of source credibility. *Speech Monographs*, **28**, 242–247.
Agard, F. B. (1971). Language and dialect: some tentative postulates. *Linguistics*, **65**, 5–24.
Agheyisi, R. and Fishman, J. A. (1970). Language attitude studies: A brief survey of methodological approaches. *Anthropological Linguistics*, **12**, 137–157.
Albert, S. and Dabbs, J. M. Jr. (1970). Physical distance and persuasion. *Journal of Personality and Social Psychology*, **15**, 265–270.
Alkire, A. A., Collum, M. E., Kaswan, J. and Love, L. R. (1968). Information exchange and accuracy of verbal communication under social power conditions. *Journal of Personality and Social Psychology*, **9**, 301–308.
d'Anglejan, A. and Tucker, G. R. (1973). Sociolinguistic correlates of speech style in Quebec. *In* "Language Attitudes: Current Trends and Prospects" (Ed. R. W. Shuy and R. W. Fasold), pp. 1–27. Georgetown University Press, Washington D.C.
d'Anglejan, A. and Tucker, G. R. (1973a). Communicating across Cultures: An Empirical Investigation. *Journal of Cross-Cultural Psychology*, **4**, 121–130.
Anisfeld, M., Bogo, N. and Lambert, W. E. (1962). Evaluational reactions to accented English speech. *Journal of Abnormal and Social Psychology*, **65**, 223–231.
Anisfeld, M. and Lambert, W. E. (1964). Evaluational reactions of bilingual and monolingual children to spoken languages. *Journal of Abnormal and Social Psychology*, **69**, 89–97.
Anshen, F. (1969). Speech variation among Negroes in a small southern community. Unpublished doctoral dissertation, New York University.
Apte, M. L. (1970). Some sociolinguistic aspects of interlingual communication in India. *Anthropological Linguistics*, **12**, 63–82.
Argyle, M. (1967). "The Psychology of Interpersonal Behaviour". Pelican, Harmondsworth.
Argyle, M. (1969). "Social Interaction". Methuen, London.
Argyle, M., Alkema, F. and Gilmour, R. (1971). The communication of friendly and hostile attitudes by verbal and non-verbal signals. *European Journal of Social Psychology*, **2**, 385–402.

Argyle, M. and Kendon, A. (1967). The experimental analysis of social performance. *In* "Advances in Experimental Social Psychology" (Ed. L. Berkowitz). vol. 3. Academic Press, New York.

Argyle, M., Salter, V., Nicholson, H., Williams, M. and Burgess, P. (1970). The communication of inferior and superior attitudes by verbal and non-verbal signals. *British Journal of Social and Clinical Psychology*, **9**, 222–231.

Asher, J. J. and Garcia, R. (1969). The optimal age to learn a foreign language. *Modern Language Journal*, **53**, 334–341.

Bales, R. F. (1950). "Interaction Process Analysis". Addison-Wesley, Cambridge, Mass.

Ball, R. S. (1952). Reinforcement conditioning of verbal behaviour by verbal and non-verbal stimuli in a situation resembling a clinical interview. Unpublished doctoral dissertation, Indiana University.

Baratz, J. C. (1970). Should black children learn white dialect? *ASHA*, **12**, 415–417.

Baratz, J. C. (1970). Teaching reading in an urban Negro school system. *In* "Language and Poverty" (Ed. F. Williams). pp. 11–24. Markham, Chicago.

Barker, G. C. (1947). Social functions of language in a Mexican-American community. *Acta Americana*, **5**, 185–202.

Beardsley, R. B. and Eastman, C. M. (1971). Markers, pauses and codeswitching in bilingual Tanzanian speech. *General Linguistics*, **11**, 17–27.

Bee, H. L., van Egeren, L. F., Streissguth, A. P., Nyman, B. A. and Leckie, M. S. (1969). Social class differences in maternal teaching strategies and speech patterns. *Developmental Psychology*, **1**, 726–734.

Bellows, R. and Estop, M. F. (1954). "Employment Psychology: The Interview". Rinehart and Co., New York.

Bender, A. and Mahl, G. F. (1960). Stress, feelings of identification and dialect usage. Unpublished. Yale University. Cited in G. F. Mahl and G. Schulze (1964).

Bender, M. L., Cooper, R. L. and Ferguson, C. A. (1972). Language in Ethiopia: Implications of a survey for sociolinguistic theory and method. *Language in Society*, **1**, 215–233.

Benney, M., Reisman, D. and Star, S. (1956). Age and sex in the interview. *American Journal of Sociology*, **62**, 143–152.

Berger, M. D. (1968). Accent, pattern and dialect in North American English. *Word*, **27**, 55–61.

Berko-Gleason, J. (1973). Code switching in children's language. *In* "Cognitive Development and the Acquisition of Language" (Ed. T. E. Moore). Academic Press, New York and London.

Bernstein, B. (1962). Linguistic codes, hesitation phenomena and intelligence. *Language and Speech*, **5**, 37–46.

Bernstein, B. (1970). A sociolinguistic approach to socialization: with some reference to educability. *In* "Language and Poverty" (Ed. F. Williams). pp. 25–61. Markham, Chicago.

Black, J. W. (1949). Loudness of speaking. I: The effects of heard stimuli on spoken responses. Joint Project No. 2, Contract N7 onr-411 T.O.I. Project No. NM 001 053, U.S. Naval School of Aviation, Medicine and Research, Pensacola, Ohio.

Bodine, A. (1971). A phonological analysis of the speech of two mongoloid (Down's Syndrome) children. Unpublished doctoral dissertation, Cornell University.

Bonaventura, M. (1935). Ausdruck der Personlichkeit in der Sprechstimme und im Programm. *Archiv für die Gesamte Psychologie*, **94**, 501–570.

Boomer, D. S. and Goodrich, D. W. (1961). Speech disturbance and judged anxiety. *Journal of Consulting Psychology*, **25**, 160–164.

Bourhis, R. Y., Giles, H. and Lambert, W. E. (1975). Social consequences of accommodating one's style of speech: A cross-national investigation. *International Journal of the Sociology of Language*, in press.

Bourhis, R. Y., Giles, H. and Tajfel, H. (1973). Language as a determinant of Welsh identity. *European Journal of Social Psychology*, **3**, 447–460.

Bourhis, R. Y., Giles, H., Tajfel, H. and Taylor, D. M. (1974). The determinants of Welsh identity. Paper read at Annual Conference of the British Psychological Society, Bangor.

Brein, M. and David, K. H. (1971). Intercultural communication and the adjustment of the sojourner. *Psychological Bulletin*, **76**, 215–230.

Brennan, E. M. and Ryan, E. B. (1973). Reported language usage and verbal fluency of bilingual Mexican American adolescents. *Anthropological Linguistics*, **15**, 398–405.

Brennan, E. M., Ryan, E. B. and Dawson, W. E. (1975). Scaling of apparent accentedness by magnitude estimation and sensory modality matching. *Journal of Psycholinguistic Research*, **4**, 27–36.

Brook, G. L. (1963). "English Dialects". Deutsch, London.

Brook, G. L. (1973). "Varieties of English", Macmillan, London.

Brophy, J. E. (1970). Mothers as teachers of their own preschool children: the influence of socio-economic status and task structure on teaching specificity. Mimeograph: University of Texas, Austin.

Brosnaham, L. F. (1963). Some aspects of the linguistic situation in tropical Africa. *Lingua*, **12**, 54–65.

Brown, B. L. (1969). The social psychology of variations in French Canadian speech styles. Unpublished doctoral dissertation, McGill University, Montreal.

Brown, B. L., Strong, W. J. and Rencher, A. C. (1973). Perceptions of personality from speech: effects of manipulations of acoustical parameters. *Journal of the Acoustical Society of America*, **54**, 29–35.

Brown, B. L., Strong, W. J. and Rencher, A. C. (1975). Acoustic determinants of the perceptions of personality from speech. *International Journal of the Sociology of Language*, in press.

Brown, B. L., Strong, W. J., Rencher, A. C. and Smith, B. L. (1974). Fifty-four voices from two: the effects of simultaneous manipulations of rate, mean fundamental frequency, and variance of fundamental frequency on ratings of personality from speech. *Journal of the Acoustical Society of America*, **55**, (in press).

Brown, R. and Ford, M. (1961). Address in American English. *Journal of Abnormal and Social Psychology*, **62**, 375–385.

Brown, R. and Gilman, A. (1960). The pronouns of power and solidarity. *In* "Style in Language" (Ed. T. Sebeok). Wiley, New York.

Bruck, M. and Tucker, G. R. (1972). "Lower Class Language: Deficient or Different?" Mimeo, McGill University.

Buck, J. F. (1968). The effects of Negro and White dialectal variations upon attitudes of college students. *Speech Monographs*, **35**, 181–186.

Burling, R. (1971). Talking to teachers about social dialects. *Language Learning*, **21**, 211–234.

Butcher, H. J. (1965). The attitudes of student teachers to education. *British Journal of Social and Clinical Psychology*, **4**, 17–24.

Byrne, D. (1969). Attitudes and attraction. *Advances in Experimental Social Psychology*, **4**, 35–89.

Cadora, F. J. (1970). Some linguistic concomitants of contactual factors of urbanization. *Anthropological Linguistics*, **12**, 10–19.

Cantril, H. and Allport, G. W. (1935). "The Psychology of Radio". Harper and Bros., New York.

Carment, D. W., Miles, C. S. and Cervin, V. B. (1965). Persuasiveness and persuasability as related to intelligence and extraversion. *British Journal of Social and Clinical Psychology*, **4**, 1–7.

Carranza, M. A. and Ryan, E. B. (1975). Evaluative reactions of bilingual Anglo and Mexican American adolescents toward speakers of English and Spanish. *International Journal of the Sociology of Language*, in press.

Carter, T. P. (1970). "Mexican Americans in School: A Case of Educational Neglect". College Entrance Examination Board, New York.

Cassotta, L., Feldstein, S. and Jaffe, J. (1967). The stability and modifiability of individual vocal characteristics in stress and nonstress interviews. *Research Bulletin No. 2*. William Alanson White Institute, New York.

del Castillo, J. C. (1970). The influence of language upon symptomatology in foreign-born patients. *American Journal of Psychiatry*, **127**, 242–244.

Catford, J. C. (1964). Phonation types: the classification of some laryngeal components of speech production. *In* "In Honour of Daniel Jones" (Ed. D. Abercrombie *et al.*). Longmans, London.

Centers, R. (1950). Social class identification of American youth. *Journal of Personality*, **18**, 402–421.

Cervin, V. (1957). Relationship of ascendant-submissive behaviour in dyadic groups of human subjects to their emotional responsiveness. *Journal of Abnormal and Social Psychology*, **54**, 241–249.

Charbonneau, R. (1955). Recherche d'une norme phonétique dans la région de Montreal. *In* "Études sur le parler francais au Canada". Quebec.

Charney, E. J. (1966). Postural configurations in psychotherapy. *Psychosomatic Medicine*, **28**, 305–315.

Cheyne, W. (1970). Stereotyped reactions to speakers with Scottish and English regional accents. *British Journal of Social and Clinical Psychology*, **9**, 77–79.

Chiasson-Lavoie, M., and Laberge, S. (1971). "Attitudes face au français parlè á—Montreal et degrés de conscience de variables linguistiques". Mimeo, University of Montreal.

Chittick, E. V. and Himmelstein, P. (1967). The manipulation of self-disclosure. *Journal of Psychology*, **65**, 117–121.

Clément, R. and Taylor, D. M. (1974). "Normative reactions to styles of Quebec French". *Anthropological Linguistics*, **16**, 202–217.

Condon, W. S. and Ogston, W. D. (1966). Sound film analysis of normal and pathological behaviour patterns. *Journal of Nervous and Mental Diseases*, **143**, 338–347.

Condon, W. S. and Ogston, W. D. (1967). A segmentation of behaviour. *Journal of Psychiatric Research*, **5**, 221–235.

Conklin, H. C. (1962). Lexicographical treatment of folk taxonomies. *International Journal of American Linguistics*. **28**, 119–141.

Cook, M. (1969). Anxiety, speech disturbances and speech rate. *British Journal of Social and Clinical Psychology*, **8**, 13–21.

Cook, M. (1971). "Interpersonal Perception". Penguin, Harmondsworth.

Cook, M., Argyle, M. and Lalljee, M. G. (1967). The effect of varying visibility on floor apportionment. Unpublished, University of Oxford.

Cook, M. and Lalljee, M. G. (1967). The effects of lack of vision on conversation. Unpublished, University of Oxford.

Cooper, R. L. and Greenfield, L. (1969). Word frequency estimation as a measure of degree of bilingualism. *Modern Language Journal*, **53**, 166–172.

Cooper, R. L. and Horvath, R. J. (1973). Language, migration and urbanization in Ethiopia. *Anthropological Linguistics*, **15**, 221–243.

Cope, C. S. (1969). Linguistic structures and personality development. *Journal of Counseling Psychology*, **16**, (Supplement), 1–19.

Costanzo, F. S., Markel, N. N. and Costanzo, P. R. (1969). Voice quality profile and perceived emotion. *Journal of Counseling Psychology*, **16**, 267–270.

Coulthard, M. (1969). A discussion of restricted and elaborated codes. *Educational Review*, **22**, 38–50.

Cowan, M. (1936). The pitch and intensity characteristics of stage speech. *Archives of Speech*, supplement.

Craig, K. D. (1966). Incongruencies between content and temporal measures of patients' responses to confrontation with personality descriptions. *Journal of Consulting Psychology*, **30**, 550–554.

Crowl, T. K. and MacGinitie, W. H. (1970). White teachers' evaluations of oral responses given by white and Negro 9th grade males. Proceedings of the 78th Annual Convention of the American Psychological Association, pp. 635–636.

Crowne, D. P. and Strickland, B. R. (1961). The conditioning of verbal behaviour as a function of the need for social approval. *Journal of Abnormal and Social Psychology*, **63**, 395–401.

Dabbs, J. M. Jr. (1969). Similarity of gestures and interpersonal influence. Proceedings of the 77th Annual Convention of the American Psychological Association.

Daniel, J. L. (1970). Facilitation of White-Black communication. *Journal of Communication*, **20**, 134–141.

Davis, L. M. (1970). Social dialectology in America: A critical survey. *Journal of English Linguistics*, **4**, 46–56.

Davis, L. M. (1970a). Some social aspects of the speech of blue-grass Kentucky. *Orbis*, **19**, 337–341.

Davis, J. D. and Skinner, A. E. G. (1974). Reciprocity of self-disclosure in interviewing: modelling or social exchange? Unpublished. University of Sheffield.

Denis, R. (1949). "Les Vingt Siècles du Français." Fides, Montreal.

Deshaies-Lafontaine, D. (1974). Sociolinguistic study of Trois-Rivières French. Paper read at Colloquium on Empirical Work on Sociolinguistics, L.S.E., London.

Deutsch, C. P. (1964). Auditory discrimination and learning: Social factors. *Merrill-Palmer Quarterly of Behaviour and Development*, **10**, 277–296.

Deutsch, M. et al. (1967). "The Disadvantaged Child". Basic Books, New York.

Dibner, A. S. (1956). Cue-counting: a measure of anxiety in interviews. *Journal of Consulting Psychology*, **20**, 475–478.

Dinoff, M., Morris, J. R. and Hannon, J. E. (1963). The stability of schizophrenic speech in a standardized interview. *Journal of Clinical Psychology*, **19**, 279–282.

Drakeford, J. W. (1967). "Integrity Therapy". Broadman Press, Nashville, Tennessee.

Duffy, E. (1957). The psychological significance of the concept of "arousal" or "activation". *Psychological Review*, **64**, 265–275.

Duncan, S. Jr., Rice, L. N., and Butler, J. M. (1968). Therapists' paralanguage in peak and poor psychotherapy hours. *Journal of Abnormal Psychology*, **73**, 566–570.

Dusenbury, D. and Knower, F. (1938). Experimental studies of the symbolism of actor and voice. *Quarterly Journal of Speech*, **24**, 67–75.

Edelman, M., Cooper, R. L. and Fishman, J. A. (1968). The contextualization of schoolchildren's bilingualism. *Irish Journal of Education*, **2**, 106–111.

Edwards, J. (1974). "Current Issues in Bilingual Education". Mimeo, St. Patrick's College, Dublin.

Ehrlich, H. J. and Graeven, D. B. (1971). Reciprocal self-disclosure in a dyad. *Journal of Experimental Social Psychology*, **7**, 389–400.

Eisenberg, P. and Zalowitz, E. (1938). Judging expressive movement. III. Judgments of dominance-feeling from phonograph records of voice. *Journal of Applied Psychology*, **22**, 620–631.

Eisenmann, R. (1966). Birth order, anxiety and verbalizations in group psycho-therapy. *Journal of Consulting Psychology*, **30**, 521–526.

Eiser, J. R. and Stroebe, W. (1972). "Categorization and Social Judgement". Academic Press, London and New York.

El-Dash, L. and Tucker, G. R. (1974). Subjective reactions to various speech styles in Egypt. *International Journal of the Sociology of Language*, in press.

Ellis, D. S. (1964). The effects of limiting the amount of exposure between inter-viewers and interviewees. Unpublished. Purdue University.

Ellis, D. S. (1967). Speech and social status in America. *Social Forces*, **45**, 431–437.

Ellis, P. M. (1965). Les phonèmes du français Maillarduillon. *Canadian Journal of Linguistics*, **13**, 94–98.

Ervin-Tripp, S. M. (1964). An analysis of the interaction of language, topic and listener. In supplement to *American Anthropologist*, **66**, 86–102.

Ervin-Tripp, S. M. (1969). Sociolinguistics. *Advances in Experimental Social Psychology*, **4**, 91–165.

Ervin-Tripp, S. M. (1971). Social dialects in developmental sociolinguistics. *In* "Sociolinguistics: A Cross-disciplinary Perspective" (Ed. R. Shuy). p. 45. Center for applied linguistics, Washington D.C.

Estvan, F. J. and Estvan, E. W. (1959). "The Child's World: His Social Perception". Putnam, New York.

Fairbanks, G. (1940). Recent experimental investigations of vocal pitch in voice. *Journal of the Acoustical Society of America*, **11**, 457–466.

Fairbanks, G. and Provonost, W. (1939). An experimental study of the pitch charac-teristics of the voice during the expression of emotion. *Speech Monographs*, **6**, 87–104.

Fasold, R. W. (1970). Two models of socially significant linguistic variation. *Language*, **46**, 551–563.

Fay, P. J. and Middleton, W. C. (1939). Judgments of Spranger personality types from the voice as transmitted over a public address system. *Character and Personality*, **8**, 144–155.

Fay, P. J. and Middleton, W. C. (1939a). Judgment of occupation from the voice as transmitted over a public address system. *Journal of Applied Psychology*, **23**, 586–601.

Fay, P. J. and Middleton, W. C. (1940). Judgment of intelligence from the voice as transmitted over a public address system. *Sociometry*, **3**, 186–191.

Fay, P. J. and Middleton, W. C. (1941). The ability to judge sociability from the voice as transmitted over a public address system. *Journal of Social Psychology*, **13**, 303–309.

Fay, P. J. and Middleton, W. C. (1942). Judgement of introversion from the trans-mitted voice. *Quarterly Journal of Speech*, **28**, 226–228.

Fay, P. J. and Middleton, W. C. (1943). Judgement of leadership from the trans-mitted voice. *Journal of Social Psychology*, **17**, 99–102.

Feigenbaum, I. (1969). Using foreign language methodology to teach Standard English: evaluation and adaptation. *Florida Foreign Language Reporter*, **7**, 116.

Feldman, R. E. (1968). Response to compatriots and foreigners who seek assistance. *Journal of Personality and Social Psychology*, **10**, 202–214.

Feldstein, S., Brenner, M. S. and Jaffe, J. (1963). The effect of subject sex, verbal interaction, and topical focus on speech descriptions. *Language and Speech*, **6**, 229–239.

Feldstein, S., Jaffe, J. and Cassotta, L. (1967). The effects of mutual visual access upon conversational time patterns. *American Psychologist*, **22**, 594 (Abstract).

Fellman, J. (1973). Sociolinguistic problems in the middle eastern Arab: an overview. *Anthropological Linguistics*, **15**, 24–32.

Fellman, J. (1973a). Language and national identity: the case of the Middle East. *Anthropological Linguistics*, **15**, 244–249.

Fellman, J. (1973b). Concerning the "revival" of the Hebrew language. *Anthropological Linguistics*, **15**, 250–257.

Ferguson, C. A. (1959). Diglossia. *Word*, **15**, 325–340.

Ferguson, C. A. (1964). Baby talk in six languages. *In* Supplement to *American Anthropologist*, **66**, 103–114.

Fertig, S. and Fishman, J. A. (1969). Some measures of the interaction between language, domain and semantic dimension in bilinguals. *Modern Language Journal*, **53**, 244–249.

Fielding, G. (1972). Participation in conversation: the phenomenon of response matching. Paper read at the Annual Meeting of the Social Psychology Section of the British Psychological Society, Brighton.

Fischer, J. L. (1958). Social influences in the choice of a linguistic variant. *Word*, **14**, 47–56.

Fishbein, M. (1967). Attitudes and the prediction of behaviour. *In* "Readings in Attitude Theory and Measurement" (Ed. M. Fishbein). pp. 477–492. Wiley, New York.

Fishman, J. A. (1969). National languages and languages of wider communication in the developing nations. *Anthropoligical Linguistics*, **11**, 111–135.

Fishman, J. A. (1969a). Language maintenance and language shift as a field of inquiry (revisited). Mimeograph: Yeshiva University, New York.

Fishman, J. A. (1970). "Sociolinguistics: A Brief Introduction". Newbury House, Rowley, Mass.

Fishman, J. A. (1972). "Language and Nationalism". Newbury House, Rowley, Mass.

Fishman, J. A. and Herasimchuk, E. (1969). The multiple prediction of phonological variables in a bilingual speech community. *American Anthropologist*, **71**, 648–657.

Fishman, J. A. and Hofman, J. E. (1964). Mother tongue and nativity in the American population. *In* "Language Loyalty in the United States" (Ed. J. A. Fishman *et al.*). Mimeo report to Language Research Section, U.S. Office of Education, Chapter 2.

Fishman, J. A. *et al.* (1966). "Language Loyalty in the United States". Mouton, The Hague.

Flavell, J. H., Botkin, P. T., Fry, C. L. Jr., Wright, J. W. and Jarvis, P. E. (1968). "The Development of Role-Taking and Cumminication Skills in Children". Wiley, New York.

Ford, C. S., Prothro, E. T. and Child, I. (1966). Some transcultural comparisons of esthetic judgment. *Journal of Social Psychology*, **68**, 19–26.

Foster, G. M. (1964). Speech forms and the perception of social distance in a Spanish-speaking Mexican village. *Southwerstern Journal of Anthropology*, **20**, 107–122.

Francès, R. and Tamba, A. (1973). Étude interculturelle des préférences musicales. *International Journal of Psychology*, **8**, 95–108.

Fraser, B. (1973). Some "unexpected" reactions to various American-English dialects. *In* "Language Attitudes: Current Trends and Prospects" (Ed. R. W. Shuy and R. W. Fasold). Georgetown University Press, Washington, D.C.

Fraser, C. and Roberts, N. (1975). Mothers' speech to children of four different ages. *Journal of Psycholinguistic Research*, **4**, 9–16.

Frender, R., Brown, B. L. and Lambert, W. E. (1970). The role of speech characteristics in scholastic success. *Canadian Journal of Behavioural Sciences*, **2**, 299–306.

Frender, R. and Lambert, W. E. (1972). Speech style and scholastic success: the tentative relationships and possible implications for lower class children. *Monograph Series on Language and Linguistics*, **25**, 237–271.

Gall, M. D., Hobby, A. K. and Craik, K. H. (1969). Non-linguistic factors in oral language productivity. *Perceptual and Motor Skills*, **28**, 871–874.

Galli de' Paratesi, N. (1974). The standardization of pronunciation in contemporary Italian. Paper read at Sociolinguistics Colloquium, L.S.E., London.

Gaertner, S. L. (1972). Helping behaviour and racial discrimination among Liberal and Conservatives. Mimeo: University of Delaware,

Gaertner, S. L. and Bickman, L. (1971). Effects of race on the elicitation of helping behaviour: the wrong number technique. *Journal of Personality and Social Psychology*, **20**, 218–222.

Gardner, R. C. and Taylor, D. M. (1968). Ethnic stereotypes: their effects on person perception. *Canadian Journal of Psychology*, **22**, 267–274.

Gardner, R. C., Wonnacott, E. J. and Taylor, D. M. (1968). Ethnic stereotypes: A factor analytic investigation. *Canadian Journal of Psychology*, **22**, 35–44.

Geertz, H. (1963). "The Javanese Family". Free Press, Glencoe.

Gendron, J. D. (1966). "Tendances Phonétique du Français Parlé au Canada". C. Klincksieck, Paris.

Geohegan, W. (1971). Information processing systems in culture. *In* "Explorations in Mathematical Anthropology (Ed. P. Kay). M.I.T. Press, Cambridge, Mass.

Giffin, K. (1967). The contribution of studies of source credibility to a theory of interpersonal trust in the communication process. *Psychological Bulletin*, **68**, 104–120.

Giles, H. (1970). Evaluative reactions to accents. *Educational Review*, **22**, 211–227.

Giles, H. (1971). Speech patterns in social interaction: accent evaluation and accent change. Unpublished doctoral dissertation, University of Bristol.

Giles, H. (1971a). Ethnocentrism and the evaluation of accented speech. *British Journal of Social and Clinical Psychology*, **10**, 187–188.

Giles, H. (1971b). Patterns of evaluation in reactions to R.P., South Welsh and Somerset accented speech. *British Journal of Social and Clinical Psychology*, **10**, 280–281.

Giles, H. (1971c). Teachers' attitudes towards accent usage and change. *Educational Review*, **24**, 11–25.

Giles, H. (1972). The effects of stimulus mildness-broadness in the evaluation of accents. *Language and Speech*, **15**, 262–269.

Giles, H. (1972a). Evaluation of personality content from accented speech as a function of listeners' social attitudes. *Perceptual and Motor Skills*, **34**, 168–170.

Giles, H. (1973). Communicative effectiveness as a function of accented speech. *Speech Monographs*, **40**, 330–331.

Giles, H. (1973a). Accent mobility: a model and some data. *Anthropological Linguistics*, **15**, 87–105.

Giles, H., Baker, S. and Fielding G. (1975). Communication length as a behavioural index of accent prejudice. *International Journal of the Sociology of Language*, in press.

Giles, H. and Bourhis, R. Y. (1973). Dialect perception revisited. *Quarterly Journal of Speech*, **59**, 337–342.

Giles, H. and Bourhis, R. Y. (in press). Racial Identification of British Blacks from Speech. *Language Sciences*.

Giles, H., Bourhis, R. Y. and Davies, A. (1975). Prestige speech styles: the imposed norm and inherent value hypotheses. *In* "Language in Anthropology. IV: Language in Many Ways" (Ed. W. C. McCormack and S. Wurm). Mouton, The Hague.

Giles, H., Bourhis, R. Y., Gadfield, N., Davies, G. and Davies, A. P. (in press). Cognitive aspects of humour in social interaction: a model and some linguistic data. *In* "Research in Laughter and Humour" (Ed. A. J. Chapman and H. Foot). Wiley, London.

Giles, H., Bourhis, R. Y., Trudgill, P. and Lewis, A. (1974). The imposed norm hypothesis: a validation. *Quarterly Journal of Speech*, **60**, 405–410.

Giles, H., Taylor, D. M. and Bourhis, R. Y. (1973). Towards a theory of interpersonal accommodation through language: some Canadian data. *Language in Society*, **2**, 177–192.

Giles, H., Taylor, D. M. and Bourhis, R. Y. (1974). "Dimensions of Welsh Identity". Mimeo, McGill University.

Giles, H., Taylor, D. M., Lambert, W. E. and Albert, G. (in press). Dimensions of Ethnic Identity: An Example from Northern Maine. *Journal of Social Psychology*.

Gimson, A. C. (1962). "An Introduction to the Pronunciation of English". Arnold, London.

Gladney, M. R. and Leaverton. L. (1968). A model for teaching Standard English to Nonstandard English speakers. *Elementary English*, **45**, 758–763.

Glasgow, G. M. (1961). The effects of manner of speech on appreciation of spoken literature. *Journal of Educational Psychology*, **52**, 322–329.

Goldman-Eisler, F. (1954). On the variability of the speed of talking and its relation to the length of utterances in conversations. *British Journal of Psychology*, **45**, 94–107.

Goldman-Eisler, F. (1968). "Psycholinguistics: Experiments in Spontaneous Speech". Academic Press, London and New York.

Gouldner, A. W. (1960). The norm of reciprocity: a preliminary statement. *American Sociological Review*, **25**, 161–178.

Grace, H. A. (1952). The effects of different degrees of knowledge about an audience on the content of communication: the comparison of male and female audiences. *Journal of Social Psychology*, **36**, 89–96.

Granowsky, S. and Krossner, W. J. (1970). Kindergarten teachers as models for children's speech. *Journal of Experimental Education*, **38**, 23–28.

Greenfield, L. and Fishman, J. A. (1970). Situational measures of normative language views in relations to person, place and topic among Puerto Rican bilinguals. *Anthropos*, **65**, 602–618.

Greenspoon, J. (1955). The reinforcing effect of two spoken sounds on the frequency of two responses. *American Journal of Psychology*, **68**, 409–416.

Griffin, D. M. (1970). Dialects and democracy. *English Journal*, **59**, 551–556.

Grimshaw, A. D. (1967). Directions for research in sociolinguistics: suggestions of a nonlinguistic sociologist. *International Journal of American Linguistics*, **33**, 191–204.

Grosz, H. J. and Wagner, R. (1971). MMPI and EPPS profiles of high and low verbal interactors in therapy groups. *Psychological Reports*, **28**, 951–955.

Gump, P. V., Schogger, P. and Redl, F. (1963). The behaviour of the same child in different milieus. *In* "The Stream of Behaviour" (Ed. R. G. Barker). Appleton-Century-Crofts, New York.

Gumperz, J. J. (1958). Dialect differences and social stratification in a North Indian village. *American Anthropologist*, **60**, 668–682.

Gumperz, J. J. (1964). Speech variations and the study of Indian civilization. *In* "Language in Culture and Society" (Ed. D. Hymes). pp. 416–423. Harper and Row, New York.

Gumperz, J. J. (1964a). Linguistic and social interaction in two communities. In *American Anthropologist*, **66** (supplements: No. 6, Part 2), 137–153.

Gumperz, J. J. (1964b). Hindi-Punjabi code-switching in Delhi. Proceedings of the

9th International Congress on Linguistics (Ed. G. Lunt). pp. 1115–1124. Mouton, The Hague.

Gumperz, J. J. (1967). Language and communication. *Annals of the American Academy of Political and Social Science*, **373**, 219–231.

Gumperz, J. J. (1970). Sociolinguistics and communication in small groups. Working Paper No. 33, Language Behaviour Research Laboratory, University of California, Berkeley.

Haas, M. R. (1951). Interlingual word taboos. *American Anthropologist*, **53**, 338–344.

Hahn, E. (1948). An analysis of the content and form of the speech of first grade children. *Quarterly Journal of Speech*, **34**, 361–366.

Haiman, F. S. (1949). An experimental study of the effects of ethos in public speaking. *Speech Monographs*, **16**, 190–202.

Halverson, C. F. and Waldrop, M. (1970). Maternal behaviour toward own and other preschool children: the problem of "ownness". *Child Development*, **41**, 830–845.

Hamilton, R. G. and Robertson, M. (1968). Examiner influence on the Holtzman inkblot technique. *Journal of Projective Techniques and Personality Assessment*, **30**, 553–558.

Hargreaves, W. A. (1960). A model for speech unit duration. *Language and Speech*, **3**, 164–173.

Hargreaves, W. A. and Starkweather, J. A. (1963). Recognition of speaker identity. *Language and Speech*, **6**, 63–67.

Hargreaves, W. A. and Starkweather, J. A. (1964). Voice quality changes in depression. *Language and Speech*, **7**, 84–88.

Hargreaves, W. A., Starkweather, J. A. and Blacker, K. H. (1965). Voice quality in depression. *Journal of Abnormal Psychology*, **70**, 218–220.

Harmer, L. C. (1954). "The French Language Today, its Characteristics and Tendencies". Hutchinson, London.

Harms, L. S. (1961). Listener judgments of status cues in speech. *Quarterly Journal of Speech*, **47**, 164–168.

Harris, M. B. and Baudin, H. (1973). The language of altruism: the effects of language, dress, and ethnic group. *Journal of Social Psychology*, **97**, 37–41.

Harris, S. and Masling, J. (1970). Examiner sex, subject sex, and Rorschach productivity. *Journal of Consulting and Clinical Psychology*, **34**, 60–63.

Hart, R. J. and Brown, B. L. (1974). Interpersonal information contained in the vocal qualities and in content aspects of speech. *Speech Monographs*, in press.

Hartford, T., Blane, H. T. and Chafetz, M. (1970). Language predictability and psychiatric interviews. *Perceptual and Motor Skills*, **31**, 725–726.

Hasselmo, N. (1961). American Swedish: a study in bilingualism. Unpublished doctoral dissertation, Harvard University.

Haugen, E. (1966). Dialect, language, nation. *American Anthropologist*, **68**, 922–935.

Heider, F. (1958). "The Psychology of Interpersonal Relations". Wiley, New York.

Heinberg, P. (1963). Relationships of content and delivery to general effectiveness. *Speech Monographs*, **30**, 105–107.

Henderson, D. (1969). Social class differences in form-class usage among five year old children. *In* "Primary Socialization, Language and Education. Vol. 1: Social Class, Language and Communication" (Ed. W. Brandis and D. Henderson). Routledge and Kegan Paul, London.

Herman, S. (1961). Explorations in the social psychology of language choice. *Human Relations*, **14**, 149–164.

Hersen, M. (1970). Controlling verbal behaviour via classical and operant conditioning. *Journal of General Psychology*, **83**, 3–22.

Herzog, A. (1933). Stimme und Personlichkeit. *Zeitschrift für Psychologie*, **130**, 300–379.

Hinchliffe, M. K., Lancashire, M. H. and Roberts, F. J. (1971). Depression: defence mechanisms in speech. *British Journal of Psychiatry*, **118**, 471–472.

Hockett, C. F. (1958). "A Course in Modern Linguistics". MacMillan, London.

Hogan, R. (1968). Preface to New York Board of Education "Nonstandard Dialect". N.C.T.E., Champaign, Ill.

Hollander, E. P. (1971). "Principles and Methods in Social Psychology". Oxford University Press, Oxford.

Hollingshead, A. B. and Redlich, F. C. (1958). "Social Class and Mental Illness: A Community Study". Wiley, New York.

Holzman, P. S. and Rousey, C. (1970). Monitoring, activation and disinhibition: effects of white noise masking on spoken thought. *Journal of Abnormal Psychology*, **75**, 227–241.

Holzman, P. S. and Rousey, C. (1971). Disinhibition of communicated thought: generality and role of cognitive style. *Journal of Abnormal Psychology*, **77**, 263–274.

Homans, G. C. (1961). "Social Behaviour". Harcourt, Brace and World, New York.

Honikman, B. (1964). Articulatory settings. *In* "In Honour of Daniel Jones" (Ed. D. Abercrombie *et al.*). Longmans, London.

Hopper, R. and Williams, F. (1973). Speech characteristics and employability. *Speech Monographs*, **40**, 296–302.

Houck, C. L. and Bowers, J. T. (1969). Dialect and identification in persuasive messages. *Language and Speech*, **12**, 180–186.

Houston, S. H. (1969). Child Black English: the school register. Paper read at the 44th Annual Meeting of the Linguistic Society of America. San Francisco.

Hovland, C. I., Janis, I. L. and Kelley, H. H. (1953). "Communication and Persuasion". Yale University Press, New Haven.

Höweler, M. and Vrolijk, A. (1970). Verbal communication length as an index of interpersonal attraction. *Acta Psychologica*, **34**, 511–515.

Howell, R. W. (1967). Linguistic choice as an index to social change. Unpublished Ph.D. thesis, University of California, Berkeley.

Hunt, J. McV. (1964). The psychological basis for using pre-school enrichment as an antidote for cultural deprivation. *Merrill-Palmer Quarterly of Behaviour and Development*, **10**, 209–243.

Hunt, C. L. (1967). Language choice in a multilingual society. *International Journal of American Linguistics*, **33**, 112–125.

Hunt, R. G. and Lin, T. K. (1967). Accuracy of judgments of personal attributes from speech. *Journal of Personality and Social Psychology*, **6**, 450–453.

Hymes, D. (1962). The ethnography of speaking. *In* "Anthropology and Human Behaviour" (Ed. T. Gladwin and W. Sturtevart). Anthropological Society of Washington, Washington, D.C.

Hymes, D. (1967). Models of the interaction of language and social setting. *Journal of Social Issues*, **23**, 8–28.

Hymes, D. (1972). Models of the interaction of language and social life. *In* "Directions in Sociolinguistics: The Ethnography of Communication" (Ed. J. J. Gumperz and D. Hymes). pp. 35–71. Holt, Rinehart and Winston, New York.

Iannuci, D., Liben, L. and Anisfeld, M. (1968). Some determinants of stylistic variations. *Journal of Verbal Learning and Verbal Behaviour*, **7**, 956–961.

Innes, G., Miller, W. M. and Valentine, M. (1959). Emotion and blood pressure. *Journal of Mental Science*, **105**, 840–851.

Iwao, S. and Child, I. (1966). Comparisons of esthetic judgment by American experts and Japanese potters. *Journal of Social Psychology*, **68**, 27–33.

Jackson, R. H., Manaugh, T. S., Weins, A. N. and Matarazzo. J. D. (1971). A method for assessing the saliency of areas in a person's current life situation. *Journal of Clinical Psychology*, **27**, 32–39.

Jaffe, J. and Feldstein, S. (1970). "Rhythms of Dialogue". Academic Press, New York and London.

Janofsky, A. I. (1971). Affective self-disclosure in telephone versus face-to-face interviews. *Journal of Humanistic Psychology*, **11**, 93–103.

Jawande, J. S. (1970). Personality and verbal conditioning. *Indian Journal of Experimental Psychology*, **4**, 22–24.

Jernudd, B. H. (1971). Social change and aboriginal speech variation in Australia. *Anthropological Linguistics*, **13**, 16–32.

Johnson, D. W. (1971). Effects of warmth of interaction, accuracy of understanding and the proposal of compromises on listeners' behaviour. *Journal of Counseling Psychology*, **18**, 207–216.

Johnson, T. J., Feigenbaum, R. and Weibey, M. (1964). Some determinants and consequences of the teacher's perception of causality. *Journal of Educational Psychology*, **55**, 237–246.

Johnson, K. R. (1971). Should black children learn standard English? *Viewpoints*, **47**, 83–101.

Johnson, K. R. (1971a). Teacher's attitude toward the nonstandard Negro dialect— let's change it. *Elementary English*, **48**, 176–184.

Johnson, W. (1944). Studies in language behaviour: I: A program of research. *Psychological Monographs*, **56**, 1–15.

Jones, D. (1956). "An outline of English Phonetics". Heffer, Cambridge.

Jones, D. (1956a). "The Pronunciation of English". Cambridge University Press, Cambridge.

Jones, D. (1956b). "An English Pronouncing Dictionary". Dent, Cambridge.

Jones, E. E. (1964). "Ingratiation". Appleton-Century-Crofts, New York.

Jones, E. E. and Davis, K. E. (1965). From acts to dispositions: the attribution process in person perception. *In* "Advances in Experimental Social Psychology" (Ed. L. Berkowitz). Academic Press, New York and London.

Jones, E. E. and Gerard, H. B. (1967). "Foundations of Social Psychology". Wiley, New York.

Jones, H. E. (1942). The adolescent growth study. VI. The analysis of voice trends. *Journal of Consulting Psychology*, **6**, 255–256.

Jones, R. G. and Jones, E. E. (1964). Optimum conformity as an ingratiation tactic. *Journal of Personality*, **32**, 4–36.

Jones, R. R. (1973). Linguistic standardization and national development. *International Journal of Psychology*, **8**, 51–54.

Joos, M. (1962). The five clocks. *International Journal of American Linguistics*, **28**, part 5.

Jourard, S. M. and Friedman, R. (1970). Experimenter-subject "distance" and self-disclosure. *Journal of Personality and Social Psychology*, **15**, 278–282.

Jourard, S. M. and Richman, P. (1963). Factors in the self-disclosure input of college students. *Merrill-Palmer Quarterly of Behaviour and Development*, **9**, 14–48.

Kanfer, F. H. (1958). The effect of a warning signal preceding a noxious stimulus on verbal rate and heart rate. *Journal of Experimental Psychology*, **55**, 73–80.

Kanfer, F. H. (1958a). Supplementary report: stability of a verbal rate change in experimental anxiety. *Journal of Experimental Psychology*, **56**, 182–183.

Kanfer, F. H. (1959). Verbal rate, content and adjustment ratings in experimentally structured interviews. *Journal of Abnormal and Social Psychology*, **58**, 305–311.

Kanfer, F. H. (1960). Verbal rate, eyeblink, and content in structured psychiatric interviews. *Journal of Abnormal and Social Psychology*, **61**, 341–347.

Kaplan, R. (1969). On a note of protest (in a minor key). *College English*, **30**, 386–389.

Karnes, M. B., Teska, J. A., Hodgins, A. S. and Badger, E. D. (1971). Educational intervention at home by mothers of disadvantaged infants. *Child Development*, **41**, 925–935.

Kasl, S. V. and Mahl, G. F. (1965). The relationship of disturbances and hesitations in spontaneous speech to anxiety. *Journal of Personality and Social Psychology*, **5**, 425–433.

Kean, J. M. (1968). Linguistic structure of second and fifth grade teachers' oral classroom language. *American Educational Research Journal*, **5**, pt. 4, 599–615.

Kelley, H. H. (1973). The process of causal attribution. *American Psychologist*, **28**, 107–128.

Kendon, A. (1970). Movement coordination in social interaction: some examples described. *Acta Psychologica*, **32**, 101–125.

Kimple, J. Jr., Cooper, R. L. and Fishman, J. A. (1969). Language switching and the interpretation of conversations. *Lingua*, **23**, 127–134.

Klapper, J. T. (1960). "The Effects of Mass Communication". The Free Press, Glencoe.

Kleiven, J. (1972). Social stereotypes elicited by linguistic differences: a Norwegian example. University of Bergen, Institute of Psychology Reports, No. 8.

Kloss, H. (1967). Bilingualism and nationalism. *Journal of Social Issues*, **23**, 39–47.

Kocher, M. (1967). Second person pronouns in Serbo-Croatian. *Language*, **43**, 725–741.

Koeske, G. and Crano, W. D. (1968). The effect of congruous and incongruous source-statement combinations upon the judged credibility of a communication. *Journal of Experimental Social Psychology*, **4**, 384–399.

Koustaal. C. W. and Jackson, F. L. (1972). Race identification on the basis of biased speech samples. *Ohio Journal of Speech and Hearing*, **6**, 48–51.

Kramer, E. (1963). Judgment of personal characteristics and emotions from non-verbal properties of speech. *Psychological Bulletin*, **61**, 408–420.

Kramer, E. (1964). Personality stereotypes in voice: a reconsideration of the data. *Journal of Social Psychology*, **62**, 247–251.

Krasner, L. (1958). Studies of the conditioning of verbal behaviour. *Psychological Bulletin*, **55**, 148–170.

Krause, M. S. (1961). Anxiety in verbal behaviour: an intercorrelational study. *Journal of Consulting Psychology*, **25**, 272.

Krause, M. S. and Pilisuk, M. (1961). Anxiety in verbal behaviour: a validation study. *Journal of Consulting Psychology*, **25**, 414–419.

Krauss, R. M. and Glucksberg, S. (1969). The development of communication competence as a function of age. *Child Development*, **40**, 255–266.

Krear, S. (1969). The role of the mother tongue at home and at school in the development of bilingualism. *English Language Teaching*, **24**, 2–4.

Kučera, H. (1961). "The Phonology of Czech." Mouton, The Hague.

Labov, W. (1964). Phonological correlates of social stratification. In Supplement to *American Anthropologist*, **66**, 164–176.

Labov, W. (1965). On the mechanism of linguistic change. *Georgetown Monograph Series on Language and Linguistics*, **18**, 91–114.

Labov, W. (1966). "The social stratification of English in New York City". Center for Applied Linguistics, Washington D.C.

Labov, W. (1966a). The effect of social mobility on linguistic behaviour. *Social Inquiry*, **36**, 186–203.

Labov, W. (1970). Language in social context. *Studium Generale*, **23**, 30–87.

Labov, W., Cohen, P., Robins, C. and Lewis, J. (1968). A study of the nonstandard English of Negro and Puerto Rican speakers in New York City. Final Report, U.S. Office of Education Cooperative Research Project No. 3288, Vols I and II, Washington D.C.: Office of Education.

Lambert, W. E. (1967). The social psychology of bilingualism. *Journal of Social Issues*, **23**, 91–109.

Lambert, W. E. (1967a). The use of *tu* and *vous* as forms of address in French Canada: a pilot study. *Journal of Verbal Learning and Verbal Behaviour*, **6**, 614–617.

Lambert, W. E., Anisfeld, M. and Yeni-Komshian, G. (1965). Evaluational reactions of Jewish and Arab adolescents to dialect and language variations. *Journal of Personality and Social Psychology*, **2**, 84–90.

Lambert, W. E., Frankel, H. and Tucker, G. R. (1966). Judging personality through speech: a French-Canadian example. *Journal of Communication*, **16**, 305–321.

Lambert, W. E., Giles, H. and Albert, G. (1975). Language Attitudes in a Rural Community in Northern Maine. *La monda linguo-problemo*, in press.

Lambert, W. E., Giles, H. and Picard, D. (1975). Language attitudes in a French American community. *International Journal of the Sociology of Language*, in press.

Lambert, W. E., Hodgson, R. C., Gardner, R. C. and Fillenbaum, S. (1960). Evaluational reactions to spoken languages. *Journal of Abnormal and Social Psychology*, **60**, 44–51.

Lambert, W. E. and Tucker, G. R. (1972). "Bilingual Education of Children: The St. Lambert Experiment". Newbury House, Rowley, Mass.

Lambert, W. E., Tucker, G. R. and d'Anglejan, A. (1973). Cognitive and attitudinal consequences of bilingual schooling: the St. Lambert project through Grade Five. *Journal of Educational Psychology*, **65**, 141–159.

Laver, J. (1968). Voice quality and indexical information. *British Journal of Disorders of Communication*, **3**, 43–54.

Lawson, E. D. and Giles, H. (1973). British semantic differential responses on world power. *European Journal of Social Psychology*, **3**, 233–240.

Lawton, D. (1965). "Social Class Language Differences in Individual Interviews". Mimeo, Institute of Education, University of London.

Lawton, D. (1968). "Social Class, Language and Education". Routledge and Kegan Paul, London.

Lay, C. H. and Burron, B. F. (1968). Perception of the personality of the hesitant speaker. *Perceptual and Motor Skills*, **26**, 951–956.

Lazure, J. (1970). "La Jeunesse du Québec en Révolution: Essai d'Interpretation". Montreal: Les Presses de l'Université du Québec.

Ledvinka, J. (1971). Race of interviewer and the language elaboration of Black interviewees. *Journal of Social Issues*, **27**, 185–197.

Ledvinka, J. (1972). The intrusion of race: black responses to the white observer. *Social Science Inquiry*, March, 907–920.

Ledvinka, J. (1973). Race of employment interviewer and reason given by Black job-seekers for leaving their jobs. *Journal of Applied Psychology*, in press. (Mimeo: University of Georgia, Athens.)

Lee, R. R. (1971). Dialect perception: a critical review and re-evaluation. *Quarterly Journal of Speech*, **57**, 410–417.

Leginski, W. and Izzett, R. R. (1973). Linguistic styles as indices for interpersonal distances. *Journal of Social Psychology*, **91**, 291–304.

Lennard, H. L. and Bernstein, A. (1960). Interdependence of therapist and patient verbal behaviour. *In* "Readings in the Sociology of Language" (Ed. J. A. Fishman). Mouton, The Hague.

Leventhal, H., Singer, R. P. and Jones, S. (1963). Effects of fear and specificity of recommendations upon attitudes and behaviour. *Journal of Personality and Social Psychology*, **2**, 20–29.

Levin, H. and Silverman, I. (1965). Hesitation phenomena in children's speech. *Language and Speech*, **8**, 67–85.

Levin, H., Silverman, I. and Ford, B. L. (1967). Hesitations in children's speech during explanations and descriptions. *Journal of Verbal Learning and Verbal Behaviour*, **6**, 560–564.

Levine, L. and Crockett, H. J. (1967). Speech variation in a Piedmont community: postvocalic/r/. *International Journal of American Linguistics*, **33**, 76–98.

Levy, M. R. (1970). Issues in the personality assessment of lower class patients. *Journal of Projective Techniques and Personality Assessment*, **34**, 6–9.

Levy, M. R. and Kahn, M. W. (1970). Interpreter bias on the Rorschach test as a function of patients' socioeconomic status. *Journal of Projective Techniques and Personality Assessment*, **34**, 106–112.

Licklider, J. C. R. and Miller, G. A. (1951). The perception of speech. *In* "Handbook of Experimental Psychology" (Ed. S. S. Stevens), Wiley, New York.

Lieberson, S. (1970). "Language and Ethnic Relations in Canada". Wiley, New York.

Lightfoot, C. (1949). Rate of speaking: I. Relation between original and repeated phrases. Joint Project NR 782004, Pensacola, Florida.

Lightfoot, C. and Black, J. W. (1949). Rate of speaking responses to heard stimuli. II. Repetitions of phrases containing logical and illogical pauses. Pensacola, Florida.

Lin, S. C. (1965). "Pattern Practice in the Teaching of Standard English to Students with a Nonstandard Dialect". Columbia University Teachers' College, New York.

Lind, G. (1972). Language gaps and language links in Scandinavia. *Anthropological Linguistics*, **14**, 62–70.

Link, L. J. and Ishii, S. (1966). Pronouns and direct address in conversation. A comparative study of Japanese and English. *Bulletin of the Institute for Research in Language Teaching*, **276**, 9–14.

Loewenthal, K. (1968). The effects of "understanding" from the audience on language behaviour. *British Journal of Social and Clinical Psychology*, **7**, 247–252.

Ma, R. and Herasimchuk, E. (1968). The linguistic dimensions of a bilingual neighbourhood. *In* "Bilingualism in the Barrio" (Ed. J. A. Fishman *et al.*) (Final report to Department of Health, Education and Welfare under contract No. OEC-1-7-062817-0297).

MacNamara, J. (1967). Introduction: bilingualism in the modern world. *Journal of Social Issues*, **23**, 1–7.

Mbaga, K. and Whiteley, W. H. (1961). Formality and informality in Yao speech. *Africa*, **31**, 135–146.

Mahl, G. F. (1956). Disturbances and silences in the patient's speech in psychotherapy. *Journal of Abnormal and Social Psychology*, **33**, 1–15.

Mahl, G. F. and Schulze, G. (1964). Psychological research in the extralinguistic area. *In* "Approaches to Semiotics" (Ed. T. A. Sebeok *et al.*) Mouton, The Hague.

Malmstrom, J. (1967). Dialects. *Florida Foreign Language Reporter*, **5**.

Manaugh, T. S., Weins, A. N. and Matarazzo, J. D. (1970). Content saliency and interviewee speech behaviour. *Journal of Clinical Psychology*, **26**, 17–24.

Mann, R. D. (1959). A review of the relationships between personality and performance in small groups. *Psychological Bulletin*, **56**, 241–270.

Mann, J. W. (1963). Rivals of different rank. *Journal of Social Psychology*, **61**, 11–28.

Markel, N. N. (1969). Relationship between voice-quality profiles and MMPI profiles in psychiatric patients. *Journal of Abnormal Psychology*, **74**, 61–66.

Markel, N. N., Eisler, R. M. and Reese, H. W. (1967). Judging personality from dialect. *Journal of Verbal Learning and Verbal Behaviour*, **6**, 33–35.

Markel, N. N., Meisels, M. and Houck, J. E. (1964). Judging personality from voice quality. *Journal of Abnormal and Social Psychology*, **69**, 458–463.

Markel, N. and Sharpless, C. A. (1972). Socioeconomic and ethnic correlates of dialect differences. *In* "Studies in Linguistics in Honor of George L. Treger" (Ed. E. M. Smith). Mouton, The Hague.

Martin, S. (1964). Speech levels in Japan and Korea. *In* "Language in Culture and Society" (Ed. D. Hymes), pp. 407–412.

Martinet, A. (1953). Introduction to "Language in Contact", by U. Weinreich. Mouton, The Hague.

Matarazzo, J. D., Weins, A. N., Jackson, R. H. and Manaugh, T. S. (1970). Interviewee speech behaviour under conditions of endogenously-presented and exogenously-induced motivational states. *Journal of Clinical Psychology*, **26**, 141–148.

Matarazzo, J. D., Weins, A. N., Jackson, R. H. and Manaugh, T. S. (1970a). Interviewee speech behaviour under different content conditions. *Journal of Applied Psychology*, **54**, 15–26.

Matarazzo, J. D., Weins, A. N., Matarazzo, R. G. and Saslow, G. (1968). Speech and silence behaviour in clinical psychotherapy and its laboratory correlates. *In* "Research in Psychotherapy: Vol. 3" (Ed. J. Schlier, J. D. Matarazzo and C. Savage). American Psychological Association, Washington, D.C.

McCroskey, J. C. and Mehrley, R. S. (1969). The effects of disorganization and non-fluency on attitude change and source credibility. *Speech Monographs*, **36**, 13–21.

McDavid, R. I. (1948). Postvocalic-r in South Carolina: A social analysis. *American Speech*, **23**, 194–203.

McDavid, R. I. and Davis, L. (1972). The dialects of Negro Americans. *In* "Studies in Linguistics in Honour of George L. Treger" (Ed. M. E. Smith). Mouton, The Hague.

McDowell, J. and McRae, S. (1972). Differential response of the class and ethnic components of the Austin speech community to marked phonological variables. *Anthropological Linguistics*, **14**, 228–239.

McGuire, W. J. (1969). The nature of attitudes and attitude change. *In* "Handbook of Social Psychology" (Ed. G. Lindzey and E. Aronson) 2nd ed. Vol. 3, pp. 136–314. Addison-Wesley, Cambridge, Mass.

McGuire, M. T. and Lorch, S. (1968). A model for the study of dyadic communication. *Journal of Nervous and Mental Disease*, **146**, 221–229.

McGuire, M. T. and Lorch, S. (1968a). Natural language conversation modes. *Journal of Nervous and Mental Diseases*, **146**, 239–247.

McIntire, M. L. (1972). Terms of address in an academic setting. *Anthropological Linguistics*, **14**, 286–292.

McIntyre, D. and Morrison, A. (1967). The educational opinions of teachers in training. *British Journal of Social and Clinical Psychology*, **6**, 32–37.

McKay, J. R. (1969). A partial analysis of a variety of nonstandard Negro English. Unpublished doctoral dissertation, University of California, Berkeley.

Mehrabian, A. (1965). Communication length as an index of communicator attitudes. *Psychological Reports*, **17**, 519–522.

Mehrabian, A. (1969). Significance of posture and position in the communication of attitude and status relationships. *Psychological Bulletin*, **71**, 359–372.

Mehrabian, A. (1971). Verbal and nonverbal interaction of strangers in a waiting situation. *Journal of Experimental Research in Personality*, **5**, 127–138.

Mehrabian, A. and Ferris, S. (1967). Inference of attitudes from nonverbal communication in two channels. *Journal of Consulting Psychology*, **31**, 248–252.

Mehrabian, A. and Wiener, M. (1967). Decoding of inconsistent communications. *Journal of Personality and Social Psychology*, **6**, 109–114.

Meisels, M. (1967). Test anxiety, stress and verbal behaviour. *Journal of Consulting Psychology*, **31**, 577–582.

Midgett, D. (1970). Bilingualism and linguistic change in St. Lucia. *Anthropological Linguistics*, **12**, 158–170.

Miller, H. A. (1924). "Races, Nations and Classes". Lippincott, Chicago.

Miller, G. R. and Hewgill, M. A. (1964). The effect of variations in nonfluency on audience ratings of source credibility. *Quarterly Journal of Speech*, **50**, 36–44.

Milmoe, S., Rosenthal, R., Blane, H. T., Chafetz, M. E. and Wolf, I. (1967). The doctor's voice: postdictor of successful referral of alcoholic patients. *Journal of Abnormal Psychology*, **72**, 78–84.

Miner, H. (1939). "St. Denis, A French-Canadian Parish". University of Chicago Press, Chicago.

Moscovici, S. (1967). Communication processes and the properties of language. *Advances in Experimental Social Psychology*, **3**, 226–270.

Moscovici, S. and Plon, M. (1966). Les situations colloques: observations théoriques et experimentales. *Bulletin de Psychologie*, **247**, 702–722.

Mosher, D. L., Mortimer, R. L. and Grebel, M. (1968). Verbal aggressive behaviour in delinquent boys. *Journal of Abnormal Psychology*, **73**, 454–460.

Moss, H. A. (1967). Sex, age and state as determinants of mother-infant interaction. *Merrill-Palmer Quarterly of Behaviour and Development*, **13**, 19–36.

Murray, H. A. (1943). "Thematic Apperception Test". Harvard University Press, Cambridge, Mass.

Naremore, R. C. (1971). Teachers' judgments of children's speech: a factor analytic study. *Speech Monographs*, **38**, 17–27.

Nicolson, H. G. (1955). "Good Behaviour". Constable, London.

O'Barr, W. M. (1971). Multilingualism in a rural Tanzanian village. *Anthropological Linguistics*, **13**, 289–300.

Olim, E. G. (1970). Maternal language styles and children's cognitive behaviour. *Journal of Special Education*, **4**, 53–68.

Omar, A. H. (1971). Standard language and the standardization of Malay. *Anthropological Linguistics*, **13**, 75–90.

O'Neil, W. (1972). The politics of bidialectalism. *College English*, **33**, 433–438.

Opler, M. and Hoijer, H. (1940). The raid and war-path language of the Chiricahua Apache. *American Anthropologist*, **42**, 617–634.

Ortego, P. D. (1970). Some cultural implications of a Mexican American border dialect of American English. *Studies in Linguistics*, **21**, 77–84.

Paivio, A. (1966). Personality and audience influence. *In* "Progress in experimental personality research" (Ed. B. A. Meher). Academic Press, London and New York.

Paulson, S. F. (1954). The effects of the prestige of the speaker and acknowledgement of opposing arguments on audience retention and shift of opinion. *Speech Monographs*, **21**, 267–271.

Pear, T. H. (1931). "Voice and Personality". Wiley, London.

Pear, T. H. (1971). Suggested subjects for students of speaking. *Bulletin of the British Psychological Society*, **24**, 185–194.

Pearce, W. B. (1971). The effect of vocal cues on credibility and attitude change. *Western Speech*, **35**, 176–184.

Pearce, W. B. and Brommel, B. J. (1972). Vocalic communication in persuasion. *Quarterly Journal of Speech*, **58**, 298–306.

Pearce, W. B. and Conklin, F. (1971). Nonverbal vocalic communication and perceptions of a speaker. *Speech Monographs*, **38**, 235–241.

Pellowe, J., Nixon, G., Strang, B. and McNeany, V. (1972). A dynamic modelling of linguistic variation: the urban (Tyneside) linguistic survey. *Lingua*, **30**, 1–30.

Petrucci, R. (1959). Social class and intraoccupation mobility: a study of the Purdue Engineering Graduate from 1911–1956. Unpublished doctoral dissertation, Purdue University.

Pinault, L. and Ladouceur, L. (1971). National language policies. Mimeograph, McGill University, Montreal.

Plant, W. T. (1958). Changes in ethnocentrism associated with a two year college experience. *Journal of Genetic Psychology*, **92**, 189–197.

Plant, W. T. (1958a). Changes in ethnocentrism during college. *Journal of Educational Psychology*, **49**. 112–165.

Pope, B., Blass, T., Cheek, J. A. and Siegman, A. W. (1970). Some effects of discrepant role expectations on interviewee verbal behaviour in the initial interview. Proceedings of the 78th Annual Convention of the American Psychological Association, pp. 527–528.

Pope, B., Blass, T., Siegman, A. W. and Raher, J. (1970). Anxiety and depression in speech. *Journal of Consulting and Clinical Psychology*, **35**, 128–133.

Pope, B. and Siegman, A. W. (1962). The effect of therapist activity level and specificity on patient productivity and speech disturbances in the initial interview. *Journal of Consulting Psychology*, **26**, 489.

Pope, B. and Siegman, A. W. (1968). Interviewer warmth in relation to interviewee verbal behaviour. *Journal of Consulting and Clinical Psychology*, **32**, 588–595.

Powesland, P. F. and Giles, H. (1975). Persuasiveness and accent-message incompatibility. *Human Relations*, **28**, 85–93.

Preston, M. S. (1963). Evaluational reactions to English, Canadian French and European French voices. Unpublished Master's dissertation, McGill University, Montreal.

Putnam, G. W. and O'Hern, E. M. (1955). The status significance of an isolated urban dialect. *Language*, **31**, dissertation supplement no. 53.

von Raffler Engel, W. (1972). Language in context: situationally conditioned style change in black speakers. Paper read at 11th International Congress of Linguistics, Bologna.

von Raffler Engel, W. and Sigelman, C. K. (1971). Rhythm, narration, description in speech of black and white school children. *Language Sciences*, December, 9–14.

Rainey, M. (1969). Style-switching in a headstart class. *In* "Studies in Interaction". Working paper No. 16, Language-behaviour research laboratory, University of California, Berkeley.

Ramanujan, A. K. (1967). The structure of variation: a study in caste dialects. *In* "Social Structure and Social Change in India" (Ed. B. Cohn and M. Singar). Aldine, New York.

Ramsay, R. W. (1968). Speech patterns and personality. *Language and Speech*, **11**, 54–63.

Ratner, S. C. and Rice, F. E. (1963). The effect of the listener on the speaking interaction. *Psychological Review*, **13**, 265–268.

Ray, M. L. and Webb, E. J. (1966). Speech duration effects in the Kennedy news conference. *Science*, **153**, 899–901.

Razran, G. (1950). Ethnic dislikes and stereotypes. A laboratory study. *Journal of Abnormal and Social Psychology*, **45**, 7–27.

Rebelsky, F. and Hanks, C. (1971). Father's verbal interaction with infants in the first three months of life. *Child Development*, **42**, 63–68.

Reinstein, S. and Hoffman, J. E. (1972). Dialect interaction between black and Puerto Rican children in New York City: implications for the language arts. *Elementary English*, **49**, 190–196.

Rémillard, L., Tucker, G. R. and Bruck, M. (1973). The role of phonology and lexicon in eliciting reactions to dialect variation. *Anthropological Linguistics*, **15**, 383–397.

Robinson, W. P. (1965). The elaborated code in working class language. *Language and Speech*, **8**, 243–252.

Robinson, W. P. (1972). "Language and Social Behaviour". Penguin, London.

Rosen, H. (1972). "Language and Class: A Critical Look at the Theories of Basil Bernstein". Falling Wall Press, Bristol.

Rosen, H. (1973). The sense of audience and research in written composition. *Educational Research*, in press.

Rosen, S. and Tesser, A. (1970). On reluctance to communicate undesirable information: the mum effect. *Sociometry*, **33**, 253–263.

Rosenthal, R. (1966). Interpersonal expectations: effects of the experimenter's hypothesis. *In* "Artifact In Behavioural Research" (Ed. R. Rosenthal and R. Rosnow). Academic Press, New York and London.

Rothbart, M. (1971). Birth order and mother-child interaction in an achievement situation. *Journal of Personality and Social Psychology*, **17**, 113–120.

Rubel, A. (1968). Some cultural aspects of learning English in Mexican American communities. *In* "Schools in Transition: Essays in Comparative Education" (Ed. A. M. Kazamias). Allyn and Bacon, Boston.

Rubin, J. (1962). Bilingualism in Paraguay. *Anthropological Linguistics*, **4**, 52–58.

Ruesch, J. and Prestwood, A. R. (1949). Anxiety: its initiation, communication and interpersonal management. *A.M.A. Archives of Neurology and Psychiatry*, **62**, 527–550.

Ryan, E. B. (1969). A psycholinguistic attitude study. *Studies in Language and Language Behaviour*, **8**, 437–450.

Ryan, E. B. (1973). Subjective reactions toward accented speech. *In* "Language Attitudes: Current Trends and Prospects" (Ed. R. W. Shuy and R. W. Fasold). Georgetown University Press, Washington D.C.

Ryan, E. B. and Carranza, M. A. (1974). Methodological approach to the study of evaluative reactions of adolescents towards speakers of different language varieties. Paper read at Annual Meeting of Southwestern Sociological Association, Dallas.

Ryan, E. B. and Carranza, M. A. (1975). Evaluative reactions of adolescents toward speakers of standard English and Mexican American accented English. *Journal of Personality and Social Psychology*, **31**, 855–863.

Ryan, E. M., Carranza, M. A. and Moffie, R. W. (1974). Reactions toward varying degrees of accentedness in the speech of Spanish-English bilinguals. Mimeograph: University of Notre Dame. Chicago, Illinois.

Sachs, J., Lieberman, P. and Erikson, D. (1973). Anatomical and cultural determinants of male and female speech. *In* "Language Attitudes: Current Trends and

Prospects" (Ed. R. W. Shuy and R. W. Fasold) pp. 74–84. Georgetown University Press, Washington D.C.

Sanford, F. H. (1942). Speech and personality. *Psychological Bulletin*, **39**, 811–845.

Sankoff, G. (1971). Language use in multilingual societies: some alternative approaches *In* "Sociolinguistics" (Ed. J. B. Pride and J. Holmes). Penguin, London.

Sapir, E. (1915). Abnormal types of speech in Nootka. Memoir 62, *Anthropological Studies No. 5*, Geological Survey of Canada, Ottawa.

Sattler, J. M. (1970). Racial experimenter effects in experimentation, testing, interviewing and psychotherapy. *Psychological Bulletin*, **73**, 137–160.

Sawyer, J. B. (1965). Social aspects of bilingualism in San Antonio, Texas. *American Dialect Society*, **41**, 7–16.

Saxman, J. H. and Burke, K. W. (1968). Speaking fundamental frequency and rate characteristics of adult female schizophrenics. *Journal of Speech and Hearing Research*, **11**, 194–203.

Scherer, K. R. (1972). Judging personality from voice: a cross-cultural approach to an old issue in interpersonal perception. *Journal of Personality*, **40**, 191–210.

Scovel, T. (1969). Foreign accents, language acquisition and cerebral dominance. *Language Learning*, **19**, 245–253.

Sechrest, L., Flores, L. and Arellano. L. (1968). Language and social interaction in a bilingual culture. *Journal of Social Psychology*, **76**, 155–161.

Secord, P. F. (1959). Stereotyping and favourableness in the perception of Negro faces. *Journal of Abnormal and Social Psychology*, **59**, 309–315.

Secord, P. F., Bevan, W. and Katz, D. (1956). The Negro stereotype and perceptual accentuation. *Journal of Abnormal and Social Psychology*, **53**, 78–83.

Seligman, C. R., Tucker, G. R. and Lambert, W. E. (1972). The effects of speech style and other attributes on teachers' attitudes toward pupils. *Language in Society*, **1**, 131–142.

Semmel, M. I. (1968). The influence of disability labels and dialect differences on the semantic differential responses of college students. *Studies in Language and Language Behaviour*, **7**, 296–307.

Sereno, K. K. and Hawkins, G. J. (1967). The effects of variations in speakers' non-fluency upon audiences ratings of attitude towards the speech topic and speakers' credibility. *Speech Monographs*, **34**, 58–64.

Shinedling, M. M. and Pedersen, D. M. (1970). Effects of sex of teacher and student on children's gain in quantitative and verbal performance. *Journal of Psychology*, **76**, 79–84.

Shuy, R., Baratz, J. and Wolfram, W. (1969). Sociolinguistic factors in speech identification. National Institute of Mental Health Research Project No. MH-15048-01. Center for Applied Linguistics, Washington D.C.

Siegman, A. and Pope, B. (1965). Effects of question specificity and anxiety-producing messages on verbal fluency in the initial interview. *Journal of Personality and Social Psychology*, **2**, 522–530.

Siegman, A. and Pope, B. (1966). Ambiguity and verbal fluency in the TAT. *Journal of Consulting Psychology*, **30**, 239–245.

Siegman, A., Pope, B. and Blass, T. (1969). Effects of interviewer status and duration of interviewer messages on interviewee productivity. Proceedings of the 77th Annual Convention of the American Psychological Association, 4, 541–542.

Silverman, S. H. (1969). The evaluation of language varieties. *Modern Language Journal*, **53**, 241–244.

Simard, L. and Taylor, D. M. (1973). The potential for bicultural communication in a dyadic situation. *Canadian Journal of Behavioural Sciences*, **5**, 211–225.

Simard, L., Taylor, D. M. and Giles, H. (in press). Attribution processes and interpersonal accommodation in a bilingual setting. *Language and Speech*, in press.
Simons, H. W., Berkowitz, N. N. and Moyer, R. J. (1970). Similarity, credibility and
attitude change: a review and a theory. *Psychological Bulletin*, **73**, 1–16.
Sledd, J. (1969). Bi-dialectalism: the linguisics of white supremacy. *English Journal*,
**58**, 1307–1316.
Slobin, D. I. (1963). Some aspects of the use of pronouns of address in Yiddish. *Word*,
**19**, 193–202.
Slobin, D. I., Miller, S. H. and Porter, L. W. (1968). Forms of address and social
relations in a business organization. *Journal of Personality and Social Psychology*, **8**,
289–293.
Smith, J. M. (1970). A note on achievement motivation and verbal fluency. *Journal of
Projective Techniques and Personality Assessment*, **34**, 121–124.
Smith, B. L., Brown, B. L. Strong, W. J. and Rencher, A. C. (1975). Effects of speech
rate on personality perception. *Language and Speech*, **18**, in press.
Smithers, A. (1970). Open-mindedness and the University curriculum. *Journal of
Curriculum Studies*, **2**, 73–77.
Sommer, B. A. and Marsh, J. (1969). Vernacular and English: Language compre-
hension by some N. Queensland aborigines. *Anthropological Linguistics*, **11**, 1–47.
Soskin, W. F. and John V. (1963). A study of spontaneous talk. *In* "The Stream of
Behaviour" (Ed. R. G. Barker). Appleton-Century-Crofts, New York.
Spencer, J. (1958). R. P.—some problems of interpretation. *Lingua*, **7**, 7–29.
Spencer, J. (ed.) (1963). "Language in Africa". Cambridge University Press, London.
Spilka, I. V. (1970). "For a Study of Diglossia in French Canada". Mimeo, Univer-
sity of Montreal.
Spiritas, A. A. and Holmes, D. S. (1971). Effects of models on interview responses.
*Journal of Counseling Psychology*, **18**, 217–220.
Spradlin. J. and Rosenberg, S. (1964). Complexity of adult verbal behaviour in a
dyadic situation with retarded children. *Journal of Abnormal and Social Psychology*, **68**,
694–698.
Stagner, R. (1936). Judgments of voice and personality. *Journal of Educational Psychology*, **27**, 272–277.
Stanley, G. E. (1971). Phonoaesthetics and West Texas dialect. *Linguistics*, **71**,
95–102.
Starkweather, J. A. (1964). Variations in vocal behaviour. *In* "Disorders of Communication". Proceedings of the Association for Research in Nervous and Mental
diseases, XLII, 424–429.
Starkweather, J. A. (1967). Vocal behaviour as an information channel of speaker
status. *In* "Research in Verbal Behaviour and Some Neurophysiological Implications" (Ed. K. Salzinger and S. Salzinger) Academic Press, New York and London.
Starkweather, J. A. and Hargreaves, W. A. (1964). The influence of sodium pento-
barbital on vocal behaviour. *Journal of Abnormal and Social Psychology*, **69**, 123–126.
Stern, H. and Grosz, H. J. (1966). Verbal interactions in group psychotherapy
between patients with similar and with dissimilar personalities. *Psychological Reports*,
**19**, 1111–1114.
Stern, H. and Grosz, H. J. (1966a). Personality correlates of high and low interactors
in group psychotherapy. *Psychological Reports*, **18**, 411–414.
Stewart, W. A. (1964). Foreign language teaching methods in quasi-foreign language
situations. *In* "Non-standard Speech and the Teaching of English". Center for
Applied Linguistics, Washington, D.C.

Stewart, W. A. (1964a). Urban Negro speech: sociolinguistic factors affecting English teaching. *In* "Social Dialects and Language Learning". Proceedings of the Bloomington, Indiana Conference, N.C.T.E., 15–16.

Stewart, W. A. (1967). Sociolinguistic factors in the history of American Negro dialects. *Florida Foreign Language Reporter*, **5**, 1–4.

Stewart, W. A. (1968). A sociolinguistic typology for describing national multilingualism. *In* "Readings in the Sociology of Language" (Ed. J. A. Fishman) pp. 531–545. Mouton, The Hague.

Stewart, W. A. (1970). Toward a history of the American Negro dialect. *In* "Language and Poverty" (Ed. F. Williams) pp. 351–379. Markham, Chicago.

Stolinski, J. H. and Thayer, F. H. (1970). If you're different from me you're no damn good. Unpublished. State University College of New York at Fredonia.

Strongman, K. T. and Woosley, J. (1967). Stereotyped reactions to regional accents. *British Journal of Social and Clinical Psychology*, **6**, 164–167.

Stroud, R. (1961). A study of the relations between social distance and speech differences of white and Negro high school students of Dayton, Ohio. Unpublished master's dissertation, Bowling Green State University, Ohio.

Tajfel, H. (1959). A note on Lambert's "Evaluational reactions to spoken language". *Canadian Journal of Psychology*, **13**, 86–92.

Tajfel, H. (1962). Social perception. *In* "Social Psychology Through Experiment" (Ed. G. Humphrey and M. Argyle). pp. 20–54. Methuen, London.

Tajfel, H. (1974). Social identity and intergroup behaviour. *Social Science Information*, **13**, 65–93.

Tajfel, H. (1974a). Intergroup behaviour, social comparison and social change. Katz-Newcomb Lectures, University of Michigan, Ann Arbor.

Tajfel, H., Sheikh, A. A. and Gardner, R. C. (1964). Content of stereotypes and the inference of similarity between members of stereotyped groups. *Acta Psychologica*, **22**, 191–201.

Tajfel, H. and Wilkes, A. L. (1963). Classification and quantitative judgment. *British Journal of Psychology*, **54**, 101–114.

Tanner, N. (1967). Speech and society among the Indonesian elite: a case study of multilingual society. *American Linguistics*, **9**, 15–40.

Tataru, A. (1969). On the specific character of pronunciation. *English Language Teaching*, **24**, 26–27.

Taylor, A. C. (1934). Social agreement on personality traits as judged from speech. *Journal of Social Psychology*, **5**, 244–248.

Taylor, D. A. (1965). Some aspects of the development of interpersonal relationship: social penetration processes. Naval Medical Research Institute, Washington D.C.

Taylor, D. M., Bassili, J. and Aboud, F. (1973). Dimensions of ethnic identity: an example from Quebec. *Journal of Social Psychology*, **89**, 185–192.

Taylor, D. M. and Gardner, R. C. (1969). Ethnic stereotypes: their effects on the perception of communicators of varying credibility. *Canadian Journal of Psychology*, **23**, 161–173.

Taylor, D. M. and Gardner, R. C. (1970). Bicultural communication: a study of communicational efficiency and person perception. *Canadian Journal of Behavioural Science*, **2**, 67–81.

Taylor, D. M. and Gardner, R. C. (1970a). The role of stereotypes in communication between ethnic groups in the Philippines. *Social Forces*, **49**, 271–283.

Taylor, D. M. and Jaggi, V. (1974). Ethnocentrism and causal attribution in a South Indian context. *Journal of Cross-Cultural Psychology*, **5**, 162–171.

Taylor, D. M., Tucker, G. R. and Gaboriault, E. (1971). Ethnic group interaction: a methodological note. *Anthropological Linguistics*, **13**, 442–447.
Taylor, D. M. and Simard, L. (1972). The role of bilingualism in cross-cultural communication. *Journal of Cross-Cultural Psychology*, **3**, 101–108.
Taylor, O. (1971). Some sociolinguistic concepts of Black language. *Today's Speech*, Spring, 19–26.
Taylor, W. (1959). Inferences about language commonality: cloze procedure. *In* "Trends in Content Analyses" (Ed. I. de Sola Pool) pp. 78–88. Illinois University Press, Urbana, Illinois.
Thananjayarajasingham, S. (1973). Bilingualism and acculturation in the Juravar community of Ceylon. *Anthropological Linguistics*, **15**, 276–280.
Thomas, C. (1971). On the Welsh language. Paper read at Annual Summer School of the International Folk Group.
Thomas, N. (1973). "The Welsh Extremist". Y Lolfa, Wales.
Timm, L. A. (1973). Modernization and language shift: the case of Brittany. *Anthropological Linguistics*, **15**, 281–298.
Tognoli, J. (1969). Response matching in interpersonal information exchange. *British Journal of Social and Clinical Psychology*, **8**, 116–123.
Tolhurst, G. C. (1955). Some effects of changing time patterns and articulation upon intelligibility and word perception. Project no. NR 145–993, U.S. Naval School of Aviation Medicine. Pensacola, Florida.
Triandis, H. C. (1960). Cognitive similarity and communication in a dyad. *Human Relations*, **13**, 175–183.
Triandis, H. C., Loh, W. D. and Levin, L. A. (1966). Race, status, quality of spoken English and opinions about Civil Rights as determinants of interpersonal attitudes. *Journal of Personality and Social Psychology*, **3**, 468–472.
Trudgill, P. (1972). Sex, covert prestige and linguistic change in the urban British English of Norwich. *Language in Society*, **1**, 179–196.
Trudgill, P. (1974). Linguistic change and diffusion: description and explanation in sociolinguistic dialect geography. *Language in Society*, **3**, 215–246.
Trudgill, P. (1974a). "The Social Differentiation of English in Norwich". Cambridge University Press, London.
Tucker, G. R. (1968). Judging personality from language usage: a Filipino example. *Philippine Sociological Review*, **16**, 30–39.
Tucker, G. R. and Lambert, W. E. (1969). White and Negro listeners' reactions to various American-English dialects. *Social Forces*, **47**, 463–468.
Tucker, G. R., Taylor, D. M. and Reyes, E. (1970). Ethnic group interaction in a multiethnic society. *International Journal of Psychology*, **6**, 217–222.
Ullrich, H. E. (1971). Linguistic aspects of antiquity: a dialect study. *Anthropological Linguistics*, **13**, 106–113.
Valin, R. (1970). Quel français devons-nous enseigner? *In* "Cahiers de l'Office de la Langue Français" No. 7. Gouvernement du Québec, Québec.
Walster, E., Aronson, E. and Abrahams, D. (1966). On increasing the persuasiveness of a low prestige communicator. *Journal of Experimental Social Psychology*, **2**, 325–342.
Warr, P. B., Faust, J. and Harrison, G. J. (1967). A British ethnocentrism scale. *British Journal of Social and Clinical Psychology*, **6**, 267–277.
Walker, R. V. and Chalmers, D. K. (1971). The use of technical and nontechnical language in communication. *Journal of Psychology*, **78**, 65–71.
Webb, J. T. (1969). Subject speech rates as a function of interviewer behaviour. *Language and Speech*, **12**, 54–67.
Webb, J. T. (1970). Interview synchrony: an investigation of two speech rate

measures in an automated standardized interview. *In* "Studies in Dyadic Communication" (Ed. A. W. Siegman and B. Pope). Pergamon, Oxford.

Webster, H. (1956). Personality development during the college years. *Journal of Social Issues*, **12**, 29–43.

Webster, H., Freedman, M. B. and Heist, P. (1962). Personality changes in college students. *In* "The American College" (Ed. N. Sanford). Wiley, New York.

Webster, W. G. and Kramer, E. (1968). Attitudes and evaluational reactions to accented English speech. *Journal of Social Psychology*, **75**, 231–240.

Weeks, T. (1971). Speech registers in young children. *Child Development*, **62**, 119–131.

Weinreich, U. (1963). "Language in Contact". Mouton, The Hague.

Weins, A. N., Jackson, R. H., Manaugh, T. S. and Matarazzo, J. D. (1969). Communication length as an index of communicator attitude: a replication. *Journal of Applied Psychology*, **53**, 264–266.

Weitz, S. (1972). Attitude, voice and behaviour: a repressed affect model of interracial interaction. *Journal of Personality and Social Psychology*, **24**, 14–21.

Weiss, W. (1957). Opinion congruence with a negative source on one issue as a factor influencing agreement on another issue. *Journal of Abnormal and Social Psychology*, **54**, 180–186.

Welkowitz, J. and Feldstein, S. (1969). Dyadic interaction and induced differences in perceived similarity. Proceedings of the 77th Annual Convention of the American Psychological Association.

Welkowitz, J. and Feldstein, S. (1970). Relation of experimentally manipulated interpersonal perception and psychological differentiation to the temporal patterning of conversation. Proceedings of the 78th Annual Convention of the American Psychological Association, **5**, 387–388.

Wells, J. C. (1970). Local accents in England and Wales. *Journal of Linguistics*, **6**, 231–252.

Whittaker, J. O. and Meade, R. D. (1967). Sex and age as variables in persuasibility. *Journal of Social Psychology*, **73**, 47–52.

Wilkinson, A. (1965). Spoken English. *Educational Review*, suppl. 6, 17,

Willcock, E. D. and Walker, A. (Eds) (1936). "The Arte of English Poesie by George Puttenham." Cambridge University Press, London.

Williams, F. (1970). Psychological correlates of speech characteristics: on sounding "disadvantaged". *Journal of Speech and Hearing Research*, **13**, 472–488.

Williams, F., Whitehead, J. L., and Miller, L. M. (1971). Attitudinal correlates of children's speech characteristics. Final Report Project No. 0-0336. Center for Communication Research, Austin, Texas.

Williams, F., Whitehead, J. L. and Miller, L. M. (1971a). Ethnic stereotyping and judgements of children's speech. *Speech Monographs*, **38**, 166–170.

Williams, J. H. (1964). Conditioning of verbalization: a review. *Psychological Bulletin*. **62**, 383–393.

Wöber, M. (1969). Distinguishing centri-cultural from cross-cultural tests and research. *Perceptual and Motor Skills*, **28**, 488.

Wolck, W. (1973). Attitudes toward Spanish and Quechua in bilingual Peru. *In* "Language Attitudes: Current Trends and Prospects". (Ed. R. W. Shuy and R. W. Fasold). Georgetown University Press, Washington D.C.

Wölff, H. (1959). Intelligibility and inter-ethnic attitudes. *Anthropological Linguistics*, **1**, 34–41.

Wolff, W. (1943). "The Expression of Personality". Harper, New York.

Wolfram, W. (1968). "A Sociolinguistic Description of Detroit Negro Speech." Center for Applied Linguistics, Washington, D.C.

Wyld, H. C. (1934). "The Best English: A Claim for the Superiority of Received Standard English." Society for Pure English, Tract No. 39, Clarendon Press, Oxford.

Yackley, A. (1969). Levels of aspiration in intergroup competition: a cross-cultural study. Unpublished Master's dissertation, McGill University, Montreal.

Zajonc, R. (1966). "Social psychology: An experimental Approach". Wadsworth, Belmont, California.

Zimbardo, P. G., Mahl, G. F. and Barnard, J. W. (1963). The measurement of speech disturbance in anxious children. *Journal of Speech and Hearing Disorders*, **28**, 362–370.

# Author Index

# Subject Index